TEXAS TERROR

CONFLICTING WORLDS
New Dimensions of the American Civil War

T. Michael Parrish, Series Edtior

TEXAS TERROR

DONALD E. REYNOLDS

THE SLAVE INSURRECTION PANIC OF 1860 AND THE SECESSION OF THE LOWER SOUTH

LOUISIANA STATE UNIVERSITY PRESS

BATON ROUGE

Published by Louisiana State University Press
Copyright © 2007 by Louisiana State University Press
All rights reserved
Manufactured in the United States of America
First Printing

Designer: Michelle A. Neustrom
Typeface: Minion Pro
Printer and binder: Thomson-Shore, Inc.

LIBRARY OF CONGRESS CATALOGING-IN-PUBLICATION DATA

Reynolds, Donald E., 1931–
   Texas terror : the slave insurrection panic of 1860 and the secession of the lower South / Donald E. Reynolds.
      p. cm. — (Conflicting worlds)
   Includes bibliographical rerferences and index.
   ISBN-13: 978-0-8071-3283-8 (cloth : alk. paper)
1. Slave insurrections—Texas—History—19th century. 2. Panic—Social aspects—Texas—History—19th century. 3. Antislavery movements—Texas—History—19th century. 4. Slavery—Texas—History—19th century. 5. Texas—Race relations—History—19th century. 6. Vigilance committees—Texas—History—19th century. 7. Texas—Social conditions—19th century. 8. Slave insurrections—Political aspects—Texas—History—19th century. 9. Texas—Politics and government—1846–1865. 10. Secession—Texas. I. Title.
   E445.T47R49 2008
   973.7'11409764—dc22

                                                                        2007013872

The paper in this book meets the guidelines for permanence and durability of the Committee on
Production Guidelines for Book Longevity of the Council on Library Resources. ∞

To William and Wayne

Oh, the horrors here in Texas
That these early settlers tell—
It will cause your hair to stand on end,
And make you think of h——.

    —From *Sixty Years in Texas,* by George Jackson

CONTENTS

PREFACE

The seed for this book was planted more than thirty years ago, while I was doing research for the dissertation that would later become *Editors Make War: Southern Newspapers in the Secession Crisis.* As I read scores of southern newspapers for the year 1860 in libraries and courthouses all over the South, I was struck by the prevalence of stories about the Texas slave insurrection panic of that summer and fall. From mid-summer until the presidential election of that year, virtually every political journal I read carried sensational accounts of abolitionism run amok in Texas. The "Texas Troubles," as many newspapers called the panic, soon became an epidemic as similar, if less extensive, scares broke out in other southern states.

Since Democratic journals and politicians tied the alleged plot to the Republican party and its presidential candidate, Abraham Lincoln, it became clear to me that the tremendous surge of excitement surrounding the Texas panic and its imitators in other states greatly benefited the secession movement in the South. I wondered why I had not read about the Texas insurrectionary scare in the best-known histories of the period.

Intrigued by the lack of attention given to the Texas slave panic by historians of the secession period, I determined to delve further into the subject. Subsequently, an examination of the letters and diaries of ordinary citizens and the speeches of southern fire-eaters confirmed my initial impression that allegations by southern rights editors and politicians of an abolitionist-inspired, Republican-sponsored, insurrectionist plot in the summer of 1860 constituted a key factor in the Lower South's decision to secede, following Lincoln's election as president.

My research continued over several decades, interrupted for far too long by the intrusion of administrative duties. Along the way, I published several articles and a book chapter on different aspects of the panic, but I planned to bring all the material together in one volume. About a decade ago, I finally began that process and wrote perhaps a third of the manuscript before I retired from academe. A move from Texas to New Mexico and the development of other priorities again interrupted my efforts. In 2004, Michael Parrish of Baylor University called to ask whether I was still planning to complete the larger work that I had alluded to in my other published pieces on the subject. If so, he said he would like to consider including it in the Conflicting Worlds Series he was editing for the Louisiana State University Press. I said "yes," and this book is the result.

Since the research for this study was conducted in numerous repositories over a lengthy period of time, it would be futile to attempt to recognize the dozens of librarians, archivists, and historians who have helped me. I nevertheless must mention a few individuals whose help has been invaluable. Professor Charles Roland was my mentor in the initial research that laid the basis for this study, and I am grateful to him for his guidance and friendship. James Conrad, archivist of Texas A&M University-Commerce, gave me valuable assistance in checking research data. The faculty research committee of East Texas State University (now Texas A&M University-Commerce) provided financial support in the early stages of the research, and the university's administration generously granted helpful teaching load reductions.

I am especially in debt to Michael Parrish for "restarting my motor" and providing valuable suggestions, in addition to sending helpful research materials. Rand Dotson and the editorial staff of the Louisiana State University Press have been most responsive to my needs as well. Finally, I must thank my wife, Martha, for her love and understanding during my extended affair with a demanding mistress—my computer. She patiently read the manuscript and made many helpful suggestions. The mistakes and shortcomings that remain, however, are entirely my own.

TEXAS TERROR

CHAPTER ONE

WHAT IS IN THE WIND?

Although slave insurrections were rare in the antebellum South, slave insurrection panics were not. Indeed, periodic scares over possible uprisings were about as familiar to most white southerners as grits and redeye gravy. Virtually from slavery's inception in North America there were frequent reports of rebellious bondsmen committing individual acts of violence against their owners. More frightening for whites were recurring rumors that cadres of slaves were plotting together to win their freedom by force. According to one historian of slavery, these reports "kept Southerners apprehensive throughout the colonial period."[1]

This sense of foreboding continued to weigh on southerners in the early national and antebellum periods, and the anxiety level rose significantly in 1831,

1. Kenneth M. Stampp, *The Peculiar Institution: Slavery in the Ante-Bellum South* (New York, 1956), 134. Winthrop D. Jordan discussed fears of insurrection in colonial America in *White Over Black: American Attitudes Toward the Negro, 1550–1812* (Chapel Hill, N.C., 1968), 110–115; see also Winthrop D. Jordan, *The White Man's Burden: Historical Origins of Racism in America* (New York, 1974), 62–64. Ulrich B. Phillips provided a brief survey of insurrectionist scares in *American Negro Slavery: A Survey of the Supply, Employment and Control of Negro Labor as Determined by the Plantation Regime* (New York, 1918), 463–488. A comprehensive discussion of slave revolts and panics in the South from colonial times to the Civil War may be found in Herbert Aptheker, *American Negro Slave Revolts* (New York, 1943). Aptheker lists scores of alleged insurrections. Although the validity of his work as history is compromised by an all-too-evident readiness to accept unsubstantiated reports from suspect sources, he nevertheless provides a valuable survey of the numerous panics that from time to time swept over various regions of the antebellum South. For other useful, but uncritical, accounts of alleged slave insurrections, see Joseph C. Carroll, *Slave Insurrections in the United States, 1800–1865* (Boston, 1938), and Harvey Wish, "American Slave Insurrections before 1861," *Journal of Negro History* 22 (July 1937): 299–320.

when Nat Turner led an insurrection in Virginia that left nearly sixty whites dead.[2] Although confined to one obscure county in Tidewater Virginia, Turner's rebellion reminded white southerners of what might happen to their own families and communities if they failed to maintain strict control of their slaves. Turner's rebellion was limited in its scope and unsuccessful in its outcome; nevertheless, in its aftermath many slave states passed laws designed to tighten controls on their slaves, thereby preventing future uprisings. These measures, however, failed to cause a reduction in the frightful reports of slave unrest. According to historian Kenneth M. Stampp, after Turner's rebellion, "Hardly a year passed without some kind of alarming disturbance somewhere in the South."[3]

Although the Southampton rebellion undeniably had an important impact on the South, pro-slavery editors, writers, and politicians looked beyond Turner's poorly executed uprising for a more frightening illustration of what could happen if the South should let down its defenses. They found their example in the Santo Domingo revolution of the 1790s.[4] In that great slave rebellion—the only successful one ever staged in either the West Indies or North America—rampaging blacks burned hundreds of plantations, murdering the whites who inhabited them and committing unspeakable atrocities in the process.[5] The blood of southerners ran cold whenever they contemplated such a scenario for the South, and the possibility was never far from their minds. One historian has written: "The violence and other excesses of the slave rebellion on

2. For more on Nat Turner and his insurrection, see Stephen B. Oates, *The Fires of Jubilee: Nat Turner's Fierce Rebellion* (New York, 1975).

3. Stampp, *The Peculiar Institution*, 136. See also Dickson D. Bruce Jr., *Violence and Culture in the Antebellum South* (Austin, 1979), 114–136. Communities did not live in a constant state of alarm, of course, but just beneath the surface there was always present an apprehension that could escalate into panic under stressful conditions. At the end of his third, and final, journey through the South in the summer of 1854, Frederick Law Olmsted observed that he had seen only a few "districts" in which the people were constantly apprehensive of slave insurrections. "Yet," he added, "there is no part of the South where the slave population is felt to be quite safe from a contagion of insurrectionary excitement" (Frederick Law Olmsted, *A Journey in the Back Country* [New York, 1860; reprint, Williamstown, Mass., 1972], 474).

4. Santo Domingo was the old Spanish name for that nation's colony on Hispaniola. After France settled the largely unpopulated western half of the island in the early seventeenth century, it used the French version of that name, *Saint-Domingue,* but Americans continued to refer to the colony as Santo Domingo.

5. Various reports spoke of many women being raped (one on the slain body of her husband), planters being dismembered, and infants being impaled on poles and carried about as standards for the rebel army. Although some of the reports undoubtedly were exaggerated or embellished,

Santo Domingo during the 1790s were stock themes of Southerners whenever the mere suggestion of emancipation arose."[6]

The South produced no Toussaint L'Ouvertures (the brilliant leader of the Haitian revolution), and Nat Turner's uprising was a feeble caricature, at best, of the earth-shaking events in Santo Domingo. Nevertheless, Turner's was the only American slave conspiracy of the nineteenth century that actually came to fruition and caused the deaths of white people. One might have thought this realization would have reassured slaveholders, but it did not. During the three decades leading to the Civil War, anxiety levels among white southerners remained high. The slightest rumor often was sufficient to cause a panic, even in cases where there was little or no evidence of a plot.

Historians can only speculate on the reasons for the South's easy susceptibility to often baseless rumors of slave conspiracies. In part, it may have been a result of a deep-seated uneasiness over the obvious contradictions between their political and religious ideals and the inequities of their "peculiar institution." It is true that a great majority of southern whites expressed no doubts whatsoever about the morality of slavery. Any white who did so—particularly if he lived in the Lower South—invited the scorn of, and perhaps physical assaults by, his fellow citizens. Planters who made their livings from the labor of their bondsmen almost never expressed qualms about the morality of slavery, at least publicly. Still, a few slaveowners expressed reservations privately, usually in wills by which they sometimes manumitted their slaves.[7] Reflecting on the reluctance of slaveholders in Virginia to free their slaves, Thomas Jefferson, in a letter to an English friend, opined that most planters "have not the courage to divest their families of a property which however keeps their consciences inquiet."[8]

Another reason for the extreme sensitivity of southerners to rumors of pending slave rebellions may have been psycho-sexual fears, which insured

---

they were circulated throughout America, causing dismay among slaveholders. Laurent Dubois, *Avengers of the New World: The Story of the Haitian Revolution* (Cambridge, Mass., 2004), 110–112.

6. William L. Barney, *The Road to Secession: A New Perspective on the Old South* (New York, 1972), 89. For other references to fears that Santo Domingo conjured up in the minds of white southerners, see Barney, *The Road to Secession*, 67, 150, 169; George M. Fredrickson, *The Black Image in the White Mind: The Debate on Afro-American Character and Destiny, 1817–1914* (New York, 1971), 9, 53–54, 69; Jordan, *White Over Black*, 380–385, 391–392; Aptheker, *American Negro Slave Revolts*, 42–44, 96–99.

7. Stampp, *The Peculiar Institution*, 95, 235–236.

8. David Waldstreicher, ed., *Notes on the State of Virginia, with Related Documents* (New York, 2002), 71. Jefferson was himself a conflicted slaveowner. Although he theoretically advocated emancipation, he never freed his own slaves, and he regarded blacks as inferior to whites. If eman-

that the hobgoblins of imagined horrors were never far beneath the level of individual and community consciousness. White women were especially vulnerable to such fears, often indicating a dread of being attacked by black men. In a letter to a friend, Fanny Kemble wrote that southern white men generally denied that "they live under a habitual sense of danger," but "every Southern woman to whom I have spoken on the subject has admitted to me that they live in terror of their slaves."[9]

Whether or not psychological factors contributed to the fears southern whites felt because of their bondsmen, the growing attacks by anti-slavery elements in the North unquestionably contributed to the cloud of insecurity that hung over the South during the three decades preceding the Civil War. After England abolished slavery in her colonies in 1833, southern Americans stood alone among Anglo-Saxon peoples in their continued dependence upon African slavery, which by the nineteenth century was firmly entrenched as the cornerstone of the South's socio-economic system. The region's isolation and self-consciousness were magnified by the rise and growth of militant abolitionism in the North. Relentless attacks upon slavery and southern slaveholders by William Lloyd Garrison and other anti-slavery radicals increased in volume and intensity during the decade leading up to the Civil War. This constant bombardment, wrote historian William Barney, "generated a pervasive sense of insecurity" and "anxiety over whether slavery could be maintained against the onslaught of its enemies."[10]

Southerners fiercely counterattacked against the growing assaults of the abolitionists. They insisted that slaves were content with their lot and loyal to

---

cipation were achieved, Jefferson believed the freedmen should be colonized in Africa, because they would never be able to achieve equality nor live up to their own potential in a society dominated by whites (Waldstreicher, ed., *Notes on the State of Virginia*, 37, 175–181).

9. Fanny Kemble to Elizabeth Sedgwick, April 13, 1839, in *Fanny Kemble's Journals*, ed. Catherine Clinton (Cambridge, Mass., 2000), 161. Kemble was a famous British actress who had settled in Philadelphia, where she met and married Pierce Butler, a wealthy Georgia slaveholder. She spent several months on Butler's plantation in 1838–1839, and her visit confirmed her own aversion to slavery. While in Georgia, Kemble recorded her correspondence in a journal; this letter was drawn from that document. For other references to the fears women felt in the South's slave society, see Jordan, *White Over Black*, 152–154, 398–399; Jordan, *The White Man's Burden*, 79–83; Francis B. Simkins and James W. Patton, *Women of the Confederacy* (Richmond, Va., 1936), 1–2; Bruce, *Violence and Culture in the Antebellum South*, 131; Kate M. Rowland and Mrs. Morris L. Croxall, eds., *The Journal of Julia LeGrand, New Orleans, 1862–1863* (Richmond, Va., 1911), 58–59; Isabella D. Martin and Myra Lockett Avary, eds., *A Diary from Dixie, as written by Mary Boykin Chesnut* (New York, 1906), 1, 24–25, 33.

10. Barney, *The Road to Secession*, 150–151.

their masters, and a good deal of southern literary talent was expended in an effort to convince anyone who would listen that this was so. Novelists and poets joined theologians, political theorists and orators, scientists, and sociologists in arguing the virtues of the South's peculiar institution and drawing invidious comparisons between the South's paternalistic labor system and the heartless "wage slavery" allegedly practiced by factory owners and other employers in the North.[11] Nevertheless, despite being bombarded from every side with reassuring editorials, literature, political speeches, and sermons, white slaveowners in their private communications often betrayed a distrust of the rhetorical assurances that their slaves were a contented, docile folk. Moreover, their actions demonstrated a chronic apprehension that unrest was endemic to the slave population. Throughout the antebellum period whites responded quickly, and often brutally, to acts of slave violence and rumors of planned uprisings.

The South's vulnerability to insurrection alarms is perhaps easier understood when one recognizes that individual acts of rebellion against slavery and slaveowners were in fact quite common and very real. Stampp has shown that bondsmen resorted to a wide variety of personal acts of resistance, including self-mutilation, vandalism, and even arson and murder. Although they surely longed for freedom, slaves had no realistic hope of mounting a successful insurrection without outside help, for they had no easy access to arms, and in most southern states they were outnumbered by their well-armed masters.[12] Slaves in the Lone Star State, where the great insurrection panic of 1860 occurred, apparently grasped this reality, for their methods of resistance followed the pattern described by Stampp. Randolph B. Campbell, the leading historian of slavery in Texas, stated that although there was little in the way of outright rebellion among the slaves in the Lone Star State, "thousands of bondsmen" resisted their condition "by being recalcitrant and 'unmanageable,' by running away, and by individual acts of violence."[13] Although most of the rebellious acts

11. For a broad sampling of sources drawn from various genres, see Thomas Daniel Young, Floyd C. Watkins, Richmond C. Beatty, *The Literature of the South*, rev. ed. (Glenview, Ill., 1968), 89–352. For shorter excerpts of such writings, see Drew Gilpin Faust, ed., *The Ideology of Slavery: Proslavery Thought in the Antebellum South, 1830–1860* (Baton Rouge, La., 1981). A perceptive analysis of the pro-slavery argument may be found in Frederickson, *The Black Image in the White Mind*, 1–96. An older but still useful survey of the pro-slavery defense may be found in William Sumner Jenkins, *Pro-Slavery Thought in the Old South* (Chapel Hill, N.C., 1935).

12. Stampp, *The Peculiar Institution*, 127, 140.

13. Randolph B. Campbell, *An Empire for Slavery: The Peculiar Institution in Texas, 1821–1865* (Baton Rouge, 1989), 185. For examples of the ways in which Texas slaves protested their condition, see ibid., 177–189.

by slaves, both in Texas and elsewhere in the South, were spontaneous reactions to the cruelties of individual masters, white southerners feared that the simmering unrest, if encouraged by abolitionists, might culminate in a concerted action against their communities and families.

Southern slaveholders continually reassured themselves by reciting the venerable axiom that the African American was naturally docile, but to lend credibility to this orthodox view they had to rationalize not only the actions of countless individual acts of resistance by generations of nameless blacks, but the deeds of such celebrated insurrectionists as Turner, Gabriel Prosser, and Denmark Vesey as well. They resolved the apparent contradiction between their theory of slave docility and the reality of slave rebelliousness by blaming outside influences for the latter. Clearly, argued slavery apologists, some sinister influence beyond the plantation community had confused malleable bondsmen by planting delusions of equality in their clouded minds. Before the rise of militant abolitionism, white southerners had usually charged free blacks with instigating slave unrest, even though, as historian Winthrop Jordan has pointed out, before Vesey's abortive effort in 1822 it cannot be positively shown that a single free black was involved in any such conspiracy in the United States.[14]

After the advent of Garrison's brand of militant abolitionism, which coincided in 1831 with the Turner insurrection, southerners almost always alleged that white abolitionists from the North were the instigators of alleged slave uprisings. Even though no abolitionist, except John Brown, had ever attempted to overthrow slavery by violence, either with or without the active cooperation of slaves, southern whites were unwavering in their conviction that Garrisons and Browns lurked in every shadow, ready at the slightest opportunity to seduce other Nat Turners from their natural loyalties and use them to destroy the South and its social system.[15]

Given the deep undercurrent of anxiety that was always present among whites, it was hardly surprising that slave panics broke out periodically throughout the slaveholding states—usually in times of great stress. They tended to reach a crescendo of excitement and then quickly subside, usually after the hanging of a few designated culprits. Such episodes seemed to calm the afflicted

14. Jordan, *White Over Black,* 122. One possible exception to this generalization was Charles Deslondes, who allegedly was a leader in the slave revolt that occurred in St. John Parish, Louisiana, in 1811 (see Eugene D. Genovese, *Roll, Jordan, Roll: The World the Slaves Made* [New York, 1974], 592).

15. Francis B. Simkins and Charles P. Roland, *A History of the South,* 4th ed. (New York, 1972), 102. See also Bruce, *Violence and Culture in the Antebellum South,* 129–130.

Harris County Public Library
Barbara Bush Branch

Check Out

***********7253   10.05 AM 2009/10/29

1. Texas terror : the slave insurrectio
34028066534653   Due 11/12/09

Total 1 article(s).

Items due by date shown
Please retain this receipt
Renew via telecirc 713-747-4763
or
online at www.hcpl.net

community and cleanse its collective psyche—at least temporarily—of demons. Bertram Wyatt-Brown has postulated that the punishment of those blacks and alleged white abolitionists who were identified as conspirators served as a psychological catharsis that reaffirmed values and class relationships, thus restoring equilibrium and normality to the community.[16]

But while slave panics may have reaffirmed southern social values and given reassurance to whites, they also constituted ideal vehicles for those southern radicals who desired a separate southern nation. Fortuitously for the disunionists, the Texas Troubles of 1860 exploded on the southern landscape in midsummer, just as emotions over the approaching presidential election were peaking. Leading advocates of a separate southern nation, such as William Lowndes Yancey, Robert Barnwell Rhett, Edmund Ruffin, Laurence M. Keitt, Louis Wigfall, and others of their ilk, would seize upon the alleged insurrection and use it to illustrate the fate that awaited the South should Lincoln become president.[17]

At first glance, Texas, with a comparatively small slave population, would seem to be an unlikely site for a slave insurrection panic. Before 1854 the Lone Star State was too preoccupied with the daunting challenges posed by its recent transition from republic to state to pay much attention to the national controversy over slavery that had been brewing ever since the Treaty of Guadalupe-Hidalgo added vast new territories to the Union in 1848. Nationalism continued to ride high in the state until shaken by the bitter quarrel over the Kansas-Nebraska Act in 1854. From that point onward, Texas became sharply divided over the issues that revolved around the question of slavery's expansion into the western territories and the perception of many Texans that powerful forces in the North desired to rid the nation of the South's cherished peculiar institution. This division was sharpened by the growing concern of southern rights Democrats that clandestine abolitionist activity might foment a slave insurrection that would jeopardize the lives and property of white Texans.[18]

Even though Texas's slave population of 182,566 in 1860 was much smaller than that of the other cotton states of the Lower South, its growth rate in the preceding decade was nothing short of spectacular. The U.S. Census of 1850 had counted only 58,161 slaves; thus, in one decade the number of slaves increased

16. Bertram Wyatt-Brown, *Southern Honor: Ethics and Behavior in the Old South* (New York, 1982), 402–434.

17. For good summaries of the careers of these and other southern "ultras," see Eric H. Walther, *The Fire-Eaters* (Baton Rouge, La., 1992).

18. Anna I. Sandbo, "Beginnings of the Secession Movement in Texas," *Southwestern Historical Quarterly* 18 (July 1914): 43–48.

at the rate of 214 percent. Although the white population also was growing rapidly, the slave population was outpacing it at a significantly higher rate.[19]

Other problems unique to Texas among the slave states combined with the growing fear of abolitionist activity to create a dangerous level of anxiety. Frontier lawlessness, frequent conflicts between Anglo Texans and Mexicans in southern and southwestern Texas, and escalating Indian raids on portions of northern and western sections of the state—when added to the concerns over possible slave insurrections—created a potentially explosive atmosphere. Divisive national, sectional, and state political conflicts further stressed the public psyche. And if these problems were not unsettling enough, in the summer of 1860 Mother Nature further frayed the nerves of Texans by inflicting upon the state a heat wave and drought of unprecedented severity.

As a raw and open frontier land, Texas attracted more than its share of ne'er-do-wells and outright criminals, who early on gave the Lone Star State a reputation for violence that it at least partially deserved. The phrase "Gone to Texas" often identified those who were fleeing a shady past in one of the other southern states. Many such characters migrated to the frontier, where horse thievery and other crimes became common. Even horse theft was tied to sectional issues, for there were persistent rumors that abolitionist "emissaries" engaged in horse-thieving forays into West Texas and drove their prizes northward to Kansas, where they presumably sold them for the benefit of their cause.[20] Texans early on developed the practice of going outside the law, often using vigilantes, to dispense quick justice to horse thieves and other lawbreakers. By 1860, Texans were well familiar with this *ad hoc* method of dealing with miscreants, and it was only natural for them to use vigilance committees during the panic of that summer to deal with those accused of insurrectionary plotting.[21]

Of considerable concern to Anglo Texans living in the southern and southwestern sections of the state was the presence of Mexican Texans, or *Tejanos*. Undoubtedly, much of the anti-Mexican bias evinced by Anglo Texans stemmed from ethnic and racial prejudices, but white Texans also worried about the *Tejanos'* attitudes toward slavery. Mexico had abolished slavery in 1829. Most

19. Campbell, *An Empire for Slavery,* 55–56. Campbell calculated the growth of the white population at 173 percent.

20. Charles W. Ramsdell, "The Frontier and Secession," in *Studies in Southern History and Politics, inscribed to William Archibald Dunning, Ph.D., LL.D, Lieber Professor of history and political philosophy in Columbia University by his former pupils, the authors* (New York, 1914), 75.

21. Donald E. Reynolds, "Vigilante Law during the Texas Slave Panic of 1860," *Locus: An Historical Journal of Regional Perspectives* 2 (spring 1990): 173.

Tejanos consequently had no use for the peculiar institution, and many of them despised it. Not only did they frequently fraternize with black bondsmen, but some even assisted runaways by transporting them to Mexico, often at the risk of their own lives.[22] Mexico was all the more inviting to runaways, because the Mexican government made no attempt to discourage them. Thinking the escaped slaves could constitute a buffer against Indian raids, Mexican authorities allowed them to settle along the Rio Grande, especially in the Eagle Pass area.[23]

One contemporary estimate held that as many as four thousand slaves had escaped to freedom south of the border by 1855. That number may have been exaggerated, but a modern scholar nevertheless has asserted that the numbers were great enough to pose a significant problem for Texas slaveholders.[24] Moreover, the loss of slave property increased during the decade leading to the Civil War. An estimated one thousand blacks made it across the Rio Grande between 1850 and 1855 alone. Slaveholders tried various means to stop the flow of their bondsmen to Mexico. After their early efforts to negotiate the return of runaways with Mexican authorities failed, they tried, unsuccessfully, to persuade the federal government to seek an extradition treaty with Mexico. Gaining no redress from the government, slaveholders offered rewards for the return of their chattel property, and some even offered bounties to slave hunters. None of these efforts bore significant fruit.[25]

Certain that Mexican Texans were aiding and abetting the runaway slaves, some towns and counties in Central and South Texas took preemptive steps to protect their slave property. For example, in September 1854 the citizens of Seguin passed a resolution forbidding Mexican "peons" from entering Guadeloupe County. The next month Austin whites gave all transient Mexicans ten days to leave the city or face compulsory expulsion.[26] Since Anglos believed that all Mexicans were abolitionists at heart, it was hardly surprising that two years later Mexican residents would instantly become suspects in the slave insurrection panic that broke out in Colorado County and spread to other areas of South Texas.

22. Arnoldo DeLeon, *They Called Them Greasers: Anglo Attitudes toward Mexicans in Texas, 1821–1900* (Austin, 1983), 49–51.

23. Alwyn Barr, *Black Texans: A History of African Americans in Texas, 1528–1995* (Norman, Okla., 1996), 29.

24. Sean Kelley, "'Mexico in His Head': Slavery and the Texas-Mexico Border, 1810–1860," *Journal of Social History* 37, no. 3 (2004): 717–718; Barr, *Black Texans,* 30.

25. Barr, *Black Texans,* 30–31

26. DeLeon, *They Called Them Greasers,* 51. See also, Paul D. Lack, "Slavery and Vigilantism in Austin, Texas, 1840–1860," *Southwestern Historical Quarterly* 85 (July 1981): 9–10.

The Anglo Texan animosity toward the Mexican population only increased in mid-1859, when Juan Cortina led an insurgency in the lower Rio Grande Valley to protest discriminatory treatment of Mexican Texans living in that region by the white establishment.[27] Cortina boldly continued his incursions into December of that year, threatening several Texas settlements and even occupying Brownsville at one point. Federal troops proved as ineffective in dealing with Cortina as they were in combating the hostile Indians on the northern frontier. Meanwhile, the press kept emotions high by publishing numerous inflammatory accounts of the "border war."[28] The national government's unwillingness to commit adequate resources to the defense of Texas's southwestern frontier would supply additional ammunition to those fire-eaters in the Democratic party who argued that the Lone Star State would be better off out of the Union.[29]

While Anglo Texans in the South and Southwest concerned themselves with the Mexicans in their midst, those of the northwestern frontier felt threatened by the presence of large numbers of hostile Indians. Seeing increasing numbers of white settlers encroach upon their hunting grounds and resenting the Texans's efforts to confine them to reservations, Comanche and Kiowa braves fought back by raiding isolated settlements and attacking bands of immigrants. As the raids increased between 1857 and 1859, Texans looked both to Austin and Washington for protection, but neither government gave them much help. The U.S. Army did allocate thirty-six hundred troops—one-fourth of its total strength—to Texas, but most of these were infantrymen assigned to garrison the numerous forts. These were useless in combating the mounted Indian marauders. Most settlers thought there were not enough troops and clamored for more. But the government in Washington repeatedly rejected the state's appeals for more troopers, forcing the settlers to depend upon their own volunteer forces and the Texas Rangers to combat the Indian threat. In their frustration, some living in the affected areas even began to question the value of remaining in a Union whose government demonstrated such indifference to the plight of the settlers; however, most frontier Texans continued to see greater benefits from remaining in the Union than in leaving it.[30]

27. DeLeon, *The Called Them Greasers,* 53–54.

28. Marilyn M. Sibley, *Lone Stars and State Gazettes: Texas Newspapers before the Civil War* (College Station, Tex., 1983), 281.

29. Walter L. Buenger, *Secession and the Union in Texas* (Austin, 1984), 46.

30. David Paul Smith, *Frontier Defense in the Civil War: Texas' Rangers and Rebels* (College Station, Tex., 1992), 3–20; Buenger, *Secession and the Union in Texas,* 46; Ramsdell, "The Frontier

Although Texans were displeased by the unresponsiveness of the federal government to their Indian problem, they found targets closer to home to blame for much for their plight. Indeed, frontier defense—or the lack of it— became an important state political issue in 1858 and 1859. Hardin R. Runnels had defeated Sam Houston for governor in 1857, but his failure to squelch the intensifying Indian attacks in the northern and northwestern sections of the state and his inability to persuade the federal government to increase the army's presence on the frontier diminished his support among voters in those areas.[31]

Even more damaging to Runnels's chances for reelection in 1859 was his alignment with the more extreme southern rights wing of the Democratic party. This element, which included John Marshall, editor of the Austin *Texas State Gazette*, Louis T. Wigfall, Guy M. Bryan, John Henry Brown, and others, had overplayed its hand by advocating such unpopular proposals as filibustering expeditions—aimed at extending slavery into the Caribbean—and by supporting the resumption of the African slave trade.[32] Some of these men, including Runnels himself, had spoken freely of the possibility of secession under certain circumstances—if, for example, Kansas were not allowed to enter the Union as a slave state.[33] Nor, in the opinion of the fire-eaters, did secession pose any threat of civil war. Thomas N. Waul, the southern rights Democratic candidate for U.S. Representative for the Western District, blithely pledged to "drink all the blood" that would be shed if the South should secede.[34]

Many Texans found such cavalier attitudes toward the Union and possible civil war disturbing. Although they generally believed in defending slavery,

---

and Secession," 68–73; Richard McCaslin, "Conditional Confederates: The Eleventh Cavalry West of the Mississippi River," *Military History of the Southwest* 21 (spring 1991): 88; Randolph B. Campbell, *Gone to Texas: A History of the Lone Star State* (New York, 2003), 203–206.

31. Indian depredations on the frontier increased dramatically during Runnels's administration. The governor's effort to force hostile Indians north of the Red River failed to reduce attacks against frontier settlements, and this may have helped seal Runnels's fate with the voters of that region. Smith, *Frontier Defense in the Civil War*, 14–17; Ramsdell, "The Frontier and Secession," 74–75.

32. Alvy L. King, *Louis T. Wigfall: Southern Fire-Eater* (Baton Rouge, 1970), 66–68; Billy D. Ledbetter, "Politics and Society: The Popular Response to Political Rhetoric in Texas, 1857–1860," *East Texas Historical Journal* 13 (fall 1975): 13–14. Less radical members of Runnels's party recognized that it was foolish to make an issue of the international slave trade. Moderate Democrat John H. Reagan, a candidate for the First Congressional District's seat in Congress, wrote to his constituents that only "very crazy" men would risk the Union "for the ignoble . . . privilege of being permitted to kidnap . . . a parcel of savages of Africa" (Dale Baum, *The Shattering of Texas Unionism: Politics in the Lone Star State during the Civil War Era* [Baton Rouge, 1999], 35).

33. Ledbetter, "Politics and Society," 12.

34. Quoted in Campbell, *Gone to Texas*, 238.

fully 70 percent of Texas families owned no slaves.[35] The insistence of Runnels and his extreme southern rights supporters on making slavery issues the centerpiece of their campaign made no sense to nonslaveholders or, for that matter, to those who owned only small numbers of bondsmen—especially since President James Buchanan's administration had followed a benign policy toward the South.[36] Even the pro-Democratic Galveston *News* admitted that the administration had been "all that Southern men could desire."[37]

Running as a self-styled "Union Democrat," Houston lambasted Runnels for his failed frontier policy and for his extreme states' rights program, which, he argued, if implemented might well result in secession and even civil war. "The Raven" contrasted the dangerous positions of Runnels and his supporters with his own unconditional loyalty to the Union. Having made clear his view that the overriding issue was the future of the Union, Houston saw no need to stump the state for votes. He made only one campaign speech in 1859, whereas in the campaign two years earlier he had delivered sixty-two. The outcome clearly showed that his confidence was warranted: Houston easily won the governorship, garnering 58 percent of the votes.[38]

Although other issues, such as Indian policy, undoubtedly played a role in the election's outcome, historians generally agree that the overriding issue was the Union. That this was so was clearly shown by the outcome of the other state and congressional elections in 1859. The "Opposition" (a term applied to unionists who had in common their opposition to the Democrats) won all but two of the major races, and the two it lost were won by moderate Democrats, who had taken a strong stand for the Union.[39] Not only did extreme southern rights candidates lose the races for governor and lieutenant governor, but they also failed to win either of Texas's two congressional seats. Andrew J. Hamilton defeated Thomas N. Waul for the Western District seat, and John H. Reagan won the Eastern District seat, outpolling William B. Ochiltree. Like Houston,

35. The frontier was especially hostile to policies that might lead to a breakup of the Union. Historian Charles W. Ramsdell pointed out that the northern and western counties were unsuited to slavery, and their inhabitants were always suspicious of the planters in the eastern part of the state, whom they identified with secession (Ramsdell, "The Frontier and Secession," 63–67).

36. Ninety percent of the state's slaveholders owned fewer than twenty-one slaves, and more than half of them held fewer than five bondsmen (Campbell, *An Empire for Slavery,* 68, 193). The small slaveholders were among Houston's strongest supporters in the election of 1859 (Baum, *The Shattering of Texas Unionism,* 24).

37. Galveston *Weekly News,* August 23, 1859, quoted in Baum, *The Shattering of Texas Unionism,* 37.

38. Ledbetter, "Politics and Society," 13–14.

39. Buenger, *Secession and Union in Texas,* 39.

both Hamilton and Reagan owed their victories primarily to their strong and unequivocal advocacy of the Union.[40]

Nevertheless, although the victorious politicians failed to realize it at the time, the conservative sweep in the elections of 1859 represented the high-water mark of unionism in Texas. Indeed, the seeds of secession had been planted several years earlier, and although they had been inhibited by the Texans' long-standing devotion to the Union, they continued to lie—dormant, but not dead—just beneath the surface, needing only the right political conditions to make them germinate and grow. The excesses of the Runnels faction in aggressively advocating the expansion of slavery, even at the risk of disunion and civil war, obscured the reality that a great majority of Texans—even of the large body of nonslaveholders—held very southern attitudes toward blacks and the peculiar institution. It could hardly have been otherwise, since most of them had migrated from other slave states. These inbred attitudes were continuously reinforced by politicians, newspaper editors, and preachers, almost all of whom held pro-slavery opinions. It was not surprising, therefore, that most Texans believed that not only was slavery important for the state's economy, but also that it was the only practical way to control African Americans, whom they regarded as little more than savages with a thin veneer of civilization. Given their pro-slavery attitudes and racial fears, Texans of all classes were always quick to respond whenever there were reports of incidents that seemed to threaten slavery.[41]

The slave insurrection panic in July 1860 was but the climactic event in a long series of lesser scares in the Lone Star State. The half decade leading up to that fateful summer witnessed a significant number of alleged insurrectionary incidents that marked an increased anxiety among the Texans over the future of the Union. The most dramatic of these early scares occurred in 1856, which, like 1860, was a presidential election year. As would be the case with Abraham Lincoln's candidacy four years later, southern rights fearmongers depicted John C. Frémont, the first candidate of the new Republican party, as an anti-slavery zealot who would encourage abolitionists to assault slavery in the South.[42]

The trouble began when reports of an abolitionist plot to free the slaves in Colorado County, located in southeastern Texas, caused a sensation throughout the state. A vigilance committee of Columbus reported that more than two

---

40. Ledbetter, "Politics and Society," 15.

41. For the attitudes of all classes toward slavery, see Campbell, *An Empire for Slavery,* 209–230.

42. Billy D. Ledbetter, "Slave Unrest and White Panic: The Impact of Black Republicanism in Ante-Bellum Texas," *Texana* 10 (1972): 337.

hundred slaves in the county had planned to slay all the whites—except the young ladies, who were to be made the wives of the "diabolical murderers." The black insurrectionists were to be abetted in their efforts by the Mexicans of the county, who allegedly had supplied the bondsmen with weapons and who, after the plot had been carried out, would help them make their way to freedom in Mexico. Having nipped the plot in the bud, the committee whipped two blacks to death and hanged three others. It then passed a resolution ordering all Mexicans to leave the county within five days on pain of death. Still not content with ridding their community of those Hispanics who were deemed guilty of supporting the alleged insurrection, the committee passed a resolution "forever forbidding any Mexican from coming within the limits of the county."[43]

Other communities that had not experienced "plots" nevertheless followed Colorado County's example. Matagorda County evicted its Mexican population, and San Antonio expelled a portion of its *Tejanos*. The next year, Uvalde's citizens resolved that Mexicans could not even pass through the county unless they had previously obtained a pass from local officials. These discriminatory actions were accompanied by numerous acts of violence against Mexicans, the most serious of which was the so-called Cart War, which cost an estimated seventy *Tejano* lives.[44]

The panic in Colorado County spawned lesser scares in several neighboring counties. In late October vigilantes charged an Ohioan named Davidson and two others with encouraging the slaves in the Lavaca County town of Hallettsville to take up arms, slay their masters, and flee to Mexico. Upon interrogation, Davidson reportedly confessed his guilt and said the uprising was scheduled for October 31. The committee gave him one hundred lashes as punishment. Vigilant citizens also reportedly uncovered plots in DeWitt and Victoria counties.[45] Communities elsewhere formed vigilance committees as a precaution to guard

43. Harvey Wish, "The Slave Insurrection Panic of 1856," *Journal of Southern History* 5 (May 1939): 208; Ledbetter, "Slave Unrest and White Panic," 340. See also David Grimsted, *American Mobbing, 1828–1861: Toward Civil War* (New York, 1998), 174.

44. This bloody conflict grew out of competition between Mexican cartmen and Anglos over the lucrative freight business between San Antonio and the coast. The Mexicans had monopolized this business, because they charged less. In the summer of 1857, Anglo freighters, motivated by economic self-interest and racism, began a campaign of harassment and assassination that came to be known as the Cart War. The conflict went on for several months. Finally, Texas officials, pressured by the Mexican government and U. S. Secretary of State Lewis Cass, took steps to provide protection to the Mexican teamsters. DeLeon, *They Called Them Greasers*, 82–83; Lack, "Slavery and Vigilantism in Austin, Texas," 19.

45. Wish, "The Slave Insurrection Panic of 1856," 208.

against similar plots in their counties. The ripple effect of the Colorado County panic did not stop at the Texas border. As would be the case in the summer of 1860, the abolitionist scare of 1856 proved to be contagious. Historian Harvey Wish wrote: "The Texas incidents were but a prelude to the more serious slave plots which soon broke out in Tennessee and Kentucky, spreading panic into every Southern state."[46]

Texas continued to experience occasional "abolitionist" incidents after the panic of 1856 had subsided. For example, Wood County expelled John E. Lemon in March 1857 for allegedly publishing anti-slavery comments in the Quitman *Free Press* under the pen name "Orange." Lemon went to Danville, Illinois, where he reportedly began publishing an "abolition paper."[47] In September of the same year, citizens of Limestone County, east of Waco, discovered an alleged plot involving some ten or twelve slaves and an unspecified number of Mexicans. The slaves were punished, but the Mexicans escaped before they could be tried.[48] The next month, in Ellis County, a committee charged a preacher named Thomas Dougan with receiving letters expressing anti-slavery opinions and "abolitionist" newspapers in the mail. This was enough to convict him in the eyes of the local citizens, who decreed that he receive five hundred lashes by the hand of a slave. The committee then expelled him, forbidding him ever to return. Reporting the story, the Marshall *Texas Republican* said that Dougan "expected death, but came off simply the best whipped man who ever went through the ordeal in Texas."[49] Other isolated incidents occurred in 1858. In Gonzales, two Mexicans were killed after being accused of aiding slaves to escape, and in West Liberty a citizens' committee charged one Herman Harlan with "slave tampering" and advocating "free-soil doctrines" and ordered him to leave Liberty County.[50]

A general meeting of the Northern Methodists in North Texas was the cause of the most significant confrontation of 1859. On March 11, the Arkansas Conference of that denomination convened its annual meeting at Timber Creek, in Collin County. Alarmed citizens in nearby Bonham met the next day at the courthouse to register their indignation. The local populace believed that even though the Methodists were meeting peacefully, their ultimate goal was to act

---

46. Ibid., 341.

47. Frank H. Smyrl, "Unionism, Abolitionism, and Vigilantism in Texas, 1856–1865" (Master's thesis, University of Texas, 1961), 33–34. See also Sibley, *Lone Stars and State Gazettes*, 277.

48. Smyrl, "Unionism, Abolitionism, and Vigilantism in Texas," 34.

49. Marshall *Texas Republican*, October 24, 1857.

50. Smyrl, "Unionism, Abolitionism, and Vigilantism in Texas," 35–36.

as an abolitionist vanguard, preparing the way for those who would come later and foment insurrection. At the protest meeting in Bonham, L. C. DeLisle, editor of the Bonham *Era*, called those attending the Timber Creek conference "wolves, dressed in sheep's clothing," who professed to preach only the gospel but who, in reality, were intent upon spreading abolitionist ideas and documents among the people. They were, in DeLisle's opinion, "but spies and forerunners of the invading army of abolitionism."[51]

Other speakers at the meeting voiced similar views, and the citizens passed a resolution declaring that "a secret foe lurks in our midst, known as the Northern Methodist Church, entertaining sentiments antagonistic to the institution of slavery, and the manifest intention of whose Northern coadjutors is to do away with slavery in these United States." The citizens chose a committee to "wait upon" the conference and warn its members to end their meeting immediately, "as its continuance will be well calculated to endanger the peace of this community." The resolution made clear the citizens' intention to rid the area of its unwanted guests by any means necessary when it declared that their motto would be: "Peaceably if we can, forcibly if we must."[52] Robert H. Taylor, one of the committee's leaders, echoed editor DeLisle's opinion when he alleged that the conference's delegates had been sent "to blaze the way for the host of abolitionists that were to follow." It therefore behooved the citizenry to use any means—whether legal or not—to suppress them, said Taylor, who warned that even though there was no law to prevent the Methodists from meeting, "there is something above all law—self-preservation."[53]

Accompanied by an estimated two hundred mounted men, a committee of three interrupted the Sunday service of the Timber Creek conference, just as the speaker was beginning his sermon. Samuel A. Roberts, a prominent Bon-

---

51. Bonham *Era*, March 19, 1860, clipped in Nashville (Tenn.) *Christian Advocate*, April 21, 1860. The Texas Southern Methodist newspaper later charged that the Timber Creek delegates had been "under the direction of Senator [William H.] Seward" (Galveston *Texas Christian Advocate*, November 3, 1860).

52. Bonham *Era*, March 19, 1860, clipped in Nashville (Tenn.) *Christian Advocate*, April 21, 1860; Charles Elliott, *South-Western Methodism: A History of the M. E. Church in the South-West, from 1844 to 1864* (Cincinnati, 1868), 127–129.

53. Wesley Norton, "The Methodist Episcopal Church and the Civil Disturbances in North Texas in 1859 and 1860," *Southwestern Historical Quarterly* 68 (January 1965): 328. Taylor was an example of how insurrection fears affected conservatives, as well as southern rights advocates. A lawyer who served in both houses of the Texas legislature during the 1850s, Taylor was a strong supporter of Sam Houston and later steadfastly opposed secession (*Handbook of Texas Online*, s.v., www.tsha.utexas.edu/handbook/online/articles/TT/fta24.html [accessed July 29, 2006]).

ham lawyer, was the spokesman for the group. He strode boldly down the aisle of the meetinghouse and delivered an ultimatum warning the delegates to stop their proceedings and cease all activity in Texas. The next day, the conference hastily wound up its business and adjourned.[54]

The Timber Creek affair was followed by other, lesser brouhahas later that year. In August, a Dallas committee charged Solomon McKinney, a minister recently arrived from Iowa, with espousing abolitionist views.[55] According to a later report, the basis for the charge was a sermon that McKinney preached on the relative duties of masters and slaves. His landlord, a slaveholder who also was a member of McKinney's church, had requested that he speak on the topic.[56] In the course of his sermon, the preacher reportedly made the mistake of saying that slaves had sometimes received inhumane treatment. Although his discourse was not critical of slavery as an institution and did not offend his congregation, other townsmen heard about his comment, and he soon found himself confronted by an angry vigilance committee. The citizens jailed McKinney and his friend William Blunt,[57] another minister who had come to his defense. Later, a mob removed both men from jail, stripped them of their clothing, "except shirt and pantaloons," and whipped them so badly that their backs were "one mass of clotted blood and gore, and bruised and mangled flesh." After robbing them of their money, the mob ordered them to leave the state.[58] Given the severity of their injuries, it was remarkable that the men—though both in their sixties—survived to make it to the North and safety. The Dallas *Herald* approvingly reported that the mob had given McKinney his "walking papers" for daring to instruct "Southern men how to manage their servants."[59]

54. Elliott, *South-Western Methodism,* 129–131.

55. Smyrl, "Unionism, Abolitionism, and Vigilantism in Texas," 37–38; Dallas *Herald,* August 17, 31, 1859.

56. McKinney's denominational affiliation is uncertain. Most contemporary editors and politicians referred to him and his ministerial friend, William Blunt, as Methodists and thus connected both men with the Timber Creek "vanguard" that allegedly sought to abolitionize Texas. However, a northern journal in Blunt's home state of Wisconsin later reported that both men were "of the Campbellite persuasion" (Madison *State Journal,* n.d., quoted in William Lloyd Garrison, *The New "Reign of Terror" in the Slaveholding States, for 1859–1860* [New York, 1860; reprint, New York, 1969], 30; see also Grimsted, *American Mobbing,* 175).

57. Also spelled "Blount" in some sources.

58. Madison *State Journal,* n.d., quoted in Garrison, *The New "Reign of Terror,"* 30; Cincinnati *Christian Luminary,* January 12, 1860, quoted in Garrison, *The New "Reign of Terror,"* 29. See also Grimsted, *American Mobbing,* 175.

59. Dallas *Herald,* August 17, 1859, quoted in Michael Phillips, "White Violence, Hegemony, and Slave Rebellion in Dallas, Texas, before the Civil War," *East Texas Historical Journal* 37, no. 2

There were other local incidents in 1859. One involved an alleged plot, un-covered in September, to help three slaves escape in Washington County.[60] Later that fall, a committee in Gainesville accused a man named E. C. Palmer of authoring a letter counseling northerners to prepare for a war "on the dam Southern sons of bitches." Palmer escaped and later denied the confession that he said the vigilantes had extorted from him.[61]

Although these localized incidents served to keep Texans alert to the pos-sibility of a slave uprising, it took an actual abolitionist invasion of a small town over a thousand miles away to make them see that their worst nightmare could become a reality. John Brown's raid on Harpers Ferry, Virginia, raised the anxieties of all white southerners to new heights. On the evening of October 16, 1859, Brown and his ragtag "army" of eighteen followers attacked and captured the largely undefended U.S. armory and arsenal at Harpers Ferry. Brown's plan was to send some of his men into the countryside to spread the word among the slaves, who presumably would flock to his banner of freedom. His patrol brought in a few hostages and a handful of slaves, but the expected legions of bondsmen failed to materialize. Within thirty-six hours of the raid's inception, local militia and a force of U.S. marines, led by Colonel Robert E. Lee, had eas-ily put down the incursion, capturing Brown and six of his followers.[62]

Brown's ill-conceived, poorly executed raid had been a fiasco, and historians might have written it off as a farce had not the aftermath raised it to the level of a tragic drama. The Virginians were outraged by Brown's violation of their state and demanded his blood and that of the other captives. State officials obliged by quickly indicting and trying Brown. Convicted of fomenting insurrection, as well as of treason and murder, he was hanged on December 2.[63]

The Harpers Ferry raid sent shockwaves through the North as well as the South. Leading Republicans, including such notables as William H. Seward and Abraham Lincoln, denounced Brown, arguing that his raid was a criminal act and that the would-be liberator deserved hanging.[64] Even William Lloyd Gar-rison, the personification of extreme abolitionism in the North, initially reacted

---

(1999): 27. See the epilogue for a fuller discussion of the case of McKinney and Blunt and their al-leged involvement in the slave insurrection panic of 1860.

60. Marshall *Texas Republican,* September 17, 1860.

61. Smyrl, "Unionism, Abolitionism, and Vigilantism in Texas," 39.

62. Stephen B. Oates, *To Purge This Land with Blood: A Biography of John Brown* (Amherst, Mass., 1984), 320–324.

63. Ibid., 349–352.

64. Ibid., 310, 353.

by describing Old Osawatomie's invasion of Virginia as "misguided, wild, and apparently insane."[65] Although a majority of northerners probably agreed with this assessment, many southern Democrats insisted that Brown in fact embodied the view of most northerners that slavery was evil and that aggressive action to abolish it was justified. They pointed to correspondence found among Brown's belongings that revealed he had received financial and moral support for his venture from a number of prominent northerners. Most white southerners dismissed the anti-Brown pronouncements of the Republican leaders as disingenuous and politically motivated. Southern Democratic leaders further alleged that the party of Seward and Lincoln secretly approved of Brown's effort to strike a blow against slavery, and the more extreme among them insisted that the Republicans had even actively participated. For example, Robert Barnwell Rhett's Charleston *Mercury* charged that the raid was an abolitionist-Republican plot, and he further asserted that the South would never have peace as long as it remained in the Union. Other fire-eaters expressed similar opinions and said that the South could remain in the Union only if it were to receive ironclad guarantees against further abolitionist assaults upon the slaveholding states.[66]

The true colors of the North, southern Democrats said, were reflected in the apparent effort of many communities and famous individuals north of the Mason-Dixon Line to bestow martyrdom on Brown. Before the old man's execution, leading transcendentalist and author Ralph Waldo Emerson prophesied that if Brown were hanged, he would make "the gallows as glorious as the cross."[67] On the day of Brown's death, church bells tolled, guns fired salutes, and preachers delivered eulogies of praise. Afterward, such well-known literary figures as Henry David Thoreau and William Dean Howells paid similar homage to the failed emancipationist, and Herman Melville and Walt Whitman memorialized him in verse.[68] William Lloyd Garrison, who earlier had questioned Brown's sanity, now called him a martyr, and, reversing his long held position of opposing violence in the cause of emancipation, now proclaimed: "Success to every slave insurrection at the South, and in every slave country."[69]

65. Boston *Liberator,* October 21, 1859.

66. Oates, *To Purge This Land with Blood,* 320–324.

67. C. Vann Woodward, *The Burden of Southern History,* 3rd ed. (Baton Rouge, 1993), 54.

68. Oates, *To Purge This Land with Blood,* 354–356. For thoughtful essays on the contrasting responses of the North and South to Brown's raid, see Paul Finkelman, "Manufacturing Martyrdom: The Antislavery Response to John Brown's Raid," and Peter Wallenstein, "Incendiaries All: Southern Politics and the Harpers Ferry Raid," both in *His Soul Goes Marching On: Responses to John Brown and the Harpers Ferry Raid,* ed. Paul Finkelman (Charlottesville, 1995), 41–66; 149–173.

69. Oates, *To Purge This Land with Blood.,* 355.

John Brown's raid—and the northern reaction to it—sharply intensified the fears of white southerners everywhere. Slaveholders believed that slave insurrections could occur only if abolitionist zealots from the North were able to infiltrate the South, create discontent among their normally docile slaves, and provide them with arms and leadership. Although Brown had failed miserably in his attempt to accomplish these goals, his raid served as an object lesson for those southerners who had tended to minimize the abolitionist threat. More important than Brown's pitifully inept raid, however, was the spontaneous outpouring of sympathy in many northern communities. The eloquent apotheosis of Brown by some of the best-known public figures in the North seemed to validate the fire-eaters' oft-repeated assertion that there existed in the free states a deep, abiding animosity toward the South and its peculiar institution.

The distrust that southerners had habitually harbored toward northerners now gave way to something like a siege mentality, and white citizens throughout the slave states exercised heightened vigilance, for fear that other John Browns were lurking in their midst. Towns from Mississippi to Virginia called upon militias to protect them from new "John Brown raids," communities activated night patrols to detect and snuff out incipient insurrections, and officials took steps to suppress all things northern. In the weeks following Harpers Ferry, people of northern origin were subject to special scrutiny. The new president of an Alabama college fled for his life, simply because he was a northerner and, ipso facto, must be unsafe on the slavery question. The legislature of the same state passed a law stating that only those who had resided in the state for at least ten years could teach in Alabama's schools. Vigilantes in Mississippi and South Carolina seized "anti-southern" books and destroyed them in public ceremonies.[70]

The Lone Star State had its own book burning. The East Texas town of Palestine, "apprehending the presence of abolition emissaries," appointed a committee "to rid the community of such characters." The town also passed a resolution ordering an examination of the textbooks in public schools, proscribing the employment of northern teachers, and instituting a "non-intercourse" policy for the local merchants, who were admonished not to trade with northern businesses, except those that were friendly to slavery. The next day, a vigilance committee presided over a public burning of "incendiary books" on

70. Ibid., 320–322. See also Ollinger Crenshaw, *The Slave States in the Presidential Election of 1860* (Baltimore, 1945; reprint, Gloucester, Mass., 1969), 89–91; Wallenstein, "Incendiaries All," 155–156.

the grounds that such "cheap literature" was part of a northern conspiracy to achieve the "ultimate overthrow and extinction of domestic slavery."[71]

As in the other slave states, Brown's raid on Harpers Ferry had a powerful impact on Texas politics. The elections of August had reflected a strong resurgence of unionism in the Lone Star State. The voters repudiated the extremist view of the "ultra" southern rights advocates that the North posed so great a threat to slavery that secession might be the best course for Texas and the South. Now, only two months later, Brown's raid came as a godsend to the floundering Democrats. As historian Dale Baum has written: "His [Brown's] actions appeared to fulfill the paranoid prophecies of pro-slavery Democratic party zealots who had warned for years that northern abolitionists might some-day come to the South to incite slave uprisings."[72]

The most dramatic evidence of the revival of the southern rights wing of the Democratic party in Texas was the resuscitation of Louis T. Wigfall's political career. Originally from South Carolina and known as one of the most extreme fire-eaters in Texas politics, the Marshall Democrat had been elected to the Texas Senate in 1857, but his brand of radicalism fell into disrepute during the conservative resurgence in 1858 and early 1859. Wigfall hoped to be elected to the U.S. Senate, but the ascendancy of the Opposition party appeared to put that goal out of reach. In the aftermath of Brown's raid, however, the Marshall fire-eater's prospects underwent a dramatic reversal, and three days after the Virginians hanged Old Osawatomie, the Texas legislature elected him to the U.S. Senate.[73]

Historians agree that Brown dealt a severe setback to unionism in Texas.[74] Nevertheless, although the momentum clearly swung to the side of the fire-eaters after Brown's raid and martyrdom in the North, conservatism in Texas was hardly dead. Wigfall won the senate seat only after three ballots—and then by just two votes—showing that his radicalism still caused concern among many. Walter Buenger has suggested that the importance of the Brown episode in shaping the political views of Texans "has perhaps been overemphasized,"

71. Palestine *Trinity Advocate*, January 4, 1860.

72. Baum, *The Shattering of Texas Unionism*, 38. For other appraisals of the damage done by Brown's raid to unionism in Texas, see Buenger, *Secession and Union in Texas*, 45; King, *Louis T. Wigfall*, 70–78.

73. King, *Louis T. Wigfall*, 67–76.

74. Baum, *The Shattering of Unionism in Texas*, 38; Buenger, *Secession and Union in Texas*, 45; King, *Louis T. Wigfall*, 70–78.

although, "together with other events it created an atmosphere of tension and stress."[75] There were indications by early 1860 that this observation was correct. After December, fewer references to Brown could be found in Texas newspapers, or in those of the other slave states for that matter. The Charleston *Mercury* later theorized that Brown's failure, "like a strong opiate, first excited, and then put Virginia to sleep; whilst it spread over the whole South a corresponding apathy."[76] Indeed, by the spring of 1860 relatively little newspaper space was being devoted to reports of slave violence in the South, as the press turned to other, more immediate political concerns.[77] At least one secessionist journal deplored this omission. In April, the Montgomery *Mail*, William Lowndes Yancey's sounding board in Alabama, expressed disgust with the general lack of concern over reports of abolitionist activity and complained that the South had become "comatose."[78]

Although the floodtide of anxiety ebbed in the first half of 1860, Texans hardly became "comatose" concerning the danger of insurrection. The schism within the Democratic party in the spring resulted in the nominations of both a northerner, Stephen A. Douglas of Illinois, and a southerner, John C. Breckinridge of Kentucky, for president. This turn of events led many to believe that Abraham Lincoln, the Republican nominee, might well win the election in November. Since many southerners believed Republicanism to be synonymous with abolitionism, such an outcome could only spell disaster for the South. The Columbia *Democrat and Planter* expressed this concern when it warned that if the Republicans gained the White House, "incendiary Abolition documents will find ready access to every village in [the South]."[79]

Some Texans worried that the abolitionist virus had already spread to the slaves. After reporting that a local slave had resisted his master's son by striking him on the head with a tree limb, the La Grange *True Issue* said, "A strict and constant watchfulness should be kept on the slaves. Our citizens know not the fearful thoughts [that] may be brooding in their hearts."[80] Such constant vigilance of course created considerable strain, and it is likely that communities like La Grange shared the view of an editor in neighboring Louisiana, who complained, "To live all the time under a continued state of anxiety is no living at all."[81]

75. Buenger, *Secession and Union in Texas*, 47.
76. Charleston (S.C.) *Mercury*, August 29, 1860.
77. Crenshaw, *The Slave States in the Presidential Election of 1860*, 91–92.
78. Montgomery (Ala.) *Mail*, April 20, 1860.
79. Columbia *Democrat and Planter*, July 3, 1860.
80. La Grange *True Issue*, March 31, 1860.
81. False River (La.) *Pointe Coupée Democrat*, December 24, 1859.

Isolated instances of slave rebellion—often connected to alleged abolitionists—nevertheless ensured that Texans would not be free of anxiety during the first half of 1860. In early February, for example, a slave woman in Collin County fell under suspicion for having set fire to her master's house. She asserted that George D. Drake, a white resident, had prodded her to do the deed, promising that he would later accompany her to a free state. B. Warren Stone, a Dallas lawyer, vigorously defended Drake against the charges, saying that his client was a model citizen, "and as little tinctured with abolitionism as any member of this society." The vigorous defense may have succeeded, since there was no subsequent report of punishment.[82]

In May, three blacks identified only as Jess, Ruben, and Emma allegedly murdered their master and his family in Fannin County, north of Dallas. Before they were hanged, they reportedly confessed that "a general uprising of the negroes of the neighborhood had been planned, and that a white man was at the head of it."[83] C. B. Moore, a Collin County diarist, recorded a similar though apparently different case on May 18: three blacks reportedly murdered a man named "Kineade" (Kennedy?) and his family near Pilot Point, north of Denton. Whereas the Fannin County slaves had been "convicted," possibly by a legal trial, the diarist said that a mob had hanged several blacks in the Pilot Point case "with out trial."[84] In the same entry on May 18, Moore wrote that there was "great excitement" in McKinney over allegations that blacks had stolen "bacon, corn, etc." and sold it to someone "named Burns or Barns." After whipping the blacks, the authorities jailed Burns (or Barns), along with his son and son-in-law, but a mob forcibly removed them at night, whipped them, and ordered them to leave the county, "which they did."[85]

The Brenham *Texas Ranger* reported that the town of Chapel Hill was thrown into a commotion on July 3 by reports that abolitionists were at work in the community. A large public meeting ensued and the suspects—"old man Clock," his son and son-in-law—were arrested and interrogated by a committee "of our most respected citizens." The committee apparently decided to its

82. Dallas *Herald*, March 7, 1860, quoted in Smyrl, "Unionism, Abolitionism, and Vigilantism in Texas," 45.

83. Galveston *News*, n.d., quoted in La Grange *True Issue*, June 28, 1860; Matagorda *Gazette*, July 4, 1860. This confession probably was the source of a rumor that persisted in June that there was a conspiracy to murder eight families in Fannin County (see Sibley, *Lone Stars and State Gazettes*, 282).

84. C. B. Moore Diary, May 18, 1860, Moore Papers, University of North Texas Library, Denton, Texas.

85. Ibid.

satisfaction "after a fair and impartial trial" that the three were guilty and ordered them to leave the state "as soon as they could arrange their business."
According to the *Texas Ranger,* Clock admitted his guilt and had been heard
to predict that within three years the abolitionists would rule Texas. The paper
concluded with what may have been the most damning evidence against him:
"Old man Clock had been seen to take negroes in his room and, with closed
doors, to converse with them."[86]

In view of these reports of abolitionist activity and rebellious slaves, it was
small wonder that even a hint of suspicious actions on the part of blacks was
enough to elicit dreadful fears in the minds of whites. Instead of using their
influence to allay such fears, the newspapers incited them. In late June, for example, next to the image of a pointing finger, the editor of the La Grange *True
Issue* wrote, "We saw a negro man practicing pistol shooting, on Sunday evening, above our residence. What is in the wind?"[87]

As if fears of abolitionist-inspired violence were not enough to keep anxiety levels high, a drought of unprecedented severity descended upon the state
in the spring and summer of 1860. The drought was by no means confined to
the Lone Star State; it plagued much of the rest of the South as well. A resident
of Nashville, Tennessee, wrote to a friend in Texas that the summer had been
"the longest, hottest, driest and altogether, the most disagreeable one I ever
passed North or South." Crops in the Volunteer State had suffered greatly, the
correspondent said, "giving the farmers and planters a glorious opportunity to
grumble, which they have improved to the utmost."[88] One historian has written that the summer of 1860 was "the hottest and driest that most southerners
could remember."[89] Citing a newspaper report from Georgia on the dire effects
of the drought in that state, the San Augustine *Red Land Express* said that the
story was a reminder "that Texas is not the only part of the country that has
suffered from the dreadful effects of the great drouth of 1860."[90]

86. Brenham *Texas Ranger,* July 20, 1860, clipped in Austin *Texas State Gazette,* July 28.

87. La Grange *True Issue,* June 21, 1860.

88. M. O. Huston to Oscar M. Addison, November 20, Addison Papers, Barker Texas History
Center Archives, University of Texas, Austin, Texas.

89. William L. Barney, *The Secessionist Impulse: Alabama and Mississippi in 1860* (Princeton,
N.J., 1974), 153–163.

90. Columbus *Times,* n.d., quoted in San Augustine *Red Land Express,* August 11, 1860. For
interesting anecdotes of the dramatic effects of the drought in South Carolina and Alabama, see
New Orleans (La.) *Picayune,* July 26, 1860.

Nevertheless, although other southern states also suffered from the dry, hot summer, Texas fared the worst by far. Since the last significant rain had fallen in April, by early June crops and livestock already were suffering. As early as June 8, a farmer in deep East Texas wrote: "Times are hard and provisions Scarce. And it is verry dry at this time and if it dont rain Shortly there will be nothing made in this country."[91] Another farmer in the same section of the state glumly confided to a friend that he had sold his cows for fear they would die of thirst, and he further lamented that his corn was in such bad shape that it would not even produce enough to make bread.[92] In late June, a newspaper in La Grange, between Houston and San Antonio, said that there had been no rain there since April 22 and added: "Our corn crops are nearly all burned up, cotton languishing, grass scorched and drying, trees drooping and dying, and everything is suffering or perishing for rain and water."[93]

Things only worsened in July, when temperatures peaked and the parched land became even more arid. Existing water supplies evaporated at an alarming rate in the blistering sun. C. B. Moore, of Collin County, noted in his diary that the water level in his cistern had fallen a full five inches in the second week of July alone.[94] The persistent dearth of moisture caused a sense of desperation, as food supplies ran low and the shortages sent prices soaring. In late July, the San Augustine *Red Land Express* wrote that the crops in East Texas were "ruinously bad, and destitution and want seem to stare the people in the face. . . . Distressing accounts reach us from all quarters, and it really seems that we are on the verge of a 'breadless crisis.'"[95] Conditions had become so bad by mid-July that some farmers considered giving up and going elsewhere. The San Antonio *Ledger and Texan* said, "We regret to learn through a letter from San Saba that there is no hope of a crop in that section this season. . . .The farmers are quite dispirited and many of them speak of leaving."[96]

The drought peaked in July, but its economic effects would be felt long after the rains had returned in late August. In November, a resident of Newton County

91. Lewis Jordan, Jasper, to Thomas B. Huling, Lampasas, June 8, 1860, Huling Papers, Barker Texas History Center Archives, University of Texas, Austin, Texas.

92. Willis West, Burr's Ferry, to Thomas B. Huling, Lampasas, June 21, 1860, Huling Papers, Barker Texas History Center Archives, University of Texas, Austin, Texas.

93. La Grange *True Issue,* June 28, 1860.

94. C. B. Moore Diary, July 15, 1860, Moore Papers, University of North Texas Library, Denton, Texas.

95. San Augustine *Red Land Express,* July 28, 1860.

96. San Antonio *Ledger and Texan,* July 17, 1860.

wrote, "Many of us are on Starvation. Notwithstanding, provisions are high and the poor have no money to buy with. Many of us are actually suffering."[97] Writing about the same time, another farmer from the same region of Texas took a more stoic approach: "Jasper County had one of Daniel Webster's blasts put on it this summer and how we are to live or work through for another year god only knows, but if we cant live we can die."[98]

Adding to the misery caused by a lack of rain was a scorching heat wave that accompanied and intensified the drought. The lack of rain, unrelenting heat, and high southwesterly winds off the Mexican desert threatened to make the entire state a dust bowl. The temperature continued to climb as spring gave way to summer, and by early July many found it almost impossible to carry on their normal activities. Years later, those who had lived through the summer of 1860 still held vivid recollections of the experience. S. B. Barron, a resident of Rusk, wrote, "It was the hottest summer ever known in Texas, the temperature in July running up to 112 degrees in the shade."[99] Z. N. Morrell said that anyone who had lived in Texas in the summer of 1860 would never forget the drought and heat: "The atmosphere, at one time, felt very much as though it issued from an oven." In retrospect, Morrell, a minister, thought the awful drought and heat wave was God's way of preparing Texans for the fiery hell of the war.[100]

The oppressive heat reached a peak at the beginning of the second week of July, and the whole state remained distressingly hot for the remainder of that month. Reports indicated that Saturday and Sunday, July 7 and 8, was the hottest two-day period of the summer. Writing on that Saturday from Mound City, east of Waco, a man said that even as he was writing his wife was cooking eggs on the stones of his front porch, and he compared the effect of the blistering south wind to "heat . . . from a burning building."[101] Writing on the same day from Fort Scott, west of Austin, another correspondent said that the birds were trying to fly into houses to escape a wind that was "more like flames from a

97. R. C. Ballams, Beckwith, to Thomas B. Huling, Lampasas, November 20, 1860, Huling Papers, Barker Texas History Center Archives, University of Texas, Austin, Texas.

98. John Hamilton, Jasper, to Thomas B. Huling, Lampasas, November 17, 1860, Huling Papers, Barker Texas History Center Archives, University of Texas, Austin, Texas.

99. S. B. Barron, *The Lone Star Defenders: A Chronicle of the Third Texas Cavalry, Ross Brigade* (New York, 1908), 16.

100. Z. N. Morrell, *Flowers and Fruits from the Wilderness; or, Thirty-Six Years in Texas and Two Winters in Honduras* (Boston, 1872), 357–358.

101. Letter of an unidentified correspondent, July 7, Macon (Ga.) *Daily Telegraph*, August 7, 1860.

burning prairie than any comparison that now serves me."[102]A resident of Long Point, east of Austin, later wrote to the New Orleans *Picayune* that he had kept a record of the high temperatures during the summer, and he confirmed that July was the hottest month, exceeding 100 degrees or higher on nineteen days, with highs for the thirty-one days averaging 101. The hottest day in Long Point was July 7, when the temperature reached 108.[103]

As hot as it was in Central Texas. it was even worse in North Texas. On July 12 a resident of Honey Grove, a small town northeast of Dallas, wrote that during the previous week the wind "has been the hottest I ever saw." He went on to say that the temperature had risen as high as 110 degrees, and the conditions had been so debilitating "even the Negroes" had been unable to work.[104] The Clarksville *Northern Standard* confirmed the Honey Grove resident's report, stating that the first week in July saw temperatures rise to unprecedented levels in North Texas. "The breeze which has passed over us from the South has been hot—like a Sirocco, and seemed to wilt the leaves of garden vegetation, and dry up the leaves of trees."[105]

Not surprisingly, the excruciating heat affected dispositions. This was true not only in Texas, and one historian has suggested that hardships caused by the high heat and drought in Alabama and Mississippi added to the tension caused by politics in those states.[106] This was probably true of the rest of the Lower South as well; a distinguished historian of the Civil War wrote: "Even the weather during the summer of 1860 became a part of the political climate: a severe drought and prolonged heat wave withered southern crops and drove nerves beyond the point of endurance."[107]

There are indications that the extreme weather conditions added to the edginess that Texans were feeling. Wiley Donathan, of Fayetteville, Texas, admitted to his brother that the blistering south winds had put him in "bad spirits."[108]

102. Letter of "Uncle Ben Brantley," July 7, 1860, Augusta (Ga.) *Chronicle and Sentinel,* n.d., clipped in Macon (Ga.) *Daily Telegraph,* August 7, 1860.

103. New Orleans (La.) *Daily Picayune,* September 14, 1860.

104. H. S. Moore to C. B. Moore, July 12, 1860, Moore Papers (letters), University of North Texas Library, Denton, Texas.

105. Clarksville *Northern Standard,* July 14, 1860. A sirocco is an extremely hot wind that frequently sweeps over the deserts of North Africa.

106. Barney, *The Secessionist Impulse,* 153–163.

107. James M. McPherson, *Battle Cry of Freedom* (New York, 1988), 228.

108. Wiley F. Donathan, Fayetteville, Texas, to his brother in Mississippi, July 20, 1860, Donathan Family Correspondence, Texas State Archives, Austin, Texas.

The San Augustine *Red Land Express* noted that everyone in its community had been put in a bad mood by the continuing hot, dry spell, and added, "If it was not for the occasional surprise parties and balls, and the election excitement, we very much fear our people would die of *ennui*."[109]

109. San Augustine *Red Land Express,* August 4, 1860. In accounting for the aggressive behavior of vigilantes during the slave panic of 1860, historians may have overlooked the effect of heat in provoking violence. Numerous psychologists have documented the increased aggressiveness of people subjected to high temperatures. For a summary of this scholarship, see William Griffitt and Russell Veitch, "Hot and Crowded: Influences of Population Density and Temperature on Interpersonal Affective Behavior," *Journal of Personality and Social Psychology* 17 (1971): 92–98. Also, in its study of the "civil disorders" of 1967, the Kerner Commission noted that a great majority of the riots occurred in mid-summer and concluded: "In most instances, the temperature during the day on which violence first erupted was quite high." That may be why the riots "occurred with increasing frequency as summer approached and tapered off as it waned" (Kerner Commission, *Report of the National Advisory Commission on Civil Disorders* [New York, 1968], 114, 123).

CHAPTER TWO

RED TORCH OVER OUR LAND

Sunday, July 8, 1860, dawned especially hot on the dusty prairies and rolling hills of northern and eastern Texas. By noon the temperature already stood at the century mark in many communities. Perhaps the hottest spot in the state was Marshall, where before the sun would spend itself the mercury would reach 115½ degrees in the shade. The Marshall *Texas Republican* later charted the high temperatures for July, and its records indicate that July 8 was easily the hottest day of that torrid month.[1] In Camden, Arkansas, northeast of Marshall, a planter noted in his diary that day that the temperature there had risen to 109 degrees and declared that it had been the "hottest day ever known in this country."[2]

Farther west, in Dallas, the early afternoon reading was variously reported at between 106 and 110. One pioneer Dallasite, who did not know the high temperature for that date, still believed many years later that the July 8 was "the hottest day we have ever had in this latitude." By midday, most of the 678 residents of the young Trinity River town had taken refuge in their houses. After finishing Sunday dinner, many of them reclined in various states of dishabille in an effort to reduce their discomfort from the sweltering heat. At about 1:30 P.M. the shrill cry of "Fire!" pierced the air, and the sleepy village bolted from its Sabbath siesta. The townspeople, some of them only half-clothed, rushed into the streets looking for the smoke that would pinpoint the danger. What they saw filled them with horror, for down on Commerce Street, near the town

1. Marshall *Texas Republican*, August 11, 1860.

2. Robert F. Kellan Diary, July 8, 1860, microfilm copy of original, General Microfilm Collection, Arkansas Historical Commission, Little Rock, Arkansas.

square, great billows of smoke rolled skyward from Wallace Peak's new drug-store. Flames had already enveloped the two-story frame structure and had spread northward, first to Smith's warehouse, then on to the office of the Dallas *Herald*. Within minutes the whole business section was an inferno.

There was little question of extinguishing the blaze. The drought had ren-dered the predominantly wooden structures tinder dry, and they burned with astonishing speed. Town officials had not yet made provision for combating fires—the community had only incorporated four years earlier—but even had they done so, the rapid spread of the conflagration probably would have ren-dered futile even the most determined efforts to save the business houses that lay in the path of the blaze. Fanned by the high winds, the flames seemed to leap from building to building, said the editor of the Dallas *Herald,* in some cases igniting structures that "were almost one hundred yards in advance of the main blaze."[3]

Echoing the *Herald*'s description, Mrs. Addie K. McDermett later recalled that the fire spread so rapidly that it seemed to break out simultaneously in a dozen places.[4] Most of the able-bodied citizens nevertheless worked desperately to salvage merchandise from doomed stores and personal belongings from threatened homes. Even in these efforts many were frustrated, since blowing sparks from the advancing flames in several instances set fire to property that had been dragged to apparent safety in the streets.[5] The intense heat also took a heavy toll on the salvagers, many of whom succumbed to heat prostration.[6] Emma Baird Brown was a young girl at the time of the fire, but she remem-bered vividly the heat, fear, and excitement that all Dallasites felt that day. With her mother and young brothers and sisters she watched anxiously from the porch of her home on the northwest corner of Houston and Elm streets and later recalled seeing "a heavy pall that cut off the rays of the sun, a licking flame that mounted high and destroyed all within its grasp."[7]

In less than two hours the fire in Dallas had run its course, leaving every building on the western and northern sides of the square, and half of those on the eastern side, in charred ruins. The town's hotels, shops, stores, ware-houses, lawyers' and doctors' offices, and the newspaper office—some eighteen

3. Dallas *Herald,* "Extra," July 11, 1860. Pryor may have borrowed the use of another journal's press to produce his "extra," which was more like a flyer than a full-sized newspaper.

4. "Reminiscences of Mrs. Addie K. McDermett," Dallas *Morning News,* June 21, 1925.

5. Dallas *Herald,* "Extra," July 11, 1860.

6. "Reminiscences of Mrs. Addie K. McDermett," Dallas *Morning News,* June 21, 1925.

7. Quoted in *Memorial and Biographical History of Dallas County* (Chicago, 1892), 75.

buildings in all—were destroyed.[8] For all practical purposes the flames had consumed the entire business section of the town; damage was estimated at $300,000. Dallas nevertheless was apparently lucky on one count—in spite of the fire's rapid spread and the blistering heat at the height of the conflagration, no fatalities were reported.

At about 3:00 P.M., just as the flames had begun to die away in Dallas, the same dreaded alarm sounded in Denton, another small town about forty miles to the north. There, fire broke out in the counting room of James M. Smoot's general store, which occupied the southeast corner of the town square. The same stiff southwesterly breeze that had abetted the destruction of Dallas quickly spread the flames to other buildings. Twenty-five kegs of powder exploded in one store, showering the square with burning debris and setting new fires.[9] There were only a few people on or around the square when the fire broke out, and although these and other citizens were quickly organized into a fire-fighting force of sorts, a shortage of water threatened to doom all efforts to control the blaze. "But the ladies (God bless them!) came to the rescue," wrote one participant, "and notwithstanding the almost intolerable heat of the sun, soon brought sufficient water to save several buildings which we had almost given up to destruction."[10] Thus Denton was more fortunate than Dallas. Although the town suffered extensive damage, particularly to the west side of the square, the total loss amounted to less than $100,000.[11]

Dallas and Denton experienced the most serious fires in North Texas on that fateful July 8, but they were not the only towns to be struck by flames. Even as fire razed much of Dallas and a portion of Denton, yet another blaze destroyed a store in Pilot Point, a tiny burg about fifteen miles northeast of Denton. Co-incidentally, James Smoot, in whose store the Denton fire had started, was also a co-owner of the ill-fated business house in Pilot Point. Taken together, the unlucky merchant's losses came to an estimated $60,000. Meanwhile, about forty-five miles south of Dallas, in Ellis County, the little village of Milford went up in flames. Still other fires reportedly did lesser amounts of damage in Ladonia, Honey Grove, and Blackjack Grove, all of which were east or northeast

---

8. Charles R. Pryor, Dallas, to E. H. Cushing, Houston, July 9, 1860, Houston *Telegraph,* July 14, 1860. For a slightly different list of destroyed structures, see Galveston *Texas Christian Advocate,* July 19, 1860.

9. Otis G. Welch, Denton, to E. H. Cushing, Houston, July 9, 1860, Houston *Telegraph,* July 21, 1860.

10. Ibid.

11. Ibid.

of Dallas. In addition, flames destroyed a flour mill in Collin County, north of Dallas, and citizens put out a house fire in Waxahachie, twenty-five miles south of Dallas, before the flames could destroy the structure. Other fires were said to have occurred at Sulphur Springs, in Hopkins County, Mount Pisgah, in Navarro County, and Fort Worth. All of this followed by one day a disastrous fire that had destroyed eight buildings in Fort Belknap, about seventy-five miles west of Dallas.[12]

In one twenty-four-hour period, more than a dozen fires (a few of them said to be devastating) were reported within a seventy-five-mile radius of Dallas. Yet there were few outward indications that the citizens of North Texas suspected arson. Every one of the confirmed fires had broken out in broad daylight—indeed during the hottest part of the day—not at night, when arsonists would have had the best chance to remain undetected. A combination of the unprecedented heat and the presence in many of the affected communities of the relatively new, highly unstable phosphorous matches initially provided most of the shocked citizens of northern Texas with a satisfactory explanation of the fiery outbreaks. These "prairie matches," as they were called, had only recently made their appearance in Texas stores, and their dangerous properties—especially when they were exposed to excessive heat—were not fully known. Consequently, many people failed to take proper precautions when storing them.[13]

Reporting the fire in Dallas, a newspaper in a neighboring county attributed it either to the "spontaneous combustion of 'prairie matches' or rats gnawing them."[14] The fire in DuPree's store in Ladonia, said the Clarksville *Northern Standard,* was "believed to have ignited from combustion of matches, resulting from the heated atmosphere." The fires in Milford and Honey Grove had also resulted from the heat-induced ignition of matches, added the *Standard.*[15] Writing in his diary a week after the fiery events of July 8, a Collin County farmer said that there was considerable excitement over the fires in the surrounding communities, but he added: "It is now supposed to have been caused by the spontaneous combustion of prairie matches."[16]

12. Ibid.; Bonham *Era,* July 17, 1860; Galveston *Civilian and Gazette,* July 31, 1860; Galveston *News,* July 24, 1860.

13. Rupert N. Richardson, *The Frontier of Northwest Texas, 1846 to 1876; Advance and Defense by the Pioneer Settlers of the Cross Timbers and Plains* (Glendale, Calif., 1963), 223. See the epilogue for a discussion of the properties of these early phosphorous matches.

14. Corsicana *Navarro Express,* July 14, 1860.

15. Clarksville *Northern Standard,* July 14, 1860.

16. C. B. Moore Diary, July 16, 1860, Moore Papers, University of North Texas Library, Denton, Texas.

The first reports from Dallas, the most devastated of the damaged towns, similarly gave little indication that anyone initially suspected foul play. The day after the holocaust Charles Pryor, the twenty-eight-year-old editor of the Dallas *Herald,* wrote of the disaster to his friend, E. H. Cushing, editor of the Houston *Telegraph.* A bachelor who lived and worked in his newspaper's office, Pryor told his friend that he was taking a nap when the fire broke out. Since the building that housed the *Herald* was one of the first to catch fire, the young journalist barely had time to grab an armful of his books and flee to safety. The flames consumed everything else, including four presses and even the editor's clothes. "We barely escaped with our lives—some like myself, without clothes, boots, shoes or anything else," wrote Pryor, who begged: "If you have an old coat, an old shoe or shirt, send it to your confrere." Despite his temporary setback, Pryor was far from discouraged; he told the Houston editor that he already had ordered a new press and expected to be publishing again within six weeks.[17]

Pryor's optimism was echoed in two letters written by John W. Swindells, publisher of the *Herald.* The first of these, dated July 10, went to Charles De-Morse, editor-publisher of the Clarksville *Northern Standard.* The Dallas fire, wrote Swindells, was "the most appalling event that has ever visited Dallas"; nevertheless, he said, most merchants had already begun taking steps to rebuild.[18] In a letter to E. H. Cushing, written the next day, Swindells reported that new fires on Monday, July 10, had destroyed two residences near Dallas, and he also mentioned that news had arrived of the fire in Denton. Still, there was no hint of suspicion that arsonists had been responsible for any of the fires; his emphasis was on the positive. He had ordered "an entire new office," Swindells said, and although his timetable was not quite as sanguine as that of his young editor, he predicted that he would be publishing again within two or three months.[19]

17. Pryor to Cushing, July 9, 1860, Houston *Telegraph,* July 14, 1860. A native of Virginia who moved to Dallas in 1850, Pryor received a medical degree from the University of Virginia. His brother Samuel was elected the first mayor of Dallas in 1856. Charles Pryor contributed articles to the *Herald* during the 1850s, and when the editor/publisher died in 1859 he became the editor of that journal and held that position until 1861, when he received an appointment as secretary of state in the Confederate state of Texas. He served in that post until the end of the Civil War. During his later years, Pryor appears to have practiced medicine in Dallas, although there is little mention of him in the available sources (*Handbook of Texas Online,* s.v., www.tsha.utexas.edu/handbook/online/articles/PP/fpr16.html [accessed January 8, 2007]).

18. John W. Swindells, Dallas, to Charles DeMorse, Clarksville, July 10, 1860, Clarksville *Northern Standard,* July 14, 1860.

19. Swindells to Cushing, July 11, 1860, Houston *Weekly Telegraph,* July 24, 1860.

Pryor, too, had failed to mention any suspicion of arson in his letter of July 9 to Cushing, but in another letter penned on the same day the young editor revealed that at least the possibility already had crossed his mind. Writing to John Marshall, editor of the Austin *Texas State Gazette*, Pryor said: "It is not known whether it was the work of an incendiary or not."[20] Otis G. Welch of Denton was less cautious about speculating on the possibility of foul play. In a long letter to Cushing, also written on July 9, Welch described the fires of Denton and Pilot Point—he apparently had not yet heard of the other fires—and concluded: "How the two fires originated at the same time in the two towns is wrapped in mystery, though we have but little doubt that they must be the work of an incendiary."[21]

Although the early letters of Swindells and Pryor had failed to reveal it, Welch's inclination to attribute the fires in Denton and Pilot Point to incendiaries clearly was already shared by many Dallasites who sought to account for their own disaster. District Judge Nat M. Burford, who lived in Dallas, had held court in Waxahachie during the week of the fire. He adjourned the session on Saturday, July 7, and started home, a distance of about thirty miles; however, he did not arrive in Dallas until Monday, the day after the fire. The judge was shocked to find most of the town's business section in smoldering ruins. Many years later, Burford still remembered the tension that permeated the town. "I remember that when I got to town everything was quiet. It was almost a death-like stillness. People talked in whispers, but they were determined looking. They were desperate. They gathered in groups and they were sure that nothing was said in the presence of anybody who was not known to be with them."[22]

The tense quiet continued for the next two days. Then, on Thursday, July 12, a fire damaged some outbuildings on Crill Miller's farm. Accounts differ as to how much damage was done, but they tend to agree generally on what happened next. Miller, a farmer who lived five miles west of Dallas, was visiting his father, who lived nearby at the time of the fire. He received word of the disaster from a young male slave named Bruce, who according to one account "came running in crying and saying: 'Oh Mars Crill, three white men came and made me fetch them some water and then they sot fire to the barn and the house.'" Unsatisfied with Bruce's account, Miller and "a committee of white men" reportedly threatened to kill the young black if he did not tell them who had burned the buildings, and they warned him that if he died with a lie on his lips,

20. Pryor to Marshall, July 9, 1860, Austin *Texas State Gazette*, July 14, 1860.

21. Welch to Cushing, July 9, 1860, Houston *Telegraph*, July 24, 1860.

22. "Judge Nat M. Burford's Version," Dallas *Morning News*, July 10, 1892.

he would surely burn in hell. Apparently convinced that he had better tell his inquisitors what they seemed determined to hear, the terrified Bruce reportedly confessed that it was he who had fired Miller's place, but he insisted that he had been induced to do so by another slave. Another source identified the second slave as "Spence," who reportedly paid Bruce a dollar to set the blaze.[23]

This "confession" led to an intensive interrogation of the blacks, first on Miller's farm and then on the other farms throughout the county. The outlines of an alleged abolitionist plot soon began to reach an alarmed populace. On July 16—four days after the fire on Miller's farm and eight days after Dallas had burned—Charles Pryor wrote excitedly to John Marshall of the *Texas State Gazette* that an exhaustive "examination" of the black suspects had "elicited" details of a far-reaching abolitionist conspiracy. According to Pryor, Solomon McKinney and William Blunt, the two preachers whom Dallasites had expelled the previous year for alleged abolitionism, had decided to take vengeance upon their persecutors. The plan was "to devastate with fire and assassination, the whole of Northern Texas," and after they had reduced the targeted region to a state of helplessness, they would signal a prearranged "general revolt of the slaves, aided by the white men of the North in our midst." The conspirators hoped to prepare North Texas for the general uprising—scheduled for August 6, the date of the state elections—by rendering the people defenseless and reducing them to starvation. In pursuit of these goals, they planned to burn the barns of the area, thereby destroying the recently harvested grain, and set fire to the stores, by which means they would not only destroy food and other necessities, but also powder and lead that whites otherwise might use to defend themselves. As if these revelations were not frightening enough, after the burnings had been successfully carried out, "assistance was expected from the Indians and Abolitionists." Concluding his letter to Marshall, Pryor said: "I write in haste, we sleep upon our arms, and the whole country is deeply excited."[24]

23. "First Account of an Old Settler in Dallas," Dallas *Morning News*, July 10, 1892. The "old settler" asserted that Miller's house and barn had burned down; however, he was eighty-five at the time he was interviewed and admitted "my memory is somewhat defective." Another Dallasite, W. P. Overton, who was seventy-one in 1892, but, according to the interviewer, still retained "a light step, lithe form and clear blue eyes," denied this report, saying: "Crill Miller's house was not burned, but his wheat stacks and cribs were burned." According to Overton, an effort had indeed been made to burn the house by placing a "chunk of fire" on a bed, "but when the mattress was turned back it smothered the fire out and the house did not burn" ("Reminiscence of W. P. Overton," *Memorial and Biographical History of Dallas County*, 177).

24. Pryor to Marshall, July 16, 1860, Austin *Texas State Gazette*, August 4, 1860. The young editor was closely allied with the Runnels-Wigfall-Marshall wing of the Democratic party, and

The Dallas editor penned a second lengthy letter to L. C. DeLisle, editor of the Bonham *Era*. This missive was in all the essentials similar to the other. The abolitionist scheme was widespread and complex, Pryor declared: "Their sphere of operations is districted and subdistricted, giving to each division a close supervision by one energetic white man who controls the Negroes as his subordinates." It was, the editor warned, nothing less than "a regular invasion and a real war," and he begged DeLisle to sound the call to arms: "You and all Bonham are in as much danger as we are. Be on your guard, and make these facts known by issuing extras to be sent in every direction. All business has ceased and the country is terribly excited."[25]

More than a week elapsed before additional details of the plot reached the outside world. In the interim, the citizens of Dallas tried to learn everything they could about the reported conspiracy, which, they were now convinced, had led to the destruction of their town and now threatened their very lives. They formed a vigilance committee to carry out the investigation, and the elected officials of the town and county readily deferred to this extra-legal body. As the tone of Pryor's two letters suggests, a state of near hysteria swept Dallas during that period, and the vigilance committee was at least as affected by the climate of irrationality as the rest of the community. The committee worked feverishly during the week following Pryor's first sensational revelations. By July 21 it had arrested and "examined" nearly one hundred blacks, who added some fearful details to the earlier accounts.

The plot was even more widespread and organized than was first thought, Pryor wrote in a letter to E. H. Cushing. The abolitionists had targeted all of North Texas, assigning a white "supervisor" to each county, then subdividing each county into "districts," which in turn were placed under "sub-agents" who

---

his emotional report in this letter and his subsequent missives on the Dallas "plot" clearly demonstrated his intention to arouse emotions that could be used to the advantage of the fire-eaters. His approach in this correspondence was typical of Pryor's reporting style, which a generation later would be called "yellow journalism." In the year preceding the Texas Troubles, Pryor filled his paper with lurid accounts of such "hot" topics as Mexican banditry on the Rio Grande and the latest Indian atrocities on the frontier. He especially embellished every report of slave violence, which he usually associated with an abolitionist-Republican plot to destroy slavery. The alleged slave insurrection in Dallas was but the final realization of his dark expectation of a John Brown-type assault upon Texas. An historian who examined the contents of the *Herald* in the months before the Dallas fire wrote: "All year long, Pryor seemingly anticipated a racial conflagration prompted by Northern outsiders" (Phillips, "White Violence, Hegemony and Slave Rebellion in Dallas, Texas," 25, 27).

25. Pryor to DeLisle, July 15, 1860, Bonham *Era*, July 17, 1860.

controlled the blacks in their areas and "by whom the firing was to be done." Moreover, it was now revealed that after the fires were set, "many of our most prominent citizens were singled out for assassination whenever they made their escape from their burning homes." Poison was to be added to the wells, presumably to take care of those who escaped the arsonists and assassins. The letter also included news of a sort that always struck the most sensitive racial nerves of white southerners and without which no southern slave panic would have been complete: While marking the white men and older white women for death, the black fiends would distribute the comely white females among themselves to gratify their bestial appetites. "They had even gone so far as to designate their choice, and certain ladies had already been selected as the victims of these misguided monsters." Pryor nevertheless made it clear in his conclusion that vengeance and lust were only incidental to the larger goal, which was nothing less than revolution: "JOHN BROWN and his few followers were *fools,* compared with the men engaged in this affair. Developments of the most alarming character and calculated to shake our Government to its very centre, are looked for. In haste, P."[26]

Pryor's letters to editors Marshall, DeLisle, and Cushing were widely reprinted, first in Texas,[27] and then throughout the South.[28] With the memory of John Brown's foray into Virginia not yet a year old, this new story of abolitionist treachery sent a thrill of horror through the hearts of southerners. The feeling was naturally most intense in Texas, where white citizens in every community wondered whether they, like the residents of Dallas, were marked for extermination by diabolical abolitionists and their black minions. The growing number of reports (many of them patently false) that other Texas towns had gone up in flames intensified this foreboding. Newspapers seized upon any report of a fire, however skimpy the details or dubious the source, and printed it as though it

26. Pryor to Cushing, July 21, 1860, Houston *Weekly Telegraph,* July 31, 1860. Cushing had acquired the *Telegraph* in 1856 and served as editor/publisher for the next thirteen years. He was a logical recipient of one of Pryor's letters, since his paper was one of the most influential southern rights journals in the state and Cushing could be counted upon to give the missive wide distribution. For a brief biography of Cushing, see *Handbook of Texas Online,* s.v., www.tsha.utexas.edu/handbook/online/articles/CC/fcu34.html (accessed July 18, 2006).

27. For examples of other Texas journals carrying one or more of Pryor's letters, see: Marshall *Texas Republican,* August 11, 1860; San Augustine *Red Land Express,* August 11, 1860; Houston *Telegraph,* August 16, 1860; Tyler *Reporter,* August 7, 1860; Corsicana *Navarro Express,* August 11, 1860; San Antonio *Ledger and Texan,* July 28, 1860.

28. See chapter 4 for a partial listing of papers outside Texas that carried at least one of Pryor's letters.

were true. In the weeks following publication of Pryor's letters to the *Era, Texas State Gazette,* and *Telegraph,* the press spawned spurious reports that at least a dozen other towns in northern and eastern Texas had burned to the ground. Within a month, terrified Texans variously read of the total destruction of such communities as Bonham, Birdville, Mount Vernon, Daingerfield, Rusk, Nacogdoches, Tyler, Dresden, Quitman, Liberty, McKinney, and Belleview.[29]

Some of these fallacious reports carried details that made them seem more believable than they might otherwise have been. For example, one account declared that one of the incendiaries who had allegedly helped to destroy Mount Vernon had already paid the ultimate penalty on the gallows. Similarly, the Marshall *Texas Republican* solemnly revealed that the discovery of a plot in Titus County had led to the hanging of several blacks and a white man. Other baseless rumors were made to seem credible by the certainty with which editors reported them. Thus, the Tyler *Reporter* on August 8 said that it had received "authentic information" (which it did not specify) that Daingerfield "was totally destroyed by fire on Sunday night."[30] Adding to the impact of such reports was the failure of most Texas papers to retract the stories once their inaccuracy had become known. The general impression therefore remained that many towns had been reduced to ashes.

Other reports indicated that some communities had barely escaped the incendiary's torch. A dispatch from Fairfield said that a watchman in that town had detected a "daring scoundrel" about to set fire "to the thickest of the business part of town." The alert official reportedly fired upon the would-be arsonist with a double-barreled shotgun, causing him to drop "an armful of shavings and a number of matches and flee."[31] In San Augustine a fire in an old, abandoned building on one side of town drew many townspeople to the site. Because there were "fresh foot prints" near the burning structure, it was somehow determined that incendiaries were responsible. Since the old building obviously could not have been the primary objective, the citizens reasoned that the arsonists must have burned it to draw the people from the center of town

29. Washington (D.C.) *Daily National Intelligencer,* September 3, 1860; Marshall *Texas Republican,* August 11, 1860; Tyler *Reporter,* August 8, 1860, clipped in Austin *Texas State Gazette,* August 25, 1860.

30. Marshall Texas Republican, August 11, 1860; Tyler *Reporter,* August 8, 1860, clipped in Austin *Texas State Gazette,* August 25, 1860.

31. Fairfield *Pioneer,* August 3, 1860, clipped in San Antonio *Daily Ledger and Texan,* August 15, 1860.

"so as to enable them to do more of their hellish work," presumably by setting fire to the business section. The townspeople were convinced that their quick thinking and the subsequent restoration of watchfulness had foiled the plan of the abolitionists. As proof, they pointed out that no attempts had been made to ignite other buildings.[32]

Still other alleged abolitionist schemes to burn, pillage, and murder were supposedly frustrated by a vigilant citizenry in such towns as Waxahachie, Sulphur Springs, Lancaster, Athens, Independence, Georgetown, Bastrop, and Austin. According to a report from Waxahachie, a black woman belonging to "Mr. Marchbanks" had revealed that a black man was to burn the town on Sunday, July 8, the day of the Dallas and Denton fires. Just as the would-be incendiary was about to carry out his assignment, however, a box of matches had accidentally caught fire in Oldham's general store, and "the alarm so frightened the Negro that he fled the town." Subsequently the determined black reportedly had returned to carry out his instructions, but before he could do so another African American cautioned him that the plot in Dallas had been discovered, "and they were hanging all the negroes, and warned him to drop the matter. This saved Waxahachie."[33] The Austin *Texas State Gazette* said that the citizens of Bastrop foiled a planned insurrection in that community on Election Day, August 6, after blacks aroused suspicion "from their conduct." Subsequently, an inspection of the slave cabins reportedly revealed "large quantities of arms and ammunition."[34] This report may have been suspect, however, since there were no reports of arrests or punishment, and the next month a member of the local vigilance committee's executive council reported that the vigilantes had not hanged anyone.[35]

The reports from Austin seemed especially shocking. The fright in the capital may have originated in a report by a Mrs. Bennett, who said that on the evening of July 21 she had seen a "sheet of flame" shoot from a neighbor's house. Writing to a friend in Houston, Mrs. Bennett said that on the next day, July 22, attempts were made to burn no fewer than twenty-five of the principal buildings of the city, including the capitol. Fortunately, she said, in every instance the flames were discovered and extinguished before any "serious damage" had been

32. San Augustine *Red Land Express,* August 25, 1860.

33. Houston *Weekly Telegraph,* July 31, 1860.

34. Austin *Texas State Gazette,* August 18, 1860, quoted in Kenneth Kesselus, *History of Bastrop County, Texas, 1846–1865* (Austin, 1987), 173.

35. Kesselus, *History of Bastrop County,* 173.

done. According to the same correspondent, the people of Austin had taken up arms and were intensely excited.[36]

Only quick, decisive action by Austin's officials prevented a full-fledged panic in the city. A search of the slave quarters, ordered by the mayor, reportedly turned up caches of powder, bullets, muskets, knives, and other weapons, which presumably were to have been used in some sort of uprising. Of course the leaders of the conspiracy, "who were doubtless white men," had fled before they could be apprehended. Although no real evidence of a plot for the capitol city ever materialized, some of Austin's citizens clearly took the rumors seriously, at least for a while. It was even alleged that some of the blacks implicated in the "conspiracy" belonged to Lieutenant Governor Edward Clark.[37]

In addition to widespread reports that abolitionists had plotted the doom of whole towns, there were numerous allegations that incendiaries had burned, or tried to burn, individual homes, barns, mills, and business houses. Indeed, whenever any structure was reported to have burned in the weeks following Pryor's exposé of the Dallas conspiracy, citizens almost reflexively blamed arsonists. This was so even though specific evidence was seldom cited indicating that the blaze might have been manmade. In such cases the press would simply report that "the evidence" indicated that an arsonist was responsible. For example, when a fire occurred in a business firm in Seguin, a newspaper reporting the story said simply that "all the collected information goes clearly to establish the fact that the burning was the work of an incendiary."[38] And when George Glasscock's steam mill burned near Austin, a local paper reported that the owner was "satisfied" that an arsonist had set the fire.[39] H. A. Hamner, editor of the Jacksboro White Man, demonstrated this general tendency to attribute all fires to arsonists in a letter that he penned to the Austin Texas State Gazette on July 30: "My printing office and entire fixtures were consumed by fire last night—the work of an incendiary, beyond the possibility of a doubt."[40] On August 6—the day of the expected "rising"—a resident of Cedar Creek,

36. Houston *Weekly Telegraph,* August 31, 1860. See also Lack, "Slavery and Vigilantism in Austin, Texas," 17–18.

37. Galveston *News,* n.d., clipped in San Augustine *Red Land Express,* August 18, 1860.

38. Seguin *Mercury,* n.d., clipped in Austin *Texas State Gazette,* September 1, 1860.

39. Austin *Texas State Gazette,* July 28, 1860.

40. H. A. Hamner to John Marshall, July 30, 1860, Austin *Texas State Gazette,* n.d., clipped in San Antonio *Daily Herald,* August 14, 1860. For still other reported incidents of alleged arson in Coryell, Houston, Lamar, and Williamson counties, see Belton *Democrat,* August 11, 1860, clipped in St. Louis *Daily Missouri Republican,* August 23, 1860; Paris *Press,* July 21, 1860, clipped in Austin *Texas State Gazette,* July 28, 1860.

southeast of Austin, said that someone had set fire to his house, and his slaves were the suspected arsonists; but the newspaper reporting the incident said: "It is probable, however, that it may have been done by abolitionists."[41]

Another essential component of the plan, as outlined by Charles Pryor, was to wage war upon and decimate the population by mass murder, principally through the use of poison. Allegations that abolitionists were systematically salting the wells and cisterns of white Texans with strychnine were almost as numerous as reports of arson. There is no indication from the newspapers or available letters of the period that poisoning was a common means of committing homicide in Texas, at least among whites; guns and knives better suited the frontiersman's penchant for a direct and immediate redress of his grievances. Still, antebellum southerners had often charged slaves with murdering, or attempting to murder, their masters with various forms of poison.[42] One historian's analysis of capital crimes cases for which slaves were convicted in Virginia between 1780 and 1864 revealed that ninety men and women had been convicted of arson, and fifty-six of poisoning. Closer to home, the same scholar found that nine of the ninety-six slaves in Louisiana's prison in 1860 had been convicted of either poisoning or attempting to poison their masters.[43] The leading historian of African American Texans wrote: "More than one slave attacked or poisoned slaveholders, despite the assurance of hanging if caught."[44]

In any case, during the panic Texans evinced a morbid fear of the deadly stuff, perhaps because of its mysterious nature, or possibly because their short supplies of water—stored in open wells and cisterns—made them so vulnerable. Pryor's assertion that abolitionists had planned to place strychnine in the wells and food supply of the Dallasites consequently was echoed in other communities. At Athens, for example, over one hundred bottles of strychnine allegedly turned up in the possession of blacks.[45] A slave arrested in Denton County reportedly possessed twenty-four bottles of the same deadly potion.[46] Other substances purported to be poisonous allegedly turned up in Anderson, Austin,

41. Austin *Texas State Gazette*, September 29, 1860, quoted in Kesselus, *History of Bastrop County*, 173.

42. For references to alleged poisonings and conspiracies to poison, see Aptheker, *American Negro Slave Revolts*, 198, 230, 236, 239, 241, and 332; Jordan, *White Over Black*, 392. All southern states included a long list of crimes for which slaves could be executed; poisoning was included, along with such felonies as murder, rape, and arson (see Stampp, *The Peculiar Institution*, 210).

43. Phillips, *American Negro Slavery*, 456–458.

44. Barr, *Black Texans*, 28.

45. Tyler *Reporter*, August 11, 1860, clipped in Marshall *Texas Republican*, August 18, 1860.

46. Quitman *Herald*, n.d., clipped in Marshall *Texas Republican*, August 25, 1860.

Cherokee, Ellis, and Washington counties, as well as in other localities.

The growing number of reports indicating that slaves had been supplied with copious amounts of strychnine by their northern sponsors evidently had a tremendous impact on the public mind. One citizen of Cherokee County wrote to a friend that he had been disposed to look with skepticism upon the accounts of rampant abolitionism until "authenticated statements came to us, that in several places, poison had been found with negroes, and confessions made, that on election day, this poison was to be administered in the food at breakfast, and deposited in the wells and springs; and that a general plot had been made, for an indiscriminate, wholesale destruction by poison and arms on that day." These startling developments had led to a search, "and on last night and this morning, poison has been found with several negroes, and they have made confessions substantially the same as the above rumors and have implicated several other negroes."[47]

Another letter, from W. L. Mann in Tyler County to Thomas B. Huling of Lampasas, provides insight into both the abolitionist psychosis and the ignorance of at least some Texans concerning the properties of strychnine. Writing of the excitement in Tyler County, Mann asserted that the conspirators had almost snuffed out the lives of his family. He charged that six men (apparently whites) living nearby on land owned by Huling, "has made three attempts in the las month to poison my whole family by putting Strichnine in my Spring." The attempts had failed, he said, only because the would-be assassins had put *too much* poison in the water, causing him and his family to vomit up the strychnine before it could take lethal effect.[48] As for those who allegedly had sought his death, the farmer said: "I can't prove that the[y] did put the poisin in my Spring But the[re] was a hoss come from that way the last time that my spring was poisoned and went back the same way." There may have been some

47. M. H. Bonner to Oze Taylor, August 4, 1860, printed in Marshall *Texas Republican*, August 11, 1860.

48. W. L. Mann, Billums Creek, to Thomas B. Huling, Lampasas, August 24, 1860, Huling Papers, Barker Texas History Center Archives, University of Texas, Austin, Texas. The notion that strychnine was an emetic was a popular misconception that apparently stemmed from the scientific name for the seed of the tree that produces the toxin: *nuxvomica*, which had been widely mistranslated as "emetic nut." In fact, strychnine is rapidly absorbed by the gastrointestinal tract and begins almost immediately its debilitating work on the central nervous system, bringing on convulsions and usually a quick death to the victim. The more potent the dose, the more deadly would be its effect. It may well be, therefore, that the real emetic in Mann's spring was some microbe, rather than poison (see Louis S. Goodman and Alfred Gilman, *The Pharmacological Basis of Therapeutics*, 2nd ed. [New York, 1958], 330–335).

economic reasons for Mann's fears that his neighbors might want to kill him. Huling had allowed the alleged would-be murderers to live rent-free upon his land, and they apparently resented Mann's efforts on behalf of the absent landlord to sell the property, since that would deprive them of their rent-free haven. Nevertheless, Mann implied that they were abolitionists, as well as ne'er-do-wells, when he wrote: "Old Abe has bin here among them and put all the devil in them he could."[49]

The wide geographical distribution of the reported fires and alleged poisoning attempts, together with the great number of such reports, seemed to confirm Pryor's earlier assertions that a widespread abolitionist plot had targeted a large portion of the state and that no community could afford to assume that it was immune from attack. A shroud of fear settled over the state. "Fires have seldom occurred in Texas," asserted the San Antonio *Herald,* thus the chances that so many conflagrations would break out accidentally in "a dozen towns" on the same day were "one in a million." In the *Herald'*s view, therefore, the fires not only had to be manmade but also constituted "one of the most diabolical plans that was ever conceived in the most depraved age or country, by the foulest fiends in human shape."[50]

Newspapers like the *Herald* fed the panic not only by their acceptance of every report of fire or conspiracy, but also by the high priority that they assigned to such stories. Some journals, such as the McKinney *Messenger,* Bonham *Era,* and San Antonio *Ledger and Texan,* published Pryor's exposé of the alleged abolitionist plot in the form of "extras," thus heightening the shock effect of the reports. Such papers apparently saw nothing wrong with aiding and abetting the panic. The *Ledger and Texan* even seemed proud of its role in stirring up San Antonio. On the day after it reprinted Pryor's letter to John Marshall in an "extra," the editor wrote: "The excitement caused by the publication was very great, and it continues to a considerable extent today. All over town, groups of persons are talking over the matter and speculating as to the causes."[51]

Many other journals gave extensive coverage in their regular editions to the developments in Dallas and to subsequent reports of abolitionist horrors elsewhere. Prominent southern rights papers, such as the Austin *Texas State Gazette,* the Houston *Telegraph,* the Galveston *News,* and the Marshall *Texas Republican* devoted column after sensational column to the latest news of

49. Mann to Huling, August 24, 1860, Huling Papers, Barker Texas History Center Archives, University of Texas, Austin, Texas.

50. San Antonio *Herald,* July 25, 1860.

51. San Antonio *Ledger and Texan,* July 23, 1860.

abolitionist activities. For six weeks after publication of Pryor's account of the alleged incendiary scheme in Dallas there were few editions of any Texas paper that failed to make some reference to the reported conspiracy.

Although it was the fire-eating editors of Texas who publicized Pryor's several accounts of the Dallas "plot" and printed the subsequent flood of allegations that blacks, inspired and directed by abolitionists, had set fires to numerous other towns, poisoned cisterns and wells, and plotted to murder white men and rape their womenfolk, conservative journals also tended to accept the horrifying stories—at least initially. The Austin *Southern Intelligencer,* the leading Opposition paper in Texas, wrote: "We have information which leaves no doubt of there being an organized band of villains in the country, who have regularly laid their plans of arson and robbery, and by preconcerted and simultaneous effort, attempted to put their diabolical plans into execution." The *Southern Intelligencer* may have betrayed reservations about Pryor's assertions that those responsible were abolitionists, however, when it wondered: "Who can they be, and what motive can they have?" Nevertheless, it called upon its readers to be vigilant.[52] Another Opposition paper, the McKinney *Messenger,* accepted Pryor's account and concluded: "It makes the blood run cold to hear the details."[53]

Some conservatives may have had their faith in the Union shaken by the reports that northern abolitionists were the instigators of the fires in North Texas. For example, the Waco *Democrat,* which, according to the Houston *Telegraph,* was "until recently opposed to the organized Democracy of Texas," ran an indignant editorial:

> "THE UNION!!"—We are its friends and supporter; but it must be a Union of political brothers. Here is how the Northern brethren are working in Texas. They must do better than this, or we will want to divide. We *hardly* think it *right* for our *Northern brothers* to burn up our houses after this fashion! We may be wrong, but we don't think they have any good cause, or any *right* to *burn* us out of the South; and we modestly and timidly venture the opinion that they ought to be *very nicely, quietly,* and *cosily* HUNG to any convenient post oak when found.[54]

Like their counterparts in Texas, unionist editors in other southern states also reacted with alarm to Pryor's letters, which were reprinted in journals all over the region; unlike the Waco *Democrat,* however, few raised the specter

52. Austin *Southern Intelligencer,* July 18, 1860.

53. McKinney *Messenger,* July 27, 1860, clipped in Austin *Texas State Gazette,* August 4, 1860.

54. Waco *Democrat,* n.d., clipped in Houston *Telegraph,* August 16, 1860.

of disunion. "Parson" William G. Brownlow's Knoxville *Whig* professed to be pleased to read that the Texas towns had formed vigilance committees and that they were keeping a strict watch "over the movements of the slaves and their white associates and spiritual advisers. The lives of innocent citizens, and their property, are alike endangered, and great alarm prevails." Brownlow, himself an ordained Methodist minister, was disgusted by reports that Northern Methodist ministers had stirred up the trouble in Dallas, and he urged the Texans to get rid of them.[55] Other notable unionist journals expressed a similar concern. The Talledega *Alabama Reporter,* a supporter of John Bell, the Constitutional Unionist candidate for president, ran a brief report of fires and allegations of abolitionist involvement and concluded: "We hope the vile insurgents may all be speedily hung up."[56] After running alarming reports from several Texas journals, the Raleigh *Register,* another Bell supporter, said: "The proof of a widespread plot in Texas to incite the negroes to insurrection is daily accumulating."[57]

Conservative journals that otherwise had reservations about printing the frightful stories from Texas lost their reluctance when rumors surfaced of insurrectionary activities in their own backyards. For example, in mid-September the Wadesborough *North Carolina Argus* wrote that it had previously avoided publishing much about the Texas Troubles, but it could be silent no longer, "as the troubles seem to be approaching our own doors, and [we] deem it our duty to call upon our citizens to be vigilant."[58] The New Orleans *Picayune,* which had expressed mixed feelings about the reported plot in Texas, noted on September 23 that three fires had occurred in or near New Orleans on September 21 and another the next day. Following the same logic as that of the Texas "conspiracy" publicists, the *Picayune* said that it was not reasonable to believe so many fires could occur by chance in such a short time frame. It concluded that "Incendiarism is surely at its diabolical work" and warned its readers to be vigilant, especially since the Texans had driven from their borders many suspicious strangers, some of whom "are known to have sailed for this city."[59]

In Texas concern intensified as August 6—the date for the election of state officials—approached. On that date, Pryor had warned, blacks everywhere

55. Knoxville (Tenn.) *Whig,* September 1, 1860.

56. Talladega *Alabama Reporter,* August 2, 1860.

57. Raleigh (N.C.) *Register,* September 12, 1860. For examples of similar views expressed by other conservative journals in the region, see New Orleans (La.) *Bee,* August 20, 24, 27, 1860; Augusta (Ga.) *Chronicle and Sentinel,* August 1, 1860; Milledgeville (Ga.) *Southern Recorder,* August 7, 1860; Charlotte (N.C.) *Whig,* August 3, 1860; Alexandria (Va.) *Gazette,* July 27, 1860.

58. Wadesborough *North Carolina Argus,* September 13, 1860.

59. New Orleans (La.) *Daily Picayune,* September 23, 1860.

would rise up and shoot, poison, and rape while the menfolk were away from their homes voting. Apprehension and foreboding increased as the fateful day neared. Two days before election day, M. H. Bonner, a lawyer who lived in Rusk, wrote to Oze Taylor of Marshall of his growing anxiety. Bonner said that he had been disposed to consider the plot stories as a "needless alarm," but new "authenticated statements" indicated that "in several places, poison had been found with negroes," and the implicated blacks had confessed "that on election day, this poison was to be administered in the food at breakfast, and deposited in wells and springs; and that a general plot had been made for an indiscriminate, wholesale destruction by poison and arms on that day."[60]

"The future is shrouded from our vision, we know not what a day will bring forth," wrote the La Grange *True Issue.* "One thing we do know, every one who loves his home, his family or his country, should be prepared for any crisis—be ready to meet the open toe or prowling assassin."[61] Most citizens hardly needed the reminder. A week before the state elections the Clarksville *Northern Standard* reported that people in that community already were afraid to leave their homes.[62]

By election eve, whole families stayed up all night in some areas, weapons at hand, ready to meet the expected assault.[63] In some communities citizens sought to prevent an election day uprising by rooting out and punishing the plotters before they could achieve their hellish goals. A farmer in Tyler County wrote to a friend in Lampasas: "I wish to inform you how badly things are going on here[.] the negros was making arrangement to rise against the whites on the 6th of Aug—But on the night of the 5th the[y] were discovered and the whole country was in arms."[64] Not surprisingly, there was reportedly a light vote in Tyler County on August 6.[65] A less-than-normal vote also seems to have characterized other counties where the excitement was greatest; for example, a

60. M. H. Bonner to Oze Taylor, August 4, 1860, Marshall *Texas Republican,* August 11, 1860. During the Reconstruction period, Micajah H. Bonner was appointed judge of the Seventh District. He later received an appointment to the Texas Supreme Court and served as chief justice from 1878 to 1882 (*Handbook of Texas Online,* s.v., www.tsha.utexas.edu/handbook/online/articles/BB/fbo19.html [accessed July 18, 2006]).

61. La Grange *True Issue,* August 2, 1860.

62. Clarksville *Northern Standard,* July 28, 1860, clipped in Marshall *Texas Republican,* August 11, 1860.

63. Hattie J. Roach, *A History of Cherokee County* (Dallas, 1934), 61.

64. Mann to Huling, August 24, 1860, Huling Papers, Barker Texas History Center Archives, University of Texas, Austin, Texas.

65. Jasper *Clarion,* August 11, 1860, clipped in Cincinnati (Ohio) *Daily Commercial,* August 27, 1860.

newspaper reported that the polls in Montgomery and Grimes counties, which had full-fledged scares of their own, "were but slimly attended."[66]

Women and children were most affected by the panic. The Austin *Texas State Gazette* noted on August 4 that a woman living on a plantation near the capital had written a letter begging the protection of friends for her family until her absent husband could return home.[67] An incident in Marshall was more dramatic. When a white woman was reported missing from her farm home on the day after the election, fears arose that she had fallen victim to the blacks. Her husband had gone into town to vote on the 6th. When he returned late that evening, his wife was gone and his slaves did not know her whereabouts. The neighbors quickly organized a search, but it was not until the next day that they located the missing woman at another farm, seven miles away from her home. The explanation for her disappearance turned out to be a simple one, but it provides insight into the mental state of the white populace at the height of the panic. The woman explained that she was outside the house when she heard gunshots fired in the distance. Thinking that these reports signaled the beginning of the expected uprising and apparently expecting to be ravished momentarily, she panicked and ran wildly into the woods, "her alarm increasing with her flight." Said the Marshall *Texas Republican,* "She was out the entire night, and arrived at Mr. Boon's barefooted and in a wretched condition." The same paper, which apparently saw no connection between its own sensational treatment of the conspiracy stories and such examples of hysteria, thought that the incident demonstrated "the necessity of prudence and caution, and the folly of unnecessary alarm."[68]

The case of the Marshall woman may not have been unusual, even in Marshall. A citizen of the same town, in a letter to the New York *Day Book* dated August 12, said: "Women and children have been so frightened by these burnings and threatened rebellion of the Negroes, that in several instances they have left their homes in their fright, and when found were almost confirmed maniacs!"[69] A letter written from Henderson on August 7 sounded a similar note: "All is alarm and excitement with our children."[70]

66. Bellville *Texas Countryman,* August 18, 1860.

67. Austin *Texas State Gazette,* August 4, 1860.

68. Marshall *Texas Republican,* August 11, 1860.

69. Letter of "W.R.D.W.," August 12, 1860, New York *Day Book,* September 8, 1860, clipped in Austin *Southern Intelligencer,* October 10, 1860.

70. M. D. Ector, Henderson, to C. A. Frazier, Marshall, August 7, 1860, Marshall *Texas Republican,* August 11, 1860.

Election day passed without the predicted calamity. Yet, far from admitting that their fears may have been groundless, some citizens argued that their extreme watchfulness on August 6 had saved their towns. Gideon Lincecum, who lived east of Austin, wrote to his nephew in Louisiana: "In this portion of the state there was no mischief done but the negroes nearly all knew of the movement, and were prevented doing anything by the timely interference of the white people."[71] One report said that while the men were voting in Athens, "two shrill blasts of a horn were heard near the town, and in a few minutes a stable was seen in flames; every man rushed to his dwelling and the town was saved."[72] A young man of Marshall wrote to his father in Houston, "Things have come to a pretty pass in Texas. . . . Yesterday the election came off, the day fixed for the Negroes and abolition dogs to poison all the water on the election grounds, so as to kill off the men at once, but they were watched so closely that they did not make the attempt. . . . Last night the guards were on the watch all night, in fact, every man in the place was on watch, and by that means the cowardly cutthroats were defeated. I would like to tell you all about this insurrection, but I am too nervous to write anymore."[73]

Also on election eve, watchful citizens reportedly discovered forty blacks and several whites planning insurrection near Paris, in Lamar County. Ten or fifteen of these were supposed to have been captured, a newspaper said, and they allegedly had confessed that on election day they intended to murder the white females in their houses and then attack their men as they returned home from the polls. Thus, careful vigilance, it was said, had saved the city.[74]

The apparent failure of the abolitionists' alleged election day plans did not allay all fears or discourage the further proliferation of rumors. Clandestine meetings of blacks, such as the one that had reportedly taken place near Paris, were rumored to be occurring in South and South Central Texas as well, and this heightened the anxiety of many who were far removed from the area where the panic began. The blacks of Grimes County, for example, were said to "have held secret meetings, and many of them are supplied with arms."[75] The Bastrop *Advertiser* reported on August 11 that the woods around that town "seem to be

71. Jerry B. Lincecum, Edward H. Phillips, Peggy A. Redshaw, eds., *Gideon Lincecum's Sword: Civil War Letters from the Home Front* (Denton, Tex., 2001), 63.

72. Letter of "D.B.M.," August 10, 1860, Anderson *Texas Baptist*, August 23, 1860.

73. James L. Craig, Marshall, to A. K. Craig, Houston, August 9, 1860, quoted in Cincinnati (Ohio) *Daily Commercial*, September 1, 1860.

74. Jefferson *Herald*, August 11, 1860, clipped in Austin *Texas State Gazette*, August 25, 1860.

75. Houston *Telegraph*, July 31, 1860.

alive with runaway slaves," several of whom had been arrested and jailed and had confessed their intention to escape to Mexico.[76]

The Austin *Texas State Gazette* on September 1 wrote of a new plot involving no fewer than two hundred Fayette County blacks, who had planned to flee to Mexico. The paper admittedly had received no details of the incident; nevertheless, it confidently stated that "the plot was no doubt concocted by the Abolitionists." Moreover, according to the same source, the revelation of the Fayette "conspiracy" made it abundantly clear that the "infernal scheme has been planned for the whole State. Lord! Deliver us from these fanatical *thieves, townburners,* and *murderers!*"[77] In neighboring Austin County, the Bellville *Texas Countryman* reported: "There are rumors about, that Negroes have been assembling together considerably on the Brazos and elsewhere in this county of late, and that plans have been concocted among them to burn, kill and murder generally."[78]

Many similarly wild rumors circulated in newspapers throughout the state. Perhaps the most far-fetched tale detailed a set battle that supposedly was fought by pro-slavery Cherokee against an army of abolitionists in the Indian Territory. In this rare instance of casting Indians in the role of heroes there was an appropriate reversal of the casualty rate that usually prevailed when whites and redskins tangled: 150 abolitionists reportedly lost their scalps, while only seven pro-slavery Indians bit the dust.[79] This account was patently suspicious. Where would the army of abolitionists have come from? Who had organized and sent them? Above all, why would any such thrust against slavery be aimed at the Indian Territory, instead of some more strategic stronghold of slavery? Yet, in spite of the absurdity of this story, many journals published it, and when later reports indicated the fictitious nature of the yarn, newspapers that had printed it as news seldom bothered to retract it.

One real event appeared to provide a more solid basis for the anxieties of white Texans. On August 5, the day before the state elections, a fire destroyed a significant portion of Henderson, the county seat of Rusk County. The blaze broke out at about 8:00 on a Sunday night, when many of the local populace were attending evening church services. Opinions differed on exactly where and how the fire began. The Tyler *Reporter* said that the flames had broken out

76. Bastrop *Advertiser,* August 11, 1860, clipped in St. Louis *Daily Missouri Republican,* August 23, 1860.

77. Austin *Texas State Gazette,* September 1, 1860.

78. Bellville *Texas Countryman,* August 11, 1860.

79. Galveston *Civilian and Gazette,* September 11, 1860.

in three or four places simultaneously.[80] Reports from the stricken town itself, however, agreed that the fire was of single origin, although they differed over the point of inception. According to Matthew D. Ector, a prominent local lawyer and editor, "the fire was put in some shape" into an old, unoccupied shop building.[81] But A. I. Hartley, a Henderson newspaperman, declared that the flames had originated behind a drugstore on the south side of the square.[82]

Although the Henderson fire's point of origin remained a mystery, the result was easy enough to see. All accounts agreed that the fire spread so swiftly that it resisted all efforts to combat it. As with the conflagrations at Dallas and Denton, a stiff southern breeze spread the flames quickly; indeed, according to Ector, the entire south side of the square was ablaze within five minutes, and those structures touched by the fire burned completely within two hours. Curiously, of the confirmed fires that plagued Texas during that fateful summer, only the Henderson fire occurred after dark. The town in flames against the backdrop of the darkening evening sky apparently presented a spectacular sight. Ector said that the driving wind flew showers of sparks for a half mile from the fire itself.[83] Many years later, a former slave who was seventeen at the time of the fire said that he still remembered the blaze "just as well as yesterday." The brightness of the fire was so great, he said, "you could see a pin on the ground at night in my master's front yard two blocks from the square."[84]

Estimates of damage ranged as high as a quarter of a million dollars, making the cost of the Henderson holocaust second only to that in Dallas. Newspaperman Hartley reported, "The whole business portion of the town is in ashes."[85] Ector's inventory of burned buildings listed fourteen stores and an estimated eight to ten law offices. But Ector indicated that his was only a partial listing by adding "&c." to it.[86] In addition to the businesses listed by Ector, other accounts

80. Tyler *Reporter,* n.d., quoted in Houston *Telegraph,* August 18, 1860.

81. M. D. Ector to C. A. Frazier, August 7, 1860, quoted in Marshall *Texas Republican,* August 11, 1860. Ector became editor of the Henderson *Democrat* in 1855 and was elected the same year to represent Rusk County in the Sixth Legislature. He joined the Confederate army during the Civil War, rising to the rank of general before a wound ended his military career in 1864 (*Handbook of Texas Online,* s.v., www.tsha.utexas.edu/handbook/online/articles/EE/fec2.html [accessed July 18, 2006]).

82. A. I. Hartley to R. W. Loughery, August 7, 1860, Marshall *Texas Republican,* August 11, 1860.

83. Ector to Frazier, August 7, 1860, quoted in Marshall *Texas Republican,* August 11, 1860.

84. Interview of Dorman H. Winfrey with Alfred Harris, June 18, 1950, Winfrey Collection, Barker Texas History Center Archives, University of Texas, Austin, Texas.

85. Hartley to Loughery, August 7, 1860.

86. Ector to Frazier, August 7, 1860, quoted in Marshall *Texas Republican,* August 11, 1860.

mention the destruction of livery stables and the burning of two newspapers, the *Texas New Era* and the *Star-Spangled Banner*.[87] The flames also destroyed large stocks of goods. A New Orleans merchant who visited Henderson after the fire reported that merchandise worth $50,000 had burned after being set out in the streets for protection. The same observer noted that all groceries and other supplies needed by Henderson and the surrounding rural area had been lost.[88]

Although witnesses differed on the fire's point of inception and the method used to start it, they all agreed that the flames had to have been the work of an arsonist, or arsonists. An incendiary had done the deed, Hartley said categorically, but although several arrests had already been made two days after the fire, no one had yet been "convicted."[89] Ector, writing on the same date, stated: "As yet we have not been able to find out who it was that did it, whether white or black. No traces have been discovered."[90]

It was perhaps a sign of the times that in spite of the admitted lack of evidence neither Ector nor Hartley considered the possibility that the fire might have originated accidentally. Indeed, Ector, who served on the vigilance committee that investigated the disaster, had already decided while the ashes still smoldered that a well-conceived plan lay behind the burning of Henderson. In support of his theory he pointed out that the fire had ignited just before the night patrol started its rounds. While the townspeople were assembling for church, said Ector, they were distracted by a fight that broke out between "two gentlemen," just before the fire started. All of this added up, at least in Ector's mind, to a well-laid plot to destroy Henderson while the townspeople were preoccupied and the community was off its guard.[91]

Ector's view that an abolitionist plot was the cause of Henderson's destructive fire was clearly shared by the town's citizens. The resultant panic was so great locally that ordinary business came to a standstill. The excitement even forced Judge C. A. Frazier to cancel the term of the district court, which had been scheduled to begin in August. Men who had scheduled business in the court were reportedly too afraid to leave their families alone. In addition,

---

87. San Augustine *Red Land Express*, August 11, 1860; Dorman H. Winfrey, *A History of Rusk County, Texas* (Waco, 1961), 39.

88. Galveston *Civilian and Gazette*, n.d., clipped in St. Louis *Daily Missouri Republican*, August 23, 1860.

89. Hartley to Loughery, August 7, 1860, quoted in Marshall *Texas Republican*, August 11, 1860.

90. Ector to Frazier, August 7, 1860, quoted in Marshall *Texas Republican*, August 11, 1860.

91. Ibid.

Henderson's lawyers had lost their offices and libraries to the fire and therefore were unable to prepare cases for trial.[92]

Leading advocates of the theory that there was a widespread abolitionist conspiracy to devastate Texas held up Henderson as an example of a town that had failed to heed earlier warnings from Dallas and therefore had suffered the terrible consequences. The Houston *Telegraph* pointedly wrote: "The people of Henderson, our informant says, put no faith in the reported conspiracy, and neglected to appoint a patrol or keep watch."[93] The implication was clear: every town, indeed every citizen, must either be vigilant or be prepared to pay in like fashion for their indifference. The lesson was not lost on white Texans. "I understand Henderson has been burned by the abolitionists," wrote a citizen of Smithland who added: "There has been some excitement up this way about the Negroes burning or trying to burn little towns &c. The people are keeping a skined eye on the Negroes at this time."[94] Another letter, written by a Methodist minister in Tyler and published in the *Texas Christian Advocate,* gave further indication of the state of mind that seems to have prevailed in Northeast Texas in the wake of the latest disaster. Saying "Henderson is in ashes," the minister reported that Tyler was in a state of "intense excitement," and "Business of every kind is almost suspended. Such a time I never saw before, and hope never to see again."[95]

There were other, more mundane lessons to be learned. Some Texans, never losing their frontier pragmatism, supported various precautionary measures to mitigate a catastrophe, should one strike their community. After hearing of the loss of the store goods in the Henderson fire, many people of Marshall began buying up large quantities of food, clothing, and other necessities for the fall and winter, in the event that a similar conflagration should wipe out their town's stores. The local paper undoubtedly pleased many of its advertisers when it endorsed such hoarding: "for these articles have to be purchased," its editor reasoned, "and in view of the incendiary spirit abroad, the sooner the better."[96] Bellville's newspaper suggested that each property owner in that town be as-

92. Henderson *Times,* clipped in Marshall *Texas Republican,* September 1, 1860.

93. Houston *Telegraph,* August 11, 1860. This comment seems to contradict Ector's account in his letter to Frazier of August 7, 1860, in which he stated that the fire had begun just before the night patrol started its rounds.

94. "E. D.," Smithland, to Mrs. Mary Tatum, Harmony Hill, August 14, 1860, James G. Gee Library Archives, Texas A&M University-Commerce, Commerce, Texas.

95. The Reverend J. W. Fields to the editor, n.d., Galveston *Texas Christian Advocate,* August 23, 1860.

96. Marshall *Texas Republican,* August 11, 1860.

sessed a "contribution," so that the town could purchase half a dozen ladders for use in fighting any fires that arsonists might set. As a further precaution, the same paper suggested that all families fill tubs and buckets with water each night and that the citizenry should be organized into units and drilled in fire-fighting procedures so that the water could be passed quickly and efficiently to the site of a fire, if one should break out.[97] The Houston *Telegraph* proudly announced that all of the offices in Houston's projected new courthouse would be fireproof.[98]

Almost lost in the excitement of the moment was the reality that election day—August 6—had come and gone without the general uprising that Charles Pryor had said was the goal of the abolitionist conspirators. Nevertheless, although no throats were cut, maidens raped, or families poisoned, the panic did not end—or even noticeably diminish—during the days that followed the election. Once the floodgates of fear had opened, the resulting outpouring of emotion had to run its course before the torrent could subside. As is often the case in such instances, the panic fed upon itself and became self-sustaining. Suspicion bred suspicion and rumor begat rumor, until there was a frenzy of fear and hatred that demanded catharsis.

S. B. Barron, a recent immigrant from Alabama, later wrote in his memoirs: "The excitement, apprehension, unrest, and the vague fear of the unseen danger pervading the minds of the people of Texas cannot be understood by persons who were not in the State at that time."[99] The Bellville *Texas Countryman* epitomized this "fear of the unseen" that gripped Texans during their long, hot summer of 1860 when it wrote: "The red torch of the incendiary demon is waving over our land and danger lurks in every passing wind."[100] Small wonder that Texans would work so feverishly to protect themselves from the danger that "lurked in every passing wind."

97. Bellville *Texas Countryman,* August 25, 1860.
98. Houston *Telegraph,* n.d., clipped in Bellville *Texas Countryman,* August 25, 1860.
99. Barron, *The Lone Star Defenders,* 6–17.
100. Bellville *Texas Countryman,* August 11, 1860.

CHAPTER THREE

BETTER TO HANG NINETY-NINE INNOCENT MEN

Although all of the panic-stricken communities possessed regularly constituted law enforcement machinery in 1860, virtually none was willing to entrust to it the investigation of the alleged insurrectionary activity. Instead, they almost exclusively resorted to the use of vigilance committees to carry out the investigations, conduct trials, and execute punishments. Such bodies had long been used on the southern frontier as a corrective for the lawlessness that was endemic to that region. First utilized by the South Carolina Regulators in 1767, vigilance committees had followed the westward march of the settlers, and by the 1850s were being convoked in Texas with a fair degree of regularity, usually to battle gangs of thieves or suspected cadres of abolitionists. Employment of vigilance committees was a national phenomenon, but nowhere in America was this tendency more prevalent than in the South, and nowhere in the South more than in Texas. By one scholar's count, Texas experienced no fewer than fifty-two separate vigilante movements in the nineteenth century.[1]

Because they deviated from—and in many ways subverted—the established legal order and clearly flouted the constitutional rights of the accused, vigilance committees never attained full respectability. During periods of social tranquility, Texans probably cherished the traditional Anglo-Saxon concept of due process as much as other Americans. Nevertheless, most citizens believed that there were times when the threat to life and property was so great that normal

---

1. Richard M. Brown, "The American Vigilante Tradition," in *The History of Violence in America: Historical and Comparative Perspectives,* ed. Hugh D. Graham and Ted R. Gurr (New York, 1969), 144–147, 153, 164.

jurisprudence must be abandoned in favor of more drastic measures. Specifically, when they became convinced that there was the threat of a servile uprising, they never hesitated to suspend the regular legal procedures and collectively usurp the power of the state.

From the standpoint of many white Texans, vigilante justice had several important advantages over the law when there seemed to be a threat to the social system, especially when there was danger of a slave insurrection. For one thing, vigilante law was swifter than regular jurisprudence. Petitions for delay of trial, postponements necessitated by the crowded dockets of itinerant district judges, and other technicalities that lawyers might use to gain time for their clients did not obtain in the proceedings of vigilante courts. Vigilance committees could act speedily, completing the investigatory, accusatory, judicial, and punitive functions all in a matter of hours, if need be. The time thus saved might mean the difference between safety and destruction. Most white citizens undoubtedly agreed with a letter writer in Hempstead who said that if the Texans detected anyone tampering with their slaves, "they will hardly wait for slow-footed justice through the courts, but a 'stake, rope, and the nearest limb,' give the aspirant his wished-for martyrdom."[2]

Conviction by vigilante courts was also more certain than in a traditional court of law. In these *ad hoc* tribunals the usual evidentiary rules did not apply. No lawyer would be present to invoke the fine points of the law to exclude weak, even illegal, evidence from the stern deliberations of these bodies. The committees were far more concerned with the safety of the community at large than with the right of the accused to be presumed innocent until proven guilty beyond a reasonable doubt. A Fort Worth correspondent of the New York *Day Book* declared: "And be not surprised when I tell you that we will hang every man who does not live above suspicion. Necessity now reverses the rule, for it is better for us to hang ninety-nine innocent (suspicious) men than to let one guilty one pass, for the guilty one endangers the peace of society, and every man coming from a northern state should live above suspicion." This view, said

2. N. N. Allen, Hempstead, to the editor, August 4, 1860, Nashville (Tenn.) *Christian Advocate,* August 23, 1860. Texans may have utilized vigilance committees more often than other slave states, but they were hardly unusual in resorting to extra-legal means when dealing with alleged abolitionists. Clement Eaton has observed that such cases rarely came before regular courts: "Indeed, one of the outstanding paradoxes of Southern life was the reverence for the Federal Constitution and the law of the Bible which Southerners displayed, while they frequently ignored the legal courts in dealing with abolitionists and Negro insurrectionists" (Clement Eaton, "Mob Violence in the Old South," *Mississippi Valley Historical Review* 29 [December 1942]: 370).

the writer, was the "universal sentiment" of his community.[3] Men capable of such logic were unlikely to become squeamish over depriving accused abolitionists of their right to due process of law.

Most Texans believed that the punitive measures provided by the law were too lenient to fit the crimes of which the alleged abolitionists and their black co-conspirators were deemed guilty. The Fifth Legislature in 1853 had established death as the penalty for conspiring to encourage a slave to rebel or engage in an insurrection, but punishment for lesser infractions was less severe.[4] The Eighth Legislature, which met in 1859, had revised the portion of the code that had established penalties for slave tampering. For example, anyone caught playing cards or other "games of chance" with either slaves or free blacks could only be fined between twenty and a hundred dollars or jailed for no more than three months. Persons who by word or "writing" endeavored to arouse in a slave discontent with his condition could be imprisoned for two to five years. Individuals who privately or publicly maintained "that masters have not right of property in their slaves" or who wrote or published anything "calculated to produce in slaves a spirit of insubordination with the intent to advise or incite insurrection" could be jailed, but only from two to seven years.[5] For citizens who believed white abolitionists and their black minions imperiled their very lives, such penalties were far too light. Only the hangman's rope or, at the very least, exile from the state would guarantee their safety.

Another important reason for abandoning legal trials in favor of vigilante law was the prohibition under Texas law of using black testimony against whites.[6] Since during the Texas Troubles black witnesses supplied virtually all of the "evidence" against alleged white abolitionists as well as against other implicated blacks, the exclusion of African American testimony from the state's courtrooms undoubtedly would have resulted in numerous acquittals of men whom the white citizens believed guilty of plotting the most heinous crimes in the southern lexicon. Exoneration of the guilty because of such a technicality was unthinkable to men whose emotions were at fever pitch and whose inclination, even in calmer times, was to take a personal hand in seeing that miscreants were punished.

3. Letter of "J.W.S.," Fort Worth, August 12, 1860, New York *Day Book,* September 8, 1860, clipped in Austin *Southern Intelligencer,* October 10, 1860. This letter may also be found in Richard Hofstadter and Michael Wallace, eds., *American Violence: A Documentary History* (New York, 1970), 202–203.

4. H.P.N. Gammel, comp., *The Laws of Texas, 1822–1897* (Austin, 1898), 3:1685.

5. Ibid., 4:1461.

6. Ibid., 2:1685. For a detailed analysis of the laws as they pertained to the slaves and slave

This stricture against using black testimony also applied in the other southern states, and some southerners believed that a revision of the rules of evidence, rather than the use of vigilance committees, was the proper course. A correspondent of the Charleston *Daily Courier* argued, for example, that the events in Texas ought to convince southerners everywhere that the law should be changed to make black evidence admissible against whites, at least in cases involving alleged abolitionism. As the law stood, the writer contended, it was virtually impossible to convict the white conspirators, since "their intercourse is exclusively with those who, by our laws and policy, are not competent witnesses, or with each other. Hence it is that in Texas and elsewhere, the people have been obliged to resort to lynch law; and so they must continue to do until the Law of Evidence shall have been changed."[7] Such a change in the legal code would have been revolutionary indeed, and there appears to have been little support for the proposal.

Some Texans wanted the legislature to expedite action in court cases involving the abolitionist conspirators by amending the law. Since the legislature was not in session at the time of the panic, the advocates of this reform urged the governor to call a special session to implement their proposal, but Governor Sam Houston, who was highly skeptical of the reports of a slave insurrection plot, ignored such requests.[8]

Still others thought a statewide convention would be the best way to deal with the crisis. The Science Hill vigilance committee, in Henderson County, passed a resolution calling for such a convention, to meet "for the purpose of adopting such united State action in regard to the continued and wide spread plot and insurrection and incendiarism as present emergencies require and our future safety shall demand."[9] The Houston *Telegraph* concurred with the resolution, arguing that the alleged conspiracy was too widespread and sinister to be combated effectively on a purely local level. This proposal nevertheless elicited little general support, since most communities and counties were content to preserve the public safety in their own bailiwicks and let their neighbors do the same.[10]

Most Texans unquestioningly supported the establishment of the familiar vigilance committees, believing them to be the most effective instruments for

---

tamperers, see Campbell, *An Empire for Slavery,* 96–114.

7. Charleston (S.C.) *Daily Courier,* August 22, 1860.

8. For examples of this suggestion, see Bonham *Era,* n.d., clipped in Marshall *Texas Republican,* August 18, 1860, and Marshall *Texas Republican,* August 25, 1860.

9. Quoted in St. Louis (Mo.) *Sunday Morning Republican,* September 30, 1860.

10. Houston *Telegraph,* August 16, 1860.

discovering and punishing the shadowy demons that threatened their lives and property. Moreover, although vigilante law amounted to a suspension of the individual rights of the accused, from another perspective it could be viewed as an exercise in democracy—after all, the citizens did elect and empower the vigilantes—and as such it accorded well with the frontier spirit.

In the wake of Pryor's sensational revelations, therefore, community leaders in every region of the state initiated action leading to the formation of vigilante groups. Citizens' committees minced no words in stating their purpose. Reporting on the meeting that established a vigilance committee in La Grange, the local paper said: "The citizens were calm, determined men, ready to meet and drive back the hoards of abolition fanatics and house-burning demons, who would pollute our soil with their presence—who would come among us for murder, rapine and plunder."[11]

The steps taken might be of an informal nature. For example, the San Augustine *Red Land Express* reported that the young men of that town, "having the public weal at heart," had met on August 8 and organized themselves into companies for patrolling the town against "the supposed incendiaries in our State."[12] The normal procedure, however, was more organized and elaborate. The usual course was to call a town or county meeting to which all of the local white male adults were invited. At this meeting the citizens discussed the dangers facing the community and passed a series of resolutions concerning them. They then elected from among their own number a vigilance committee, which they charged with detecting and punishing the abolitionist culprits. The newspapers, as well as private citizens, invariably reported that only the leading citizens of the communities were chosen to man the committees. The Galveston *News,* reporting the formation of numerous vigilance committees in the state, said: "and everywhere only the most respectable and influential citizens have been allowed to form these committees."[13] The emphasis placed upon the high standing of those who participated may have reflected a desire to lend respectability to the usurpation of legal authority by those bodies.

Unfortunately for the scholar who would test these assertions of respectability, vigilance committee membership lists almost always were withheld from publication, ostensibly to prevent white abolitionists from knowing the identities of their pursuers. A citizen of Ellis County wrote: "No one but those immediately interested knows who compose the committees, nor where or when they

11. La Grange *True Issue,* August 2, 1860.
12. San Augustine *Red Land Express,* August 11, 1860.
13. Galveston *News,* August 21, 1860.

meet, or what they are doing."[14] Typical was an article in the Corsicana *Navarro Express* describing a citizens' organizational meeting at Chatsfield. Wherever the names of elected officers were mentioned in the resolutions, the newspaper substituted blanks. It was just as secretive with the names of the rank and file of the committee, reporting that the citizens had resolved "that an investigation committee of seventeen be appointed, to be composed of the following named gentlemen, to-wit: [Here follows seventeen names]."[15]

Newspapers nevertheless occasionally identified individuals who acted as leaders of the committees, and the names thus revealed tend to support Richard Maxwell Brown's generalization that the elite of the community typically furnished the leadership for vigilante movements.[16] For example, Isaac Parker, who had served many years as a member of the Texas legislature and for whom Parker County was named, became chairman of the Tarrant County committee.[17] Benjamin Barkley, a physician and lawyer, headed the committee in Birdville.[18] John M. Crockett, who chaired the Dallas vigilantes, was a prominent lawyer and community leader. He had served in the legislature and was mayor of Dallas at the time of the panic. In 1861 he would be elected lieutenant governor of the state.[19]

Support given to the movement by prominent Texans also undoubtedly added to the respectability of the committees. Congressman John H. Reagan wrote to his brother that he had attended a meeting in Palestine "in relation to the Negro disturbances." Reagan, who the previous year had won re-election to the House as a committed unionist,[20] reiterated some of the charges of

---

14. Galveston *Weekly News,* n.d., clipped in New Orleans (La.) *Daily Delta,* July 30, 1860.

15. Corsicana *Navarro Express,* August 11, 1860. The bracketed phrase is the editor's. It demonstrates the prevailing desire to keep vigilance committee membership secret.

16. Brown, "The American Vigilante Tradition," 157.

17. Marshall *Texas Republican,* August 25, 1860. Parker was the uncle of Cynthia Ann Parker, who had been captured by Indians in 1836. For more information about Parker, see *Handbook of Texas Online,* s.v., www.tsha.utexas.edu/handbook/online/articles/PP/fpa22.html (accessed July 29, 2006).

18. B. F. Barkley, Birdville, to D. M. Barkley, Louisville, Kentucky, quoted in Louisville *Courier,* n.d., clipped in Washington (D. C.) *Constitution,* August 9, 1860. For more on Barkley, see *Handbook of Texas Online,* s.v., www.tsha.utexas.edu/handbook/online/articles/BB/fba67.html (accessed July 18, 2006).

19. William S. Speer and John Henry Brown, eds., *The Encyclopedia of the New West* (Marshall, Tex., 1881), 161. For additional information on Crockett, see *Handbook of Texas Online,* s.v., www.tsha.utexas.edu/handbook/online/articles/CC/fcr25.html (accessed July 29, 2006).

20. In his memoirs, Reagan told of the strong opposition of the Democratic establishment to his candidacy on account of his opposition to filibustering expeditions (designed to add slave ter-

Charles Pryor and told his brother that he now was convinced that an abolitionist plot lay behind the mischief, and he asserted that none of those responsible "ought to be permitted to leave the State alive where his complicity can be clearly shown."[21] Louis T. Wigfall later told his colleagues in the U.S. Senate that he had personally supported and participated in the efforts of the vigilantes in his hometown of Marshall.[22]

Although secrecy was the rule, at least one vigilance committee had its entire membership published in a newspaper. The Bellville *Texas Countryman* named the members of the Austin County Committee in a story on the citizens' meeting that had elected them.[23] There were ninety members, and seventy-seven of them appear on the U.S. Census rolls of 1860. Analysis of the membership confirms that at least in Austin County the vigilantes tended to be mature and substantial citizens. Virtually all of the members held property; indeed, by the standards of the day, most of them were well-to-do men. The median value of personal and real property for the seventy-seven identifiable vigilantes was $15,000. Thirty-one were worth over $20,000, and nineteen, or about one-fourth of the listed members, possessed holdings valued at more than $50,000. Nine members held property valued in excess of $100,000, and the wealthiest member estimated his worth at $460,000.[24]

Without exception, the richest men on the committee were farmers, but this was hardly surprising since Austin County was predominantly rural. Of the seventy-seven identifiable vigilantes, there were sixty farmers, eight merchants, four lawyers, three hotel keepers, one stock raiser, one doctor, and one brick mason. The chairman of the committee, however, was neither a farmer nor for that matter one of the wealthiest members: He was "Z. Hunt," a lawyer whose estimated worth was $18,000. It seems likely that the apparent penchant for placing lawyers at the head of the vigilance committees was due to a need

ritory at the expense of Mexico, Cuba, and Central America) and to reopening the slave trade. At the time, he said: "I repudiate all sectional heresies. I repudiate everything that is not national. . . . I denounce fanaticism in the South with the same distinctness that I denounce the fanaticism of abolitionism in the North. They are both heresies." Although the press overwhelmingly opposed him, most of the voters agreed with him, he said, and he won re-election by a landslide (John H. Reagan, *Memoirs, With Special Reference to Secession and the Civil War* [New York, 1906], 70–71, 73).

21. John H. Reagan, Palestine, to Morris Reagan, August 10, 1860, Austin *Texas State Gazette*, weekly ed., August 18, 1860.

22. *Congressional Globe*, 36th Cong., 2nd Sess., December 18, 1860, 74–75.

23. Bellville *Texas Countryman*, August 25, 1860.

24. U. S. Bureau of the Census, *Population of the United States in 1860: Compiled from the Original Returns of the Eighth Census* (Washington, D. C., 1864), 1:154–218.

to give some semblance of law to the judicial proceedings of these bodies. Since the chairman of the typical committee was roughly analogous to the judge in a regular court of law, it was presumably of some advantage for him to know the law, even though his "court" was not bound by it.[25]

As one might suspect from the healthy economic status of the group as a whole, the Austin County committee was hardly composed of rash, young hot bloods looking for excitement. The ages of committee members ranged from twenty-three to sixty-five, but the vast majority—sixty-nine to be exact—were between twenty-five and fifty-five years of age. The median and average ages were 40 and 41.3, respectively, indicating that by the life-expectancy standards of the day at least, the committee was definitely made up of mature men, if not graybeards.[26]

AGES	NUMBER OF COMMITTEEMEN
20–24	2
25–29	11
30–34	9
35–39	13
40–44	12
45–49	10
50–54	14
55–59	3
60–64	2
65	1

The citizens who, in their called meetings, established the vigilance committees and elected their members usually vested these bodies with sweeping powers. Citizens' resolutions normally spelled out the authority of the committees in broad terms, virtually giving the vigilantes carte blanche in dealing with the crisis. The committee in Brenham, for example, received "full power to act for the safety and defense of the people."[27] The citizens instructed the Tarrant County committee "to examine suspicious strangers, and take such other action as they may deem proper in case of emergency."[28] A Fort Worth resolution

25. Ibid.
26. Ibid.
27. Brenham *Texas Ranger*, n.d., clipped in Marshall *Texas Republican*, August 11, 1860.
28. Cincinnati (Ohio) *Daily Commercial*, August 20, 1860.

mandated the compilation of two lists that would include "black Republicans, abolitionists and higher law men of every class; List No. 1, all suspected persons; List No. 2, black list, to be exterminated by immediate hanging."[29] And the citizens of Mill Creek delegated to their "Committee of Safety" the power "to take such measures in the premises, as in their judgement may seem proper, and whatsoever the said committee may determine ought to be done, we pledge our honors, as good citizens, to carry out by all means and exertions in our power, and stand by them, even to the risk of our lives."[30]

While the mandates given the committees were virtually limitless, some citizens' resolutions did attempt to establish loose guidelines for the punishment of "convicted" abolitionist malefactors. If the evidence against the accused were "conclusive," said the citizens of Rush Creek, then "it shall be the duty of this committee to hang or burn such person, or persons, as the evidence in the case may determine." If, on the other hand, it was shown only that the accused individuals had "entertained and expressed sentiments against the institution of slavery," as opposed to actually tampering with slaves, then the penalty was to be "expatriation."[31] The Chatsfield resolution, while empowering the local committee to investigate charges and "take such action in reference thereto as they may deem best," nevertheless counseled calmness and prudence, and it laid down certain ground rules. A quorum of the committee (nine members), by unanimous approval, could inflict "any punishment they may deem proper"; however, abolitionists could receive only one of two possible sentences: "Death if found guilty of tampering with Negroes; expatriation upon well founded suspicion of guilt." On the other hand, any five members of the seventeen-man committee could investigate and inflict punishment in "Negro cases."[32]

The resolutions establishing the vigilance committees were adopted by vote of the citizens attending the meetings, but all citizens of the community or county, depending upon the type of committee involved, were expected to sup-

29. Quoted in Hofstadter and Wallace, eds., *American Violence*, 201.

30. Brenham *Enquirer*, August 11, 1860, clipped in Austin *Texas State Gazette*, weekly ed., August 25, 1860.

31. Corsicana *Navarro Express*, August 11, 1860.

32. Ibid. The citizens' resolutions rarely listed any qualifications for membership on the vigilance committees, but there were exceptions. For example, the Mill Creek resolution forbade membership to men of "intemperate habits" and further declared: "no person under the influence of liquor shall be permitted to accompany the patrol on any of their expeditions." It is worth noting that while the other resolutions were reported to have passed unanimously, the temperance resolution was said simply to have passed, indicating perhaps that there were in the crowd a few bibulous aspirants to the high calling of vigilante.

port the provisions. Failure to do so was certain to invite scrutiny by the committees. The citizens of Telico, in Ellis County, were "requested" to sign the resolution, "and any person objecting or refusing to sign said resolutions may be justly regarded as at least entertaining principles treasonable to the South, and will merit our suspicion."[33]

On matters involving the alleged abolitionist conspiracy, regular law officers and judges generally yielded all authority to the vigilantes. Until the panic had largely run its course in mid-September, there is no evidence that law enforcement officials attempted to exercise their responsibilities either to conduct investigations or to protect the rights of those persons accused by the committees. In the prevailing climate of excitement, it would have been risky, possibly dangerous, for public officials to assert their authority, even had they been so inclined. Thus in most communities law enforcement officers and court officials either cooperated with the vigilantes or remained discreetly in the background. When the vigilantes came to suspect African American conspirators in Montgomery County, a newspaper reported: "The Sheriff had resigned to be out of their way, the Committee by common consent of the people having all the authority."[34] A report on the secret vigilante proceedings in Dallas and Ellis counties said pointedly: "No one else interferes in the investigation."[35]

There were considerable differences in the sizes, structures, and procedures of the vigilance committees. Numbers of members varied greatly, depending upon the size of the community and wishes of the citizens. Villages such as Denton and Dallas, which had committees of fifty and fifty-two respectively, could muster fewer members than the larger towns and counties, whose committees often approached or even exceeded a hundred members. In sparsely settled rural communities the entire male population might serve on the committee and participate in its deliberations. Such was the case in Pine Grove, Austin County, where the committee chairman was empowered to call a meeting of all adult male residents whenever any allegations were made of insurrectionary activity. The citizens, or those who were able to attend the scheduled meeting, would then hear charges, examine evidence, and render a decision on the guilt or innocence of the accused.[36] In larger towns and counties, committee organization tended to be more elaborate and procedures were a bit more formal than they were in the small towns and villages. For example, the vigilantes

33. Austin *Southern Intelligencer,* October 10, 1860.
34. Marshall *Texas Republican,* August 25, 1860.
35. Galveston *News,* July 28, 1860, clipped in New Orleans (La.) *Daily Delta,* July 30, 1860.
36. Bellville *Texas Countryman,* August 25, 1860.

of Bellville not only had a president and secretary, but also an executive committee, which appointed night patrols and apparently performed other leadership functions for the larger group.[37]

In addition to giving the vigilance committees a broad mandate to deal with the abolitionist threat, the various citizens' meetings usually passed numerous resolutions spelling out specific dangers with which the vigilantes should concern themselves. Although there were naturally variations from town to town and county to county in the number and content of such resolutions, there were also many similarities. Invariably, the committees called upon the slaveholders and vigilantes to exercise stricter control over the bondsmen. Slaves caught off their plantations without a pass were subject to arrest and punishment. This requirement, which was already a part of the slave code in Texas, was laxly enforced in normal times, but during the panic it was rigorously applied. For example, Hattie Joplin Roach wrote that the slaves of Cherokee County who were caught off their plantations without the proper authorization received severe whippings. Even an elderly black woman taken up by the "Pat-Rollers" suffered thirty lashes for her indiscretion.[38]

During the panic some communities suspended all passes for slaves. A citizens' committee in Bastrop resolved that such permits should be disregarded by night patrols and ordered the arrest of "all Negroes found away from their owners' premises."[39] Vigilantes made it clear that they expected the cooperation of slaveowners in the crackdown on the slaves. For example, the Matagorda committee decided to search slave quarters for arms and declared that it would "prosecute" any slaveholders who stood in their way.[40] San Antonio's committee was even more explicit: It would fine and whip any slaveowner who refused to enforce new restrictions on the movement of their slaves.[41]

Although the committees concentrated their attention upon slaves, they also regarded free blacks with suspicion and in some cases applied restrictions to them as well. San Antonio's vigilantes, for example, prohibited both slaves and "Free Persons of Color" from drinking, gambling, and unsupervised assembly. The La Grange *True Issue* undoubtedly voiced the belief of many Texans when it wrote that the free black population constituted "the most ruinous element of dissatisfaction in any slave community. We have too many such cattle in our midst."[42]

37. Ibid., August 18, 1860.
38. Roach, *A History of Cherokee County*, 61.
39. Bellville *Texas Countryman*, August 25, 1860.
40. Austin *Texas State Gazette*, August 11, 1860.
41. San Antonio *Ledger and Texan*, August 30, 1860.
42. La Grange *True Issue*, August 2, 1860.

Slaves and free blacks were easily identified by their color; not so the white abolitionists who had allegedly planned the conspiracy and were providing direction to the misguided blacks. These mysterious figures apparently were moving among other whites, doing business with them and otherwise giving few, if any, outward signs of their perfidy. Small wonder that the citizens' resolutions stressed the need to investigate with extreme diligence all white strangers and new residents, particularly those who had come from the North. Indeed, identifying and rooting out white abolitionists became a mania in some parts of the state, and immigrants from northern states often were considered guilty of harboring anti-slavery principles unless they could prove otherwise. Typical was the ominous-sounding resolution adopted by the citizens of Guadalupe County: "We hold persons born and educated North of Mason and Dixon's line, whose antecedents are not known, and whose means of support are not visible, as enemies to our peace and welfare until the contrary is proved, and advise them, if they have a prudent regard for their personal safety to give us a wide berth, as they will be dealt with according to a law which we have established for our own protection."[43]

Charging that there was a disposition among blacks "to revolt and be insubordinate," a public meeting in the Grimes County town of Anderson blamed "certain white persons" and stipulated: "Northerners coming into the country under pretence of being ministers, teachers, drummers, etc., are to be regarded with suspicion and received with caution."[44] On the same subject, another group of citizens pledged "not to give aid, countenance or employment to any man coming from abolition States unless he be well known or comes recommended in such a manner as places his character and sentiments above suspicion."[45]

The citizens of Paris even seriously discussed whether steps should be taken to expel all northerners from Texas. Thomas J. Crooks, publisher of the Paris *Press,* took vigorous exception to this proposal, however, pointing out that Texas had been settled in large measure by northerners; indeed, he reminded his fellow citizens that the state's capital—Austin—was named after one. Northerners who had settled in Texas and had identified themselves with southern interests should no more be suspect than native-born southerners, Crooks argued. Reporting this controversy in Paris, A. B. Norton, editor of the Austin *Southern Intelligencer,* agreed with Crooks. Himself an Ohio man, Norton

43. Seguin *Union Democrat,* August 6, 1860, clipped in Austin *Texas State Gazette,* September 8, 1860.

44. Anderson *Central Texian,* July 28, 1860, clipped in Marshall *Texas Republican,* August 11, 1860.

45. Bellville *Texas Countryman,* August 25, 1860.

asserted that every Democratic editor in the state was either foreign-born, from the North, or northern-educated. The same was generally true, he said, of the state's preachers, lawyers, and merchants. Norton denounced "this spirit of intolerance, based upon geographical division of birth place."[46]

Most newspapers nevertheless agreed with the vigilantes where northerners were concerned. Several editors reprinted the citizens' warnings to white strangers and reinforced them with admonitions of their own. The Corsicana *Navarro Express* said: "Northern men of recent emigration, of all classes, trades, and professions must in justice to ourselves, be watched, until they have proven themselves reliable."[47] Sounding a similar note, the Bellville *Texas Countryman* declared: "There are many itinerating strangers among us. Some pretending to follow one occupation and some another. They will bear watching these times. They may be spies and fiends intent on the destruction of our homes, our property and our lives."[48] The Galveston *News* obviously agreed with this view when it said, "There are at this time a larger number of suspicious characters in our midst than we have ever known before," and it too called for a careful scrutiny of strangers.[49]

Northerners traveling in the Lone Star State during the panic were in special danger from vigilance committees. Warned one Texas correspondent of the New York *Herald*: "Texas is no place for Northern people just now, especially for itinerant pedlars, and so forth. Such a class had better keep away. Their necks would be in great danger of breaking. It is in the character of pedlars or preachers that these abolitionists have mostly been travelling throughout Texas."[50] Even northerners who had lived in Texas for years were often suspect. Vigilance committees frequently "waited upon" such men, interrogating them concerning their slavery views and harassing them generally. Since the burden of proof rested upon the immigrant, rather than upon his interrogators, the northerner was in a difficult, and potentially perilous, predicament unless he possessed sound credentials indeed. In view of the many reports of harsh treatment of itinerants by vigilantes, newspapers warned outsiders against travel in the Lone Star State. For example, the Wellsburg *Herald* wisely said: "It strikes us Texas would be a very unwholesome State just now for emigrants."[51]

46. Austin *Southern Intelligencer,* September 5, 1860.

47. Corsicana *Navarro Express,* August 25, 1860.

48. Bellville *Texas Countryman,* July 28, 1860.

49. Galveston *News,* n.d., clipped in Marshall *Texas Republican,* August 4, 1860.

50. Anonymous letter, dated August 20, 1860, New York *Herald,* n.d., clipped in Charleston (S.C.) *Mercury,* September 8, 1860.

51. Wellsburg (Va.) *Herald,* September 14, 1860.

Some of the frustration that all northerners of recent immigration must have felt was revealed in a letter written at the height of the panic and published in the New York *Tribune*. The writer understandably chose to remain anonymous, and he gave as his location only "somewhere near the seacoast in Texas." The author—a businessman who had been in Texas only three months— complained bitterly that the abolitionist scare had aggravated Texans' "insane opposition to everything Eastern (except goods, wares, and merchandise)." Even northern men of "permanent residence" were distrusted, the writer continued: "It is said their education, previous residence, hereditary influences, &c., render them unsafe for reliance on that 'tender vital question to the South.'" Patrols closely questioned every stranger, the disgruntled northerner wrote, and if they detected a northern accent, its unfortunate possessor "is continually questioned and annoyed, and distrusted. So a residence here in Texas is at this time exceedingly unpleasant, and were it not for the delay incident to disposing of my goods, I should depart hence without delay at once."[52]

In many communities vigilantes intercepted travelers as they passed through town, interrogating them and searching their person and baggage for incriminating evidence. These "examinations," as they were euphemistically called by the press, could be rough. In his reminiscences of the panic in East Texas, a resident of Rusk wrote that patrols guarded the towns day and night: "Every passing stranger was investigated and his credentials examined. The poor pedlar, especially was in imminent danger of being mobbed at any time on mere suspicion."[53] A young man of Marshall gave a similar account in a letter to his father: "Every man that travels this country is taken up and examined, and if he does not give a good account of himself, he is strung up to the nearest tree."[54]

This harsh treatment of strangers, so alien to the hospitality that many Texans habitually afforded travelers in peaceful times, was a regrettable necessity in the eyes of some. The Anderson *Central Texian* spoke for this element in a story that told of vigilantes stopping a traveler and subjecting him to an "examination" before allowing him to continue his journey. "The duty (for we esteem it a duty) is a painful one; but the preservation of our property, as well as the lives of our woman [*sic*] and children, leaves us no alternative. We are bound to act and exercise the most rigid scrutiny towards strangers, and woe to the man who may be found moving in our midst with the least suspicion attached to him."[55]

52. New York *Daily Tribune*, August 22, 1860.

53. Barron, *The Lone Star Defenders*, 17, 1860.

54. James L. Craig, Marshall, to A. K. Craig, Houston, August 9, 1860, Houston *Petrel*, August 24, 1860, clipped in Cincinnati (Ohio) *Daily Commercial*, September 1, 1860.

55. Anderson *Central Texian*, n.d., clipped in Galveston *The Crisis*, August 27, 1860.

Woe indeed! Even native Texans and other southerners whose foursquare views on slavery were familiar to the people of their own communities took their lives in their own hands when they ventured into those parts of Texas where they were unknown. The prudent man postponed all travel during the period of greatest vigilante activity. If one could not delay a journey, it was essential that he go armed—not only with a handy weapon, but also with full identification and preferably a "pass" from the vigilance committee of his community, attesting that he was a trustworthy citizen holding "southern" principles. James Craig, of Marshall, who in early August planned a trip to Red River County, reported that he would have to obtain a "passport" before he could safely make the journey, "and even then, I expect to have a hard time getting through, for a man's word is nothing in these critical times."[56]

Whether any pro-slavery travelers actually lost their lives or suffered serious injury at the hands of vigilantes is unknown, but it is a matter of record that some of them underwent harrowing experiences. One such unfortunate was a man named J. M. Peers (also spelled Pierce), a cabinetmaker by trade who had lived in Shreveport and, more recently, in Marshall. Peers was in Sulphur Springs when the panic broke out, and he even assisted the local vigilantes in "routing out an abolitionist." For some reason—perhaps because he was new in town and had arrived from the east—Peers fell under suspicion of being the abolitionist who had allegedly burned Henderson. After receiving rough handling in Sulphur Springs, he was taken to Paris, where he was finally released, possibly because the Henderson committee had already found an "abolitionist" to blame for that city's destruction.[57]

Peers then started out on foot for Marshall, only to be overtaken by two of the men who had previously "examined" him. His tormentors reportedly brandished a rope and threatened to hang him; they settled instead for his money ($67.50) and left him free to continue his trek to Marshall. He finally stumbled into the office of the Marshall *Texas Republican,* alive and well but "somewhat the worse for wear." R. M. Loughery, editor of the *Texas Republican,* professed to be "startled at his appearance," commenting that Peers had "evidently suffered a great deal." The irony was that Peers, far from feigning his pro-slavery opinions in Sulphur Springs, was in fact a staunch southern rights man. Noting that the mistreated itinerant was a subscriber to the New Orleans *Delta,* Richmond *Enquirer,* and Galveston *News,* as well as several other southern rights

56. James L. Craig, Marshall, to A. K. Craig, Houston, August 9, 1860, Houston *Petrel,* August 24, 1860, clipped in Cincinnati (Ohio) *Daily Commercial,* September 1, 1860.

57. Marshall *Texas Republican,* August 25, 1860.

journals, Loughery said: "If he is sound upon anything we should suppose it was the 'nigger' question." Peers himself reportedly blamed no one for arresting and interrogating him; still, he believed that he had been treated with "unnecessary and unjustifiable cruelty."[58]

Another incident involved a wealthy slaveowner from Louisiana named Savers. According to the New Orleans *Picayune*, Savers was on a business trip to Texas when Dallas burned. Arriving in Palestine, in Anderson County, shortly after that disaster, the Louisianan failed to make his stage connection to Crockett. In danger of missing a business appointment, he desperately tried to rent a private rig so that he could resume his journey. Savers's obvious anxiety and the fact that he had arrived from the direction of Dallas aroused the suspicions of local vigilantes, and a crowd quickly gathered. Savers's story failed to satisfy the mob, which determined to hang him on the spot. Acting quickly, the imperiled traveler drew his revolver and declared that if he must die he would sell his life "as dearly as possible." A tense stalemate ensued until Savers had the presence of mind to reveal that he was a member of the Masonic Lodge and to call upon any fellow Masons in the crowd to protect him until his identity could be established. This tactic succeeded. The hanging was postponed, and Savers subsequently obtained his release.[59]

Although all northerners were instantly suspect, preachers headed the citizens' lists of suspicious persons. The principal religious denominations had divided on a sectional basis years before over the slavery question. Time had only served to widen the breach. The recent, highly publicized effort of the Northern Methodists to establish churches in the Lone Star State, climaxing in the abortive Timber Creek Conference of 1859, had strengthened the animosity of Texans toward northern churchmen. Thus, when Pryor asserted that the infamous preachers Blunt and McKinney had provided the leadership for the new conspiracy, suspicion became phobia. There were but few preachers affiliated with any of the northern churches, and these appear to have been among the vanguard of northerners who fled Texas in increasing numbers as the panic intensified. For example, Anthony Bewley, a Northern Methodist minister in Johnson County, gathered up his family and fled immediately upon hearing of the alleged abolitionist plot. Having experienced great hostility from Texans

58. Ibid. Another journal described Peers as follows: "A cabinet workman by trade, heavy built, about 30 or 35 years old, dark complection, talks politics, and sometimes speaks of having been engaged in the mercantile business—Is ordinarily dressed" (Galveston *News*, n.d., clipped in Bellville *Texas Countryman*, September 8, 1860).

59. New Orleans (La.) *Daily Picayune*, August 25, 1860.

in more peaceful times, he knew that he would be unlikely to survive a full-fledged abolitionist scare, particularly one that singled out members of his denomination as the principal plotters.[60]

In the absence of any significant number of ministers representing northern sects, vigilantes turned to investigating preachers of their own denominations. The Galveston *News* reported, for example, that the vigilance committee of Magnolia, Anderson County, had exonerated "the Rev. Mr. Martin" on charges of holding anti-slavery views and was "satisfied with his opinions on the subject."[61] Such interrogations of preachers may have been common, judging from the many rumors in circulation concerning possible ministerial involvement in the alleged abolitionist activities. Oscar M. Addison, a circuit-riding Methodist preacher whose territory was in South Texas, indicated how irresponsible some of the rumors were in a letter to the Reverend L. Whitworth in Waxahachie: "My dear Bro: 'The Fool Killer' has not been around for some time and his legitimate subjects in some of the neighboring Counties are improving their short day of grace, by circulating all kinds of stories in relation to the reported abolition movement in your County—among them, that you have been hung as an abolition emmissary, and that your dying confession implicated 2000 ministers and school teachers in Texas engaged in this nefarious work &c."[62]

Addison suggested that Whitworth publish a card in the *Texas Christian Advocate* "stating the true condition of affairs in the upper counties, for some of the women are being frightened out of their wits by what I am satisfied are unmitigated lies."[63] Addison went on to say that he had previously heard it "authoritatively reported" that a Baptist preacher named Buffington had been hanged in Anderson County for abolitionist activities; however, upon visiting that area, he had learned that the story was groundless.[64]

Walter S. South, another Methodist preacher, who lived near Belknap, may have been another of the North Texas ministers rumored to be abolitionists. On July 26, South confided to his diary: "Wrote to my mother concerning a false report circulated in that country about myself and Brother."[65] In a letter to the

60. Elliott, *South-Western Methodism*, 149–158. See chapter 7 for a full account of Bewley's story.

61. Galveston *News*, n.d., clipped in Bellville *Texas Countryman*, September 8, 1860.

62. Oscar M. Addison, Caldwell, to the Reverend L. Whitworth, Waxahachie, August 15, 1860, Oscar M. Addison Papers, Barker Texas History Center Archives, University of Texas, Austin, Texas.

63. Ibid.

64. Ibid.

65. Walter S. South Diary, typescript, Barker Texas History Center Archives, University of Texas, Austin, Texas.

Texas Baptist, a correspondent who identified himself only as "D. M. B." may well have been hinting at the rumored ministerial involvement in the alleged conspiracy when he wrote: "We shall not be surprised to find that there are men engaged in this thing, whose position in society claims an unusual share of public confidence."[66]

One sure means of defeating the elusive parson-abolitionists was to cut off all contact between them and the blacks that they were supposed to lead. A common stipulation in the citizens' resolutions prohibited unsupervised black worship services. Some communities even forbade black services entirely. For example, a committee in Grimes County resolved that "preaching to the Negroes in the county be stopped, at least for one year."[67] A similar moratorium suspended African American religious services in Huntsville.[68] More usually, blacks could continue to meet for worship, but only under the strict supervision of whites. In San Antonio, they were forbidden to congregate in groups of more than five, save on the plantations; moreover, the only African American services allowed in the Alamo City were those attended by "at least one respectable slave holder."[69] In like manner, the Austin County citizens' meeting resolved "That the ministers of all religious denominations are requested to desist for this year, from preaching at public places to Negroes except religious worship be tolerated on plantations under the eye of masters and overseers."[70]

The question of whether blacks should continue to worship publicly at all apparently sparked a vigorous debate in some quarters. The Elm Fork Association of the Baptist denomination met in McKinney in early September, and, according to one minister who attended the conclave, the subject of preaching the gospel to blacks "called forth quite an animated discussion." The association finally passed a resolution endorsing the practice and even suggesting that white ministers give more time to the task than they had done formerly. The association further urged all the slave-owning brethren to bring their slaves to church "on all occasions." It was clear, however, that the spiritual welfare of the bondsmen was not uppermost in the minds of the Elm Fork Baptists, for the minister who reported on the meeting concluded: "Our brethren have taken the right view of this matter—that the present excitement creates a particular necessity for instructing the people in the truths of the gospel, that they are tempted to

66. Letter of "D. M. B.," Anderson *Texas Baptist,* August 23, 1860.

67. New Orleans (La.) *Daily Picayune,* August 7, 1860.

68. Marshall *Texas Republican,* August 25, 1860.

69. San Antonio *Daily Ledger and Texan,* August 30, 1860.

70. Bellville *Texas Countryman,* August 25, 1860.

disobedience and rebellion renders more necessary that they should be taught the relative duties of life."[71] A committee at Jamestown in Smith County noted allegations that religious services for blacks had been the source of the abolitionist trouble. Nevertheless, although the committee conceded that "some mischief" might have resulted from the "injudicious assemblage" of bondsmen for worship, it argued that no harm would come from such meetings if slaveholders would take the trouble to supervise them adequately.[72]

There was greater unanimity on curtailing other kinds of activities by blacks. In his letter to the Houston *Telegraph* of July 25, Charles R. Pryor wrote: "The danger of suffering Negroes to go out to celebrations, to hear political speeches and to hold meetings of their own, is rendered apparent by the developments connected with this matter. We have learned a lesson, and will profit by it."[73] The San Antonio *Ledger and Texan* agreed that the slaves had been allowed too much freedom and said "a strict eye" should be kept on them.[74] Hence, not only did blacks suffer increased restrictions in their religious practices, but they also found that other favorite activities, such as balls and card playing, were forbidden.[75]

Whites placed severe limitation on the movements of blacks. If caught off their master's premises, they had better have a pass signed by their owner or overseer. Some communities placed even more rigorous restrictions on the comings and goings of bondsmen. For example, the Travis and Forkston "beats" in Austin County decreed: "And if any slave shall be caught after the time allowed in his or her permit has expired, or any other place, except the one designated in the permit, or off of the main or direct route too [*sic*] or from that place, said slave shall be dealt with in the same manner as though it had no permit."[76] A Houstonian wrote to a friend in New England that the abolitionists, by their plotting, had forced the slaveholders to grind the black man down and take away many of his freedoms. "One year ago all was peace and quietness here," the Texan said. "The negro was allowed to go out to have dances and frolics; to-day, one dare not show his head after 9:00 in the evening."[77]

To enforce these restrictions upon slaves and protect their communities from the fiery torches of abolitionists, vigilantes depended upon specially

71. J. F. Johnson, McKinney, to George W. Baines, Anderson, September 10, 1860, Anderson *Texas Baptist,* August 23, 1860.

72. Galveston *Texas Christian Advocate,* September 27, 1860.

73. Houston *Telegraph,* August 7, 1860.

74. San Antonio *Daily Ledger and Texan,* August 6, 1860.

75. Ibid., August 30, 1860.

76. Bellville *Texas Countryman,* August 18, 1860.

77. Hartford (Conn.) *Weekly Times,* September 8, 1860.

appointed patrols. Every "beat" of each county in the affected areas usually mounted a patrol to watch for suspicious activity. The patrols operated both night and day during the panic, but they were especially active at night, when the towns and countryside were thought to be the most vulnerable to arsonists and assassins. Thus seventy-six of the "leading citizens of Rusk" so closely watched that town that one reportedly could not go "fifty steps in any direction" without being challenged.[78] Twenty-four watchmen took up stations each night in Jefferson, and it was said that no one could venture out upon the streets there after dark without being called upon "to give an account of himself."[79] A "political force" of between sixty and ninety men reportedly watched night and day over the capitol city of Austin.[80] Tyler had been spared, said the Tyler *Reporter*, only because of the great vigilance of its citizens: "Over one hundred citizens are on patrol duty every night. Every man who is met by one of them is hailed, and if he fails or refuses to answer his life would not be worth a straw."[81]

Even towns near the Texas coast, though far removed from the center of the alleged plot, kept a sharp lookout for abolitionists. Admitting that no attempt had yet been made to destroy Matagorda, the *Gazette* of that city nevertheless endorsed the establishment of a patrol for the town and warned that anyone caught trying to fire the town "need not expect a trial."[82] The Houston *Telegraph* observed that virtually every town in the state was under heavy guard each night, and although the editor did not believe that the evidence had indicated a bona fide plot in the southern half of the state, he added: "Still, these vigilant guards have done much good in arresting vagabond white men and runaway Negroes."[83] A resident of the same city wrote to a friend that no fewer than seven companies of patrols had been formed to guard Houston every night; moreover, "Sixteen horse patrol scour the country around. Forty-eight vigilance men say live, banish or die, as the proof may go to show. And so it is all over the country."[84]

The maintenance of large night patrols often required that a sizable proportion of a town's white male population participate. Apparently few were spared

78. Rusk *Enquirer*, n.d., quoted in San Augustine *Red Land Express*, August 18, 1860.

79. Jefferson *Herald*, August 17, 1860, clipped in Galveston *Civilian and Gazette*, weekly ed., August 28, 1860.

80. Letter of "Mrs. Bennett," n.d., Houston *True Southron*, July 28, 1860, clipped in St. Louis *Daily Missouri Republican*, August 10, 1860

81. Tyler *Reporter*, August 8, 1860, clipped in Austin *Texas State Gazette*, August 25, 1860.

82. Matagorda *Gazette*, August 22, 1860.

83. Houston *Telegraph*, n.d., clipped in Jackson *Semi-Weekly Mississippian*, August 21, 1860.

84. Hartford (Conn.) *Weekly Times*, September 8, 1860.

this duty, regardless of their station. Senator Louis T. Wigfall later told his colleagues in Washington that he had returned to his home in Marshall following the adjournment of Congress, expecting to refresh himself with an extended rest. Instead, he had found the town caught up in intense excitement over the alleged abolitionist plot: "And from the day I reached home until I left—between six weeks and two months—there was a guard of twenty-four men every night in a small village of between two and three thousand inhabitants. I myself had to shoulder my gun, and stand guard."[85]

For those who had to work all day, the requirement that they stand guard at night as well was almost too much to bear. In Tyler, where a hundred men stood watch nightly, the strain was evident in an editorial that appeared in the local newspaper: "For four nights, every man connected with the 'Reporter' has been on duty and we are all completely worn out, and if this excitement still continues to exist, we must stop our regular issues, and furnish the news in the form of extras, for it is impossible for us to watch all night and work all day. We shall keep up, however, as long as possible."[86] A similar note was sounded in a report from Waxahachie, where it was said, "The people were constantly watching, and were almost worn down with their vigilance."[87]

The presence of large numbers of anxious night patrolmen inevitably led to incidents that must have been as startling to the sleepy townspeople as they were to the victims. In Tyler, night patrolmen reportedly shot at a man they thought was preparing to set fire to the town. The man was later found dead.[88] A man in Houston wrote to his wife in Alabama about an encounter in that city:

> Last night [August 10] we had quite an alarm. The patrol had taken up a negro and were taking him to the calaboose, when he broke and ran; five or six shots were fired at him in rapid succession, accompanied with loud shouting of the pursuers, barking of dogs, &c. Mr. —— and his wife were badly scared. . . . I found that the fool nigger had jumped into the bayou in order to escape—one of the white men plunged in after him, and there they had it in the water, and the night as dark as pitch.
>
> the negro got the white man by the foot and tried to drown him. At length both were rescued, and the negro taken to jail. You can imagine, from what I have written, that we have quite lively times in Texas.[89]

85. *Congressional Globe*, 36th Congress, 2nd Sess., December 13, 1860, 74–75.
86. Tyler *Reporter*, August 8, 1860, clipped in Austin *Texas State Gazette*, August 25, 1860.
87. Houston *Telegraph*, July 31, 1860, clipped in Austin *Texas State Gazette*, August 11, 1860.
88. San Antonio *Daily Ledger and Texan*, August 15, 1860.
89. Anonymous letter of August 11, 1860, Montgomery (Ala.) *Mail*, n.d., clipped in Charleston (S.C.) *Daily Courier*, August 24, 1860.

In their relentless search for abolitionists, the vigilantes often turned to the post offices for assistance. If there was a statewide conspiracy afoot, the conspirators obviously must communicate with one another; therefore, postal officials carefully watched the mails for suspicious missives that might contain incriminating evidence. The Eighth Legislature had decreed that anyone who wrote or published any material calculated to inculcate a spirit of insubordination or incite rebellion among the slave population, or "knowingly circulate[d]" such writings or publications, could be sentenced to the penitentiary for up to seven years. The same law required postmasters who detected such seditious literature in the mails to turn over the materials to a local law enforcement officer or magistrate for examination. Persons subscribing to such publications could be fined the sum of $500 or jailed for up to six months, or both. If a postmaster failed to report the arrival of the proscribed publications, he was liable to be fined up to $200.[90] Following this law, some communities passed formal resolutions calling upon postmasters to aid the vigilance committees in the battle against the abolitionists. For example, the residents of Travis, in Austin County, admonished the postmaster in that community "not to deliver any Abolition or Incendiary documents from their offices, should any come to [him]."[91] In Denton the citizens' resolution even "authorized" the vigilantes themselves to examine the mail in the post office.[92]

Postmasters took the vigilante admonitions—and perhaps the threat of a fine—seriously. The Nacogdoches *Chronicle* reported that a large number of packages "bearing the frank of Charles Sumner" had been detained at the local post office. Broken open and examined, the packages were found to contain reprints of the Massachusetts senator's infamous speech, "Barbarism of Slavery."[93] The *Chronicle* dutifully published the names of the addressees, who it said were "nearly all preachers." But the Galveston *Civilian and Gazette,* which increasingly opposed what it thought to be excesses by the vigilantes, counseled caution in the investigation, pointing out that Senator Sumner very easily could have obtained the names from some church publication and therefore might have sent the copies out unsolicited to men who did not welcome them.[94]

In at least one instance, postal snooping resulted in public embarrassment for a postal employee and the newspaper that published his "revelations." W. O. Campbell, deputy postmaster in the Austin County town of Travis, wrote to

90. Gammel, *The Laws of Texas,* 2:99–100.
91. Bellville *Texas Countryman,* August 18, 1860.
92. Austin *Texas State Gazette,* August 11, 1860.
93. Ibid.
94. Galveston *Civilian and Gazette,* October 9, 1860.

the Bellville *Texas Countryman*: "Sir: I write hastily while the mail is waiting. . . . It is no trivial matter to find, in the post office, a paper published by Black republicans, and bearing upon its first page the names of Abraham Lincoln and [his running mate] Hannibal Hamlin. Such a paper I find in the office of this place, published at St. Louis, Missouri, in the Bohemian language, with no less than three agents in Austin County and one in Colorado [County]." The excited postman went on to reveal the last names of the "agents"—Leschikar, Reimershofer, Schiller, and Piskacek—and declared that his discovery had caused much excitement in the towns involved.[95]

Fortunately for the so-called "agents," they were well established in their communities and were able to convince the local vigilantes that they were innocent of harboring abolitionist views. The Bohemians said that they had received unsolicited invitations to subscribe to a new paper, published in their native language at St. Louis. They had accepted the offer, without realizing that the journal was Republican in its politics; moreover, they had done so without authorizing the paper to list them as its agents. Aspersions cast upon the alleged "agents" by the *Texas Countryman* clearly offended the sizable Bohemian population in Austin County. In a meeting of the county's citizens, held on August 20, a resolution was passed criticizing the paper's reporting of the allegation and absolving the Bohemians of any implication in the alleged abolitionist conspiracy.[96]

The Bohemians who so fiercely defended their own against the insinuations made against them nevertheless demonstrated their southern loyalty by "recommending" that all persons "desist from taking or circulating [abolitionist] documents," and warning all postmasters not to deliver such materials, "if any shall come to their offices." They further urged Texans to quit subscribing to "all Northern publications of whatever character except such as advocate our equality in the Union."[97] The few who might have been tempted to subscribe to such publications probably needed no such admonition, given the dire consequences that likely would result. The New York *Tribune*, widely regarded by southerners as an abolitionist newspaper, complained: "Now our subscribers in Texas are asking us not to send their papers, because they are subjected, by the new Sedition Law of that State, to punishment as felons if they receive them."[98]

95. Bellville *Texas Countryman*, August 4, 1860.
96. Ibid., August 25, September 15, 1860.
97. Ibid., August 25, 1860.
98. New York *Daily Tribune*, July 30, 1860.

Many alleged abolitionists did not fare as well as the Bohemians of Austin County. For nearly two months vigilantes reaped a terrible harvest in lives and expelled many other more fortunate souls from the state. In the process, they created such a reign of terror that hundreds chose to flee the Lone Star State rather than face the possibility that they, too, might become the helpless victims of fear-crazed vigilantes.

CHAPTER FOUR

SAVAGE DEEDS OF BLOOD AND CARNAGE

Having taken measures to protect their homes from the incendiary's torch and their families from the assassin's hand, the vigilance committees proceeded apace with the grim business of discovering and punishing the conspirators. Obtaining evidence against the enemies of slavery, however, was by no means an easy task. With few exceptions, those whites charged with having caused the mischief had stayed in the background, allegedly inducing the blacks to do the dirty work and take all the risks.

Not that there was a shortage of suspicious white persons. Most communities in this frontier land could count a generous sprinkling of white settlers who had only recently arrived from other states, and some of those from northern climes were thought to be entirely too friendly with African Americans. In some instances, so it was said, these familiarities had taken the form of trading liquor to slaves, gambling with them, and instilling in them an unhealthy dissatisfaction with their enslaved condition. Such a flaunting of the law—for recent revisions of the slave code forbade such activities—was regarded by some as *prima facie* evidence that the whites involved were at least untrustworthy, if not downright abolitionist in their views.[1] While those exemplifying more orthodox southern racial attitudes always held such men in contempt, during the panic suspect northerners were in mortal danger.

Vigilantes everywhere depended on frightened blacks to reveal the particulars of the "plots," and they usually induced confessions by threats and by forceful applications of the lash. According to one report, blacks in Tennessee

---

1. Gammel, *The Laws of Texas*, 4:1459, 1467.

Colony "were taken up and severely whipped, and made to divulge much in relation to insurrectionary movements." In consequence of their confessions, the vigilantes arrested two white men.[2] A resident of Billums Creek reported that the committee in Tyler County had whipped four blacks "very severely and one of them has died sinse from the whiping."[3] The Rusk *Enquirer* said that the vigilantes of that town had "severely whipped" some blacks, and, not surprisingly, this action appears to have led other blacks to confess their guilt "with little or no punishment."[4] A report from Athens announcing the discovery of "over one hundred bottles" of strychnine among the local blacks said: "After severe punishment [the blacks] revealed the particulars of the plot."[5] A similar report came from Judge Nat Burford of Dallas, who wrote: "Under the lash the negroes have admitted that they had in their possession deadly poisons to be administered to their masters' families in food; and when demanded of them, they have gone to the kitchen and produced the poison."[6]

The white populace generally demanded a quick and terrible punishment for those whose names were extorted from the blacks. There should be no hesitation, many believed, in putting the culprits to death. They agreed with the Corsicana editor who hoped that the incendiaries "may be swung up to the limb of a post oak."[7] There could be no punishment terrible enough to match the monstrous horrors that the abolitionists allegedly had planned for white Texans; nevertheless, some believed that an awful retribution should fall upon the guilty, not only because of the enormity of their crimes, but also because other would-be conspirators might be deterred by the fearful consequences. The Houston *Telegraph* said: "Let their crimes be washed out by their blood. And if they are insane, their insanity is of a nature that burning alive will cure, as well as prevent the spread of."[8] Hanging was "too reputable a death" for such "devil worshippers," wrote an Austin woman: "Fire, the element they invoke for the consummation of their wicked aims and purposes, should be the avenging agent for the punishment of their atrocious crimes."[9]

2. Galveston *Civilian and Gazette Weekly,* August 14, 1860.

3. W. L. Mann, Billums Creek, Tyler County, to Thomas B. Huling, Lampasas, August 24, 1860, Huling Papers, Barker Texas History Center Archives, University of Texas, Austin, Texas.

4. Rusk *Enquirer,* n.d., clipped in Marshall *Texas Republican,* August 18, 1860.

5. Tyler *Reporter,* August 11, 1860, clipped in Marshall *Texas Republican,* August 18, 1860.

6. Waco *Democrat,* n.d., clipped in Houston *Telegraph,* July 31, 1860.

7. Corsicana *Navarro Express,* August 25, 1860.

8. Houston *Telegraph,* n.d., clipped in San Antonio *Daily Ledger and Texan,* July 23, 1860.

9. Anonymous letter, printed in Houston *True Southron,* July 28, 1860, clipped in St. Louis *Daily Missouri Republican,* August 10, 1860.

Even men of the cloth apparently were not immune to the bloodlust that consumed white Texans. The *Texas Baptist,* after expressing its thanks to God for staying "the murderous hands of our enemies," said: "We would not encourage the taking of human life, or the shedding of man's blood, when it can be avoided, but if any of these demons are caught in our county, they will be shot like wolves or hung like dogs, just as they ought to be."[10] The same journal reminded those who might think it "unchristian-like" to hang the guilty that it was God Himself who had ordained the principle of an "eye for an eye" and a "tooth for a tooth."[11]

It is fitting that Dallas, the town where it all began, was among the first communities to exact retribution from those who had allegedly ravaged it. Since vigilantes were unable in this case to capture the white abolitionists who allegedly had inspired the destruction of the community, the hand of vengeance fell instead upon the blacks who had been charged with setting the fire. The only question in the minds of the Dallasites was how far they should go in punishing the black population, for it was generally believed that there was widespread involvement among the black community. "Negroes never before suspected are implicated," Pryor had written to Cushing; indeed, the conviction soon prevailed that virtually every black in the county at least knew of the conspiracy, even if they had not all directly participated in it.[12] One element of the town wanted to hang all those who were privy to the conspiracy, as well as those directly involved, but the slaveowners, who stood to bear the financial burden for this Draconian measure, naturally opposed the proposal. Since the vigilantes' investigation had implicated all but three of the county's 1,074 slaves, the cost to slaveholders of hanging all of the accused, at least by one historian's estimation, would have amounted to a staggering $820,000.[13]

On Monday, July 23, a large crowd gathered in Dallas to await the vigilance committee's decision concerning the fate of the accused. With so much at stake, a resolution of the conflicting viewpoints obviously did not come easily, for the vigilantes met all day and on into the evening. Judge Nat Burford's recollection of the vigilance committee's deliberations provides interesting insight into the procedures of such bodies in general and gives evidence that irrational fears were sometimes tempered by practical considerations. It also shows that in

10. Anderson *Texas Baptist,* August 16, 1860, clipped in Austin *Texas State Gazette,* August 25, 1860.

11. Anderson *Texas Baptist,* September 13, 1860.

12. Houston *Weekly Telegraph,* August 21, 1860.

13. Michael Phillips, *White Metropolis: Race, Ethnicity, and Religion in Dallas, 1841–2001* (Austin, 2006), 29.

Dallas, as elsewhere, men of property firmly controlled the vigilante machinery. Judge Burford recounted:

> A little after dinner T. C. Hawpe, the sheriff, came to my house and told me that a meeting was being held in the courthouse. He was afraid they were going to hang all the negroes in the county and so entail a great loss of property. He said that three were known to be guilty and he did not think that any more should hang. He asked me to go down and address the crowd and do what I could to hold violence in check. I went and when I got to the courthouse door . . . I encountered a doorkeeper. The guards were admitting only those whom they knew to be all right. The doorkeeper asked me if I would abide the action of the people's meeting. I replied that I would and went in. The first man I found inside said: "Now, we must vote to hang them three negroes, but it won't do to hang too many. We can't afford it. After we get the three let's call up some rich man's negro and make a fight to save him. If we save a rich man's negro the meeting will not then turn around and vote to hang the poor man's negro." I saw that he had an eye to business and I thought it was a good suggestion. I went up to the courtroom and talked about three-quarters of an hour. Being a judiciary officer I then left the meeting and took no part in subsequent proceedings.[14]

Sometime following Burford's departure, a "jury" of fifty-two men voted to hang the three blacks in question. Next, as if working from a script, the committee considered the case of a slave belonging to the richest man in the county. "Sure enough," recalled Burford, "a fight was made to save him and succeeded." Nevertheless, although they lacked the strength to secure the execution of all the accused blacks, the more militant vigilantes did win one concession. According to Burford, "The moderation wing of the meeting compromised with the other faction by offering and voting a resolution to whip every negro in the county. The resolution was adopted and a committee was appointed to do the whipping." Following this action the committee adjourned with the announcement that the three condemned men would hang the next day.[15]

14. "Judge Nat M. Burford's Version," Dallas *Morning News,* July 10, 1892. Burford had resided in Dallas since 1848. Soon after his arrival, he formed a law partnership with John H. Reagan, and he was elected district attorney in 1850 and again in 1852. He drafted the charter for Dallas that was accepted by the legislature in 1856, and that same year he became judge of the new Sixteenth Judicial District (*Handbook of Texas,* s.v., www.tsha.utexas.edu/handbook/online/articles/BB/fbu27. html [accessed July 18, 2006]).

15. "Judge Nat M. Burford's Version," Dallas *Morning News,* July 10, 1892.

Humming with excitement, a large crowd gathered around the courthouse the next afternoon to watch the show. At 4:00, the three black "ringleaders," Sam Smith, "Old Cato," and Patrick Jennings, emerged from the smoke-blackened building and, escorted by heavily armed vigilantes, began their walk toward the north bank of the Trinity River, just south of town, where a hastily improvised gallows awaited them. Little is known about the unfortunate trio. Sam Smith was a slave preacher, whom Charles Pryor called "a hardened old scoundrel" and who allegedly had "imbibed most of his villainous principles" from Blunt and McKinney, the two preachers whom the Dallasites had expelled the previous year. There were mixed opinions about the other two condemned slaves. Pryor said that Cato "had always enjoyed a bad reputation," but another source said he was so highly regarded by the Overton family, which owned him, that Rachel Overton had given him primary responsibility for running one of her businesses. Patrick Jennings had been brought to Texas from Virginia and was sold to a Dallas attorney. One resident of Dallas would later recall that the whites in general and the children in particular had always liked him, but the son of a former owner said: "Old Pat continued to be an agitator in Texas as he had been in Virginia." According to Pryor, it was Patrick who had set fire to Peak's drugstore and, after Dallas had burned, bragged about the deed.[16]

The condemned men showed remarkable composure as they walked to their deaths through the scorched ruins of the town they were supposed to have destroyed. Each appears to have held his emotions in check to the end. Wrote Pryor: "Pat positively refused to say anything, and died with as much indifference as if he had been about his ordinary occupation. With apparent nonchalance, he retained his chew of tobacco in his mouth, and died with it there." Still, for all his stoicism on the gallows, Patrick was not as lucky as his companions. Both of them died quickly and "without a struggle"; he, on the other hand, reportedly died "very hard"—by strangulation, because the fall failed to break his neck. The executioners left the bodies hanging for about twenty minutes and then buried them beneath the gallows.[17] It is entirely possible that the three still lie somewhere near the foot of Commerce Street and not far from the site of President John F. Kennedy's assassination in what is now downtown Dallas.

The committee appointed to whip the other blacks of the county appar-

16. Pryor to Cushing, July 28, 1860, Houston *Telegraph*, n.d., clipped in Marshall *Texas Republican*, August 25, 1860; Phillips, *White Metropolis*, 29; "Reminiscence of Mrs. Addie K. McDermett," Dallas *Morning News*, June 21, 1925.

17. Pryor to Cushing, July 28, 1860, Houston *Telegraph*, n.d., clipped in Marshall *Texas Republican*, August 25, 1860.

ently worked expeditiously to carry out its grim mission. A resident of South Texas who had visited Dallas in July reported to the Houston *Telegraph* that the Dallasites had whipped the blacks "who knew of the conspiracy but failed to inform on the conspirators."[18] David Carey Nance, a teenager who had moved to Texas from Illinois some eight years earlier, witnessed some of the whippings and was horrified by what he saw. He said that hundreds of blacks "were rounded up like cattle" and "whipped without mercy." Young Nance later wrote that it "made his blood run cold" to see human beings treated so brutally.[19]

The first white northern immigrant to feel the wrath of Texas vigilantes was a thirty-nine-year-old common laborer named William Crawford, who lived on a farm near Fort Worth. The Maine native had resided in the Minnesota Territory some five or six years before moving to Texas in December 1859, where he apparently had hoped to acquire a farm of his own.[20] Prior to the outbreak of the panic, Crawford had "excited some remarks," according to one newspaper, because of "his familiarities with the Negroes," but no one had paid much attention to his indiscretions until after Charles Pryor's sensational revelations in neighboring Dallas.[21]

Crawford's downfall reportedly came when a slave belonging to Colonel Nat Terry revealed under interrogation that the northerner had sold a gun to him and had tried to incite him to use it on his master and flee to a free state.[22] There was some question about how many arms Crawford was supposed to have cached for distribution among the blacks. One paper said that he had provided no less than fifty rifles and a like number of revolvers to blacks in the vicinity.[23] B. F. Barkley, who lived in nearby Birdville, asserted, on the other hand, that Crawford's house had yielded twenty-five Sharps rifles, twelve Colt revolvers, fifteen muskets, and eight "common rifles." Even more sinister, according to Barkley, the searchers had found an invoice for twenty-four more Colts and forty-eight additional Sharps, which had been dispatched "from a house in Boston" but had not yet arrived. Moreover, said the same source, additional unspecified evidence seemed to indicate the involvement of unnamed "prominent republicans at the North."[24] A third version of the size of Crawford's

18. Houston *Weekly Telegraph*, August 31, 1860.

19. B. P. Gallaway, *The Ragged Rebel: A Common Soldier in W. H. Parsons' Texas Cavalry, 1861–1865* (Austin, 1988), 10.

20. Bath (Me.) *Sentinel*, n.d., clipped in New York *Times*, September 4, 1860.

21. Weatherford *News*, n.d., clipped in Galveston *Civilian and Gazette*, August 14, 1860.

22. Ibid. Nat Terry, reputedly the largest slaveholder in Tarrant County, would later serve as a delegate to the Texas secession convention.

23. San Augustine *Red Land Express*, August 11, 1860.

"arsenal" was provided by an unnamed citizen of Fort Worth, who wrote to a resident of Marshall that the accused white man had brought thirty or forty guns to Texas with him. In contradiction of Barkley's allegation that Crawford's house was full of guns, this last account asserted that the alleged abolitionist had already disposed of most of his firearms by the time of his arrest, and it said nothing about an invoice for an expected shipment of additional weapons.[25]

Although there seems to have been confusion about the size of Crawford's arsenal—if indeed there was an arsenal[26]—there was neither confusion nor hesitation in deciding his fate. Indeed, those whites who had satisfied themselves as to Crawford's guilt apparently did not even bother to refer the case to the vigilance committee. The Fort Worth *Chief* of July 25 reported:
"On the 17th ult. was found the body of a man by the name of William H. Crawford suspended on a pecan tree about three-quarters of a mile from town. A large number of persons visited the body during the day. At a meeting of the citizens the same evening strong evidence was adduced proving him to have been an abolitionist. The meeting endorsed the action of the party who hung him."[27]

The posthumous endorsement of Crawford's lynching failed to mollify the dead man's wife, who reportedly declared vengeance against those who had hanged her husband and bravely, though perhaps foolishly, cried out that Fort Worth would yet be burned.[28] A newspaper in Bath, Maine, where Crawford had formerly resided, was equally indignant, calling his hanging a "villainous act." According to the same journal, Crawford "was a quiet person, not much disposed to take part in public affairs, but the Texans, knowing him to come from the North, concluded he was an abolitionist . . . and they took his life. It was an outrage which will recoil upon the perpetrators."[29]

Crawford was but the first of many white "abolitionists" who met their deaths at the hands of mobs during the long, hot summer of 1860. In most instances, the victims, like the farmer from Maine, were men of northern backgrounds who had lived only for a short time in the communities that took their lives. Typical was a young man named Morrison, who was hanged at Gilmer

24. Fort Worth *Chief,* July 25, 1860, clipped in Washington (D.C.) *Constitution,* August 15, 1860.
25. Marshall *Texas Republican,* August 11, 1860.
26. In view of the wildly varying reports of the number and types of weapons in Crawford's possession, it is worth noting that there is no record that the vigilantes ever publicly displayed the "arsenal."
27. Fort Worth *Chief,* July 25, 1860, clipped in Washington (D.C.) *Constitution,* August 15, 1860.
28. Marshall *Texas Republican,* August 11, 1860.
29. Bath (Me.) *Sentinel,* n.d., clipped in New York *Times,* September 4, 1860.

for "slave tampering." He had moved from Kansas to Texas only a few months prior to his death.[30] Two other victims, Antney Wyrick and his cousin, Alford Cable, had worked at wagon making and blacksmithing for about three years in Tennessee Colony before the panic began. Since the local white citizenry reportedly had warned them previously about "harboring and selling liquor to negroes," they were naturally prime suspects when the excitement broke out in 1860. Charged with providing blacks with arms and strychnine, they were arrested and beaten until they confessed their guilt. Some two hundred citizens, including "some of the coolest, most impartial and respectable men in the county," condemned the cousins to death, and they "expiated their crimes" on the gallows.[31]

At Ioni Post Office, near Crockett, citizens seized an amputee schoolteacher named William Staten and charged him with "tampering with negroes." Staten had only recently come to the area—the reports do not say from where—and his "familiarities" with blacks had aroused the suspicions of local whites. According to the charges brought against him, Staten had urged the blacks to "burn and steal all they could" and had assured them that he would remain ready to advise them. Convinced that the charges were true, the vigilantes hanged Staten on August 17. Undoubtedly most of the citizens concurred with the action, although the Crockett *Printer* seemed to betray some doubt when it wrote: "His [Staten's] death *may* have saved our town—though mob law is terrible—terrible!"[32]

Vigilantes in Henderson accused a small tavern operator named Green Herndon of burning that town. Like Crawford, Morrison, and other whites charged with abolitionist activities, Herndon was a northerner, and he previously had been accused of trafficking with blacks in stolen goods.[33] Moreover, to these sins Herndon added another: he was reportedly an outspoken opponent of secession. Herndon's servant, a black woman, confessed under interrogation that she had set the fire that destroyed Henderson, and she further admitted that her master had instructed her to do it. In mid-August the vigilance committee, which included some of those men whose businesses had burned,

30. Quitman *Herald,* n.d., clipped in Galveston *Civilian and Gazette Weekly,* September 4, 1860.

31. Palestine *Trinity Advocate,* August 8, 1860, clipped in Marshall *Texas Republican,* August 18, 1860. For other references to Wyrick and Cable, see Galveston *Civilian and Gazette Weekly,* August 14, 1860, and Galveston *Texas Christian Advocate,* August 16, 1860.

32. Crockett *Printer,* n.d., clipped in Clarksville *Northern Standard,* September 22, 1860.

33. Galveston *Civilian and Gazette,* n.d., clipped in St. Louis *Daily Missouri Republican,* August 23, 1860.

arrested Herndon and condemned him to be hanged on August 27. Apparently unable to wait until the appointed day, a mob seized the hapless prisoner two days before he was to hang, tied a rope around his neck, and allowed a horse to drag him to his death around what remained of the town square. Its rage apparently unsatisfied, the mob then hanged Herndon's lifeless body to a tree and used it for target practice.[34] The vigilantes also hanged the servant woman. According to an account published many years after the incident, she admitted before her death that she had falsely accused her master, in the hope of saving herself from the hangman's noose.[35]

In addition to these widely publicized killings there were many that received little or no mention in the papers. The Austin *Texas State Gazette*, for example, briefly reported that one Richard Boardwright and his nephew were hanged in Robertson County on August 19 for "tampering with slaves."[36] The editor of the Houston *Telegraph* wrote that he had seen a letter from Waxahachie stating that two whites had been hanged in that town on July 21.[37] A few weeks later, vigilantes in the same community hanged another unidentified young man, the employee of a drugstore, "for giving strychnine to slaves to put in wells."[38] Less than two weeks after a mob had hanged Crawford in Fort Worth, a diarist living in nearby Palo Pinto County cited a report that vigilantes had dispatched two other alleged abolitionists in Tarrant County and added: "I can scarcely believe it."[39] George W. Flournoy of Austin, who had been campaigning in North Texas for the office of state attorney general, nevertheless confirmed the report.[40] A laconic announcement in the Jacksboro *White Man* may have been all that the public at large would know about the fate of one apparent victim of vigilante justice: "ANOTHER MAN HUNG.—A man was found hung at Hannah's Tank, on Big Creek, in McClellan County, on Sunday, last—supposed to be an abolitionist. [41]

34. Marshall *Texas Republican,* August 18, 1860; Henderson *Times,* August 27, 1860, clipped in Marshall *Texas Republican,* September 1, 1860; interview of Alf Harris, by Dorman Winfrey, June 1950, and interview of John S. Crow, by Dorman Winfrey, March 5, 1951, both in Winfrey Collection, Barker Texas History Center Archives, University of Texas, Austin, Texas.

35. Henderson *Times,* November 25, 1937.

36. Austin *Texas State Gazette,* September 15, 1860.

37. Houston *Telegraph,* n.d., clipped in Galveston *Texas Christian Advocate,* August 2, 1860.

38. San Augustine *Red Land Express,* August 18, 1860.

39. James H. Baker Diary, typescript, part 1, page 153, Barker Texas History Center Archives, University of Texas, Austin, Texas.

40. Belton *Democrat,* n.d., clipped in Cincinnati (Ohio) *Daily Commercial,* August 20, 1860.

41. Jacksboro *White Man,* September 15, 1860.

Deaths of blacks in particular often received little publicity during the panic. One incident that escaped mention in the press was recorded by James Buckner Barry, who was on a search for horse thieves in Central Texas when the abolitionist excitement broke out. On July 13 he recorded his arrival in Cameron, "where I saw a Negro hung for setting fire to the town."[42] The hanging of another black at Science Hill on August 14 received only a few lines in the Galveston *Civilian and Gazette*.[43] Another paper of the same city routinely reported that on August 9 vigilantes had mobbed black suspects in Ellis County and had hanged one of their "ringleaders" at Red Oak.[44] Another newspaper briefly announced that vigilantes in Danville had sentenced a black man named Allen to death for alleged insurrectionary activity.[45]

The reported hangings actually may represent only a small sampling of the awful fruit of vigilante justice. There are indications that the grim guardians of the public safety may have taken more lives in secret than in public. This was not because the executions caused any sense of shame, but because those who guided the investigations believed that the activities of the committees should be unpublicized for security purposes. If the abolitionists were kept ignorant of what the committees were doing, even of whom they were executing, presumably they would be kept off balance and would be prevented from carrying out their bloody scheme in Texas. The Belton *Democrat* wrote: "We understand that several abolitionists have been quietly hung in Northern Texas—the object being not to spread such facts until they secure many others, whose names have not been revealed to the appropriate committees."[46]

These "quiet" hangings undoubtedly added significantly to the number of executions specifically reported by the press. Very early in the crisis Colonel Nat Terry, a leading participant in the Tarrant County investigation, appears to have been referring only to his own area of North Texas when he wrote to a friend in Rusk: "Some seven white men hung, and I expect before it is over, not less than fifty Negroes will be hung."[47] An anonymous letter from San Antonio to the New York *Herald*, dated August 20, estimated that "not less than twenty

42. James Buckner Barry Diary, typescript, James Buckner Barry Papers, Barker Texas History Center Archives, University of Texas, Austin, Texas.

43. Galveston *Civilian and Gazette Weekly*, August 14, 1860.

44. Galveston *Texas Christian Advocate*, August 9, 1860.

45. Henderson *Times*, n.d., quoted in San Augustine *Red Land Express*, August 25, 1860.

46. Belton *Democrat*, n.d., quoted in Cincinnati (Ohio) *Daily Commercial*, August 20, 1860.

47. Colonel Nat Terry, Fort Worth, to D. B. Martin, Rusk, July 24, 1860, Rusk *Examiner*, n.d., clipped in St. Louis *Daily Missouri Republican*, August 23, 1860.

abolitionists" had been strung up by that date, "and every mail brings us accounts of fresh hangings."[48]

Another letter writer in Marshall, who identified himself as "W.R.D.W.," lamented to the New York *Day Book*: "But unfortunately up to this time [August 12] Judge Lynch has had the honor to preside only in ten cases of whites (northern Lincolnites) and about sixty-five of Negroes, all of whom were hung or burnt, as to the degree of their implication in the rebellion or burning." The writer went on to say: "Unless the churches send out new recruits of John Brown's, I fear the boys will have nothing to do this winter, (as they have hung all that can be found)." According to the same source, the excitement around Marshall was intense and it clearly affected the young quite as much as their elders: "The school boys have become so excited by the sport in hanging Abolitionists that the schools are completely deserted, they having formed companies, and will go 15 or 100 miles on horseback to participate in a single execution of the sentence of Judge Lynch's Court."[49]

Although W.R.D.W.'s letter may have exaggerated the number of fatalities, his report was similar to that found in a private letter written by Benjamin Enloe of Collin County, some 150 miles west of Marshall. Noting that "the negroes and abolitionists has been doing all the devilment they could," Enloe wrote that the vigilantes had nevertheless "hung nrly all the negros and abolitian that they could find."[50] Writing a few days after W.D.R.D. sent his letter to the *Day Book*, Gideon Lincecum, of Long Point, gave a more conservative number of victims, estimating that "30 or 40 negroes and 10 or 12 whites have been hung or shot."[51]

Dallas, the fountainhead of the panic, may have been the site of some of

48. Anonymous writer, San Antonio, to New York *Herald*, August 20, 1860, clipped in Charleston (S.C.) *Mercury*, September 8, 1860.

49. New York *Day Book*, September 8, 1860, clipped in Austin *Southern Intelligencer*, October 10, 1860. The full text of the letter may also be found in Hofstadter and Wallace, eds., *American Violence*, 202–203.

50. Benjamin Enloe, Collin County, to John Enloe, August 30, 1860, Enloe Collection, Barker Texas History Center Archives, University of Texas, Austin, Texas.

51. Gideon Lincecum, Long Point, to "Nephew John," Bear Creek, La., August 18, 1860, quoted in Lincecum, Phillips, and Redshaw, eds., *Gideon Lincecum's Sword*, 63. Lincecum was an eccentric doctor, philosopher, and naturalist who argued that abolitionists were infected with "nigger-mania," a malady that, he believed, was due to a brain defect that he called "amativeness." Lincecum argued that the condition could be cured by castrating the abolitionists, which he thought preferable to executing them. There is no evidence that any vigilantes accepted his theory or followed his advice; hanging continued to be the preferred method of dealing with insurrectionists.

the unpublicized deaths. In one of his letters to E. H. Cushing, Charles Pryor stated: "Our jail is filled with the villains, many of whom will be hung and that very soon."[52] The subsequent decision of the vigilance committee to hang only three African Americans obviously dissatisfied those who believed that all of the implicated blacks, and perhaps some white suspects as well, should die. There is at least tenuous evidence that the dissidents may have taken steps to compensate for the vigilance committee's leniency. In mid-August the Marshall *Texas Republican* printed a report that a mob in Dallas had hanged two white men, burned two blacks to death, and fatally whipped another—an incident which even that staunch southern rights paper called "shameful."[53] Apparently speaking about the same lynchings, the Bonham *Era* declared: "When the citizens of Dallas trampled upon the law by taking men from legal custody, and subjected them to unlawful violence, we regretted their conduct; and by this time *they* no doubt appreciate fully the necessary consequences of their misguided action."[54]

The fate of numerous suspects who were arrested in some panic-stricken Texas communities remains unknown. For example, twenty-one or twenty-two blacks (the reports vary on the number) were jailed in Waxahachie in late July, and according to newspapers and private reports their hanging was imminent—yet there was no published account of the executions.[55] Similarly, there is no information concerning the disposition of an unspecified number of imperiled blacks in the Brenham jail. In late July, the Brenham *Texas Ranger* reported that a mob had gathered for the purpose of lynching the unfortunate African Americans, "but, for certain considerations, [they] have postponed the matter until after the election."[56] An Alabamian in Houston wrote to his wife that vigilantes in that city had apprehended a number of whites and blacks and had "examined" them. Three of the blacks—identified only as Dick, Handy, and John—were alleged to be the ringleaders in a plot "to burn the city, murder the citizens, and arm themselves; and with the aid of white men, to escape to Mexico." Although he was unsure how the matter would be resolved, the same correspondent said that in view of the excitement among the local whites, he would not be surprised if the accused blacks were hanged within twenty-four

52. Houston *Telegraph,* July 21, 1860, clipped in Marshall *Texas Republican,* August 11, 1860.

53. Marshall *Texas Republican,* August 18, 1860.

54. Bonham *Era,* n.d., clipped in Marshall *Texas Republican,* August 18, 1860.

55. Houston *True Southron,* July 23, 1860, clipped in Marshall *Texas Republican,* August 11, 1860.

56. Brenham *Texas Ranger,* n.d., clipped in Marshall *Texas Republican,* August 11, 1860.

hours; however, there is no mention in the Texas press of these arrests, let alone of the black prisoners' fate.[57]

Still other cases apparently never found their way onto the pages of the newspapers at all. For example, C. G. Forshey, of Rutersville, wrote to a friend in Louisiana concerning the excitement in his community. Many blacks had been whipped and some had died, he said. Specifically, he cited the shooting of one black that had been accused of setting fire to a former master's barn and gin. In addition there had been allegations of a plot to poison the whites of the community, and, perhaps as a result of these charges, Forshey said that he expected that a black cook and her husband would be hanged "in a quiet way." One nevertheless searches the existing newspapers in vain to find any mention of these incidents.[58]

There is also an absence of published information regarding the fate of an alleged abolitionist referred to in a letter written by Malcolm H. Addison to his brother on September 4: "Perhaps you remember something of a man they had in Caldwell as a "babolitionist": they have him again, having previously taken him to Cameron. What they have done, or what horrible developments they have made, I do not know; but I heare in town to day . . . that they were satisfied of his guilt, that the vigilance committee had called a mass-meeting of the country. How it will eventuate, "quien sabe?" End in smoke it is likely."[59] Nor does one find any mention in the press of the events in Bosque County referred to by frontiersman James Buckner Barry, who in an entry in his diary dated "July 23, 24, 25" noted that there was much excitement locally about "horse thieves, murders and Abolitionists hanging them without law."[60]

One should not assume, however, that all such meetings as that in Cameron resulted in executions. For various reasons a mob occasionally had a change of heart that resulted in a narrow escape for an accused abolitionist. For example, in August a man named Simmons, who had earlier been expelled from the state, returned to Quitman. After an arsonist had allegedly attempted to burn the town, vigilantes arrested Simmons as a likely suspect. According to the Corsicana *Navarro Express,* "his life would have paid the forfeit, had not his wife's

57. Letter of an unidentified man, Houston, to his wife in Montgomery, Alabama, August 11, 1860, Montgomery (Ala.) *Mail,* n.d., clipped in Charleston (S.C.) *Daily Courier,* August 24, 1860.

58. C. G. Forshey, Rutersville, to St. J. R. Liddell, August 18, 1860, quoted in Crenshaw, *The Slave States in the Presidential Election of 1860,* 95.

59. Malcolm H. Addison, Fairmount, to Oscar M. Addison, September 4, 1860, Addison Papers, Barker Texas History Center Archives, University of Texas, Austin, Texas.

60. James Buckner Barry Diary, typescript, James Buckner Barry Papers, Barker Texas History Center Archives, University of Texas, Austin, Texas.

tears and supplications prevented it."[61] In Caddo, where blacks had named one Cawly as the instigator of a planned insurrection, the vigilantes arrested the accused, and its members hotly debated his fate. According to one report, "Some were in favor of hanging, some banishing. The rope was placed around his neck and all was ready for a swing, when those opposed to this method of disposing of him prevailed, and he was released with the positive order to immediately leave the country."[62]

Other whites still had difficulty condemning one of their own race purely on African American testimony, even though the vigilante courts were not bound by the law proscribing such evidence. This reluctance worked to the advantage of a white man arrested in Navasota for "slave tampering." Wrote the Marshall *Texas Republican*: "On being brought to trial, none but Negro evidence appeared against him, in consequence of which he was not convicted, though it was perfectly evident that he had received stolen property from Negroes for months, and that the Negroes by his instigation were to have set fire to the town and made their escape on Sunday night." The Navasota vigilantes resolved their dilemma by expelling the alleged abolitionist from the state.[63]

The Navasotans' solution was hardly unusual. Although the publicized hangings naturally attracted the greatest attention throughout Texas and the nation, expulsion was usually the preferred method of ridding the state of suspected white abolitionists. Vigilantes not only expelled those who were allegedly guilty of specific acts of abolitionism, but also ordered out of the state those whites who for one reason or another were deemed untrustworthy on the slavery question. By sending a suspect out of Texas, a community could protect itself from danger without having the blood of a possibly innocent victim on its hands. Fears were thus allayed without pricking consciences. Texans had used this approach in the past, but never so extensively as in 1860.

Reports of expulsions often failed to mention any specific evidence against the unfortunate victims. A report from a Rusk County community, for example, simply noted that "certain suspicious persons" had come under the scrutiny of local vigilantes, and "Sundry individuals were ordered to 'leave the county.'"[64] Following the uncovering of an alleged plot to burn Indianola, the local committee took into custody "a suspicious young man, a loafing stranger, named Edward King," who was "given to understand that a change in locality might

61. Corsicana *Navarro Express*, August 25, 1860.

62. Cameron *Sentinel*, August 11, 1860, clipped in New York *Times*, August 30, 1860.

63. Marshall *Texas Republican*, August 25, 1860.

64. Henderson *Times*, August 11, 1860.

be better for his health. He went to New Orleans on the first Steamer."[65] Most newspaper accounts nevertheless gave at least some of the particulars of the offenses of those whites that were expelled. Most reports specified "slave tampering," which might mean anything from inciting the blacks to rebel to playing cards with them. Often the alleged miscreants were charged with a combination of such iniquities. A typical case was that of three men in Chapel Hill who were expelled after a citizens' committee had found them guilty of "attempting to incite the slaves to run off, improper familiarity with Negroes, repeated thefts, and lastly of threatening assassination."[66]

Sometimes it was a combination of deeds and words that proved the undoing of those who were ordered to leave. A committee commanded a man named Tyson and his son to leave Lamar County within thirty days after it had received information that the son "was in the habit of playing cards with the slaves," while the father allegedly had "justified the raid of John Brown, and boasted that he would have assisted to rescue him had he been present at his execution."[67] In another case, A. P. Deland, of Lynchburg, was given a month to leave Texas after a vigilance committee charged him with selling liquor to the blacks and "using very disorganizing and incendiary language in the presence of a slave."[68] Vigilantes in Anderson County expelled William Slaton from the state after finding him guilty of "inciting the servile population to rebellion and . . . committing deeds of incendiarism."[69]

Itinerant peddlers, many of whom traditionally came from the North selling northern-made wares, were favorite targets of the vigilance committees. A "German Jew pedlar" named Rotenburg barely escaped with his life when he ran afoul of a citizens' committee in Rusk County. Excited no doubt by the recent destruction of Henderson, the county seat, local vigilantes seized Rotenburg and a traveling companion. The companion was soon released, but Rotenburg was interrogated for a full week, after which the county vigilance committee of fifty men found him guilty of "improper conduct towards negroes." Eighteen of the jurors voted to hang the interloper, but thirty-two were against it. The "jury" then ordered their prisoner to leave the county within

65. Jefferson *Herald*, n.d., clipped in Jackson *Semi-Weekly Mississippian*, August 31, 1860.

66. Galveston *Civilian and Gazette Weekly*, September 18, 1860.

67. San Augustine *Red Land Express*, August 18, 1860.

68. Galveston *Civilian and Gazette Weekly*, September 25, 1860.

69. Palestine *Trinity Advocate*, August 22, 1860, clipped in Galveston *Civilian and Gazette Weekly*, August 28, 1860.

forty-eight hours and to be out of the state within four days. The harried peddler made an understandably hasty departure.[70]

Another widely reported incident in Fort Bend County is interesting because it illustrates the efforts made by some committees to enhance the legitimacy of their actions by clothing their decisions in legalistic language. Two peddlers from Illinois had the misfortune of passing through South Texas in August, just at the height of the Texas Troubles, and they soon found themselves to be the principal order of business before an official meeting of the county vigilance committee. The Bellville *Texas Countryman* published the following resolution of the committee:

> Be it resolved that Dr. A. M. D. Hughes and James L. Parker, map peddlers, having been strongly suspected of being abolition spies, and the proof before us satisfying us of their guilt, we hereby order them to leave the State of Texas for some State north of Mason and Dixon's line, and that they never again return to Texas or any southern State under penalty of death. Be it further resolved; that they be placed in the custody of some competent person or persons, to be appointed by the Chairman of the meeting, whose duty it shall be to conduct them to Galveston and have them placed upon some vessel going direct to some port north of Mason and Dixon's line.[71]

Accordingly, the chairman of the committee appointed James Hyams to see that the convicted men left Texas in the prescribed manner. Hyams dutifully escorted his charges to Galveston, placed them on board a ship bound for New York, and watched until the vessel and its unexpected passengers were safely out to sea.[72]

Another case involved J. E. Lemon, the journalist who was expelled from Wood County in 1857 for allegedly publishing "abolitionist views." He had since returned but now was once again escorted from the county by a specially appointed committee.[73] Before he was allowed to leave, however, Lemon, in the presence of the committee, signed what amounted to a quitclaim upon his right to reside in the county:

70. Rusk *Enquirer*, n.d., clipped in Marshall *Texas Republican,* August 25, 1860.

71. Bellville *Texas Countryman,* September 8, 1860.

72. Ibid.

73. Smyrl, "Unionism, Abolitionism, and Vigilantism in Texas," 33–34; Marshall *Texas Republican,* August 18, 1860.

THE STATE OF TEXAS

County of Wood

Know all men by these present that I, J. E. Lemon, do hereby pledge my sacred honor not to harm person or property within the above named county and State, and never to promulgate abolition incendiary doctrines, and that I will never return to said Wood county again under forfeiture of my life.

July 30, 1860   J. E. Lemon[74]

Such expulsions appear to have been commonplace in North Texas throughout the panic, although Lemon's case was probably more ceremonious than most. One paper in East Texas reported: "They are now driving from all the upper counties every individual upon whom rests the least suspicion of abolitionism."[75] The number of expatriates appears to have been augmented by many northerners who preferred to leave the state voluntarily, rather than risk an "examination" by unpredictable vigilantes. On arriving at St. Louis, passengers on the Overland Mail, which had crossed North Texas, reported that the road north of the Red River was lined with people leaving the Lone Star State.[76] A report from Fort Smith, Arkansas, estimated that even in late September an estimated three hundred wagons containing "suspected incendiaries" were "strung along the road" north of the Red River, heading for Kansas or Missouri.[77]

Of course, not all of the expatriates were leaving because of their fear of being associated with alleged abolitionist activities. Some had given up their battle with the frontier because of the severe drought. In mid-August a resident of Camden, Arkansas, noted in his diary that he had observed a steady stream of emigrants from Texas passing through town, "in consequence of the famine."[78] The Fayetteville *Arkansian* reported in late August that the extended dry spell in Texas had motivated at least some of the "great number" of migrating Texans

74. Galveston *Texas Christian Advocate*, August 16, 1860. Whether Lemon ever made it to safety is unclear. A subsequent report stated: "The abolitionist J. E. Lemon, who recently was escorted out of Wood County under order to leave the State, it is reported has been prevented, by a material impediment, from obeying instructions. We presume he climbed a tree and hurt himself coming down" (Galveston *News*, n.d., clipped in New York *Times*, September 6, 1860).

75. Jefferson *Herald*, n.d., clipped in Jackson *Semi-Weekly Mississippian*, August 31, 1860.

76. New Orleans (La.) *Daily Picayune*, October 19, 1860.

77. San Augustine *Red Land Express*, October 20, 1860.

78. Robert F. Kellan Diary, Camden, August 13–18, 1860, microfilm copy of original, General Microfilm Collection, Arkansas Historical Commission, Little Rock, Arkansas.

to return to friendlier climes.[79] Nevertheless, it is clear that a sizeable percentage of those who headed their family wagons north across the Red River did so to escape another kind of heat—that generated by the fires in Dallas, Denton, Pilot Point, and elsewhere.

Some of those who left barely escaped the clutches of vigilantes. One such individual was Frederick Anthon, a native of Germany who had become a naturalized U.S. citizen and had lived in Texas for four years when the Texas Troubles erupted. When vigilantes in Henderson fatally whipped a young man who had made the mistake of criticizing slavery, Anthon denounced their action. Local vigilantes thereupon turned their ire against Anthon and nearly lynched him. Barely escaping with his life, Anthon made it to the North, where he later wrote a letter to the Chicago Press and Tribune detailing his harrowing experience.[80]

Although forcing alleged incendiaries to leave Texas may have eased the consciences of those vigilantes who did not want the blood of merely suspicious men on their hands, the practice troubled many others, both inside and outside the state. Simply to send a suspect north of the Red River or east of the Sabine begged the question of guilt or innocence in the minds of those who criticized this solution. Even worse, to exile suspected abolitionists was to inflict upon unsuspecting fellow southerners a mortal danger. If a man were found guilty on the evidence, he should be given death, argued a Texas correspondent of the New Orleans Picayune: "If not, on what grounds can he be ordered to leave? Is it justice, after having discovered firebrands in your own house, to throw them on your neighbors'?"[81]

It was this last point concerning security, rather than any deep concern for justice, that bore most heavily upon the critics of exile. A correspondent of a Texas journal, in denouncing the reported expulsions of alleged abolitionists from Navasota and Galveston, argued that a community that had saved itself from the incendiary's torch should not, "for mercy sake," allow the culprit safe passage elsewhere. Not only would he be a threat to other unsuspecting towns, but he would be free to return to do fatal mischief to the very community that had shown him compassion: "Is he confined beyond the limits of this State? Is there an 'impassable gulf' by means of which he cannot return?" The answer obviously was "no." "Then," continued the letter writer, "where is the benefit of

79. Fayetteville Arkansian, August 31, 1860.

80. Letter of Frederick Anthon, September 18, 1860, to Chicago (Ill.) Press and Tribune, n.d., cited in Grimsted, American Mobbing, 176.

81. New Orleans (La.) Evening Picayune, August 18, 1860.

sending him away? Is it that he may return in disguise next month or next year and burn down the town which treated him thus?"[82]

Others living well beyond the border of the Lone Star State agreed with this logic. A newspaper in Virginia likened the practice of banishing "incendiary agents" to bailing water from a sinking boat without attempting to repair the leak, and it warned that "a short shrift and a long rope" was the only sure cure for the "sickness" plaguing Texas.[83] A Philadelphian wrote to E. M. Pease, in Austin, of his "utmost astonishment" that the people of Texas had shown so many leniencies toward "the fiendish abolitionists." He could scarcely believe that the villains charged with plotting to destroy property and murder "your families" were allowed to leave the state, instead of being hanged.[84]

Although there can be little question that more suspected persons left the state than lost their lives there, it is also clear that the terrified Texans exacted a fearful toll of lives between July 8 and the end of September 1860. Unfortunately, the absence of either vigilance committee records or dependable data on mob action makes it impossible to estimate with any degree of accuracy the total number of alleged conspirators who paid the ultimate penalty for their "crimes." Utilizing eyewitness reports, both published and unpublished, it is possible to document more than thirty deaths; however, the actual number of fatalities was probably much greater, and a variety of sources indicate that killings were commonplace occurrences that had become entirely acceptable to a majority of the population. One sensitive Texas minister confided the horror that he felt over the bloody deeds of his fellow Texans when he wrote in his diary: "Here where the mind [has been] so long familiarized with savage deeds of blood and carnage, the most tender hearted naturally become relentless and cruel. God of Heaven! Pity this people!"[85]

Others were also uneasy about denying accused men their legal rights, and some of them said so; however, they almost invariably conceded that the preservation of their communities, their property, and their lives took precedence over the law. They agreed with B. F. Barkley, chairman of the vigilance committee in Birdville, when he said, "It is true that it may seem hard to hang a man

82. Bellville *Texas Countryman*, August 25, 1860. For similar views, see letters published in the Galveston *News*, July 24, 1860, and Marshall *Texas Republican*, August 25, 1860.

83. Richmond (Va.) *Daily Dispatch*, September 4, 1860.

84. John J. Sinickson, Philadelphia, to E. M. Pease, Austin, September 13, 1860, Pease-Graham-Niles Family Papers, Austin Public Library, Austin, Texas.

85. Walter S. South Diary, August 9, 1860, typescript, Barker Texas History Center Archives, University of Texas, Austin, Texas.

without judge or jury; but when the lives of our families are at stake—when those that are most dear to us are in danger of being not only murdered in cold blood, but perhaps to meet a worse fate, then it is time to take the law into our own hands, and to protect our families."[86]

One anonymous letter writer said that although he feared that "some innocent persons have suffered and will yet suffer," the blame should fall upon the "abolitionists of the North, who are producing this work," and not upon the Texans who were merely defending themselves. It was too much to expect a people "in the midst of a servile insurrection, with their property burning down on their heads, and their wells being filled with poison" to "always act with judgment."[87] Yet another correspondent admitted that the law had been violated by the vigilantes but contended: "A people who would lie supinely upon their backs until their enemies had burned down their towns and houses, murdered by poison, or with Abolition pikes and spears, their wives and children, and forced their fair daughters into the embrace of buck negroes for wives . . . deserve to be enslaved."[88] Men tormented by such visions had little difficulty suppressing any regrets they might otherwise have felt over committing "savage deeds of blood and carnage."

86. B. F. Barkley, Birdville, to D. M. Barkley, Louisville, Ky., Louisville *Courier,* n.d., clipped in Washington (D.C.) *Constitution,* August 9, 1860.

87. New York *Herald,* n.d., clipped in Charleston (S.C.) *Mercury,* September 8, 1860.

88. R. S. Finley to the editor, August 18, 1860, Galveston *Texas Christian Advocate,* August 30, 1860.

CHAPTER FIVE

GREAT NEWS FROM TEXAS

Ollinger Crenshaw has written: "During the summer of 1789, a vague feeling of unrest swept the rural provinces of France, where it was said that 'the brigands are coming.' It seems that some kind of similar feeling existed in the states of the old South in the summer and fall of 1860, a feeling of tenseness which led Southerners to hang peddlers and piano tuners, and see abolitionists swarming everywhere."[1] The malaise that permeated the whole South may explain why the excitement and fear that spread from Texas into Arkansas and Louisiana did not stop there. Within a matter of weeks the whole South was buzzing over editor Pryor's various sensational accounts of the events in Dallas, at least one of which appeared in a large percentage of the region's newspapers. The assertion of some scholars that southern editors habitually suppressed stories of slave unrest for fear they might provide the bondsmen with dangerous models to emulate may have been valid for some slave panics, but it does not apply to the Texas Troubles of 1860.[2] William Barney has written, "Highlighted by the press and political orators, the news reached into every corner of the South."[3] The excitement engendered by the frightening stories coming out of the Lone Star State increased dramatically when Texas-like "plots" were exposed in several other slave states of the Lower South.

Just as the press played the leading role in publicizing the alleged plot in Texas and in warning other communities in all sections of the Lone Star State, so did the Fourth Estate trumpet the shocking reports to other Americans,

1. Crenshaw, *The Slave States in the Presidential Election of 1860*, 107.
2. Wish, "The Slave Panic of 1856," 206; Aptheker, *American Negro Slave Revolts*, 155.
3. Barney, *The Secessionist Impulse*, 167.

both above and below the Mason-Dixon Line. Arguing that the Republican party either was behind the incendiary business in Texas or would support similar assaults on slavery if it were to gain control of the White House, the more radical southern rights advocates insisted that Abraham Lincoln's election must signal the South's withdrawal from the Union. The dire reports pouring out of Texas thus provided the secessionist editors and fire-eating politicians an ideal weapon with which to advance their own cause and attack their political opponents—the defenders of the Union, whose caution and skepticism often made them appear wishy-washy at best, and at worst, as traitors to the South.

Newspapers of all persuasions carried one or more of the Pryor letters; however, the prominence that a given editor assigned to the sensational reports from Texas and the extent and tone of his editorializing generally depended upon his politics. Breckinridge supporters usually gave high visibility to the reports and printed them under such eye-catching headlines as: "Great News From Texas—Abolitionists Shot and Hung, etc."; "John Brownites in Texas"; "The Reported Diabolical Plot in Texas;" "Conspiracy to Set Fire to the Whole of Northern Texas."[4] Given the southern rights newspapers' sensational stories of rampant abolitionism in Texas, it was not surprising that friends and relatives of people living in the Lone Star State expressed concern for the safety of their loved ones. In the midst of a newsy letter to her relations in Texas, a resident

4. Des Arc (Ark.) *Weekly Citizen*, August 8, 22, 1860; Jacksonville (Ala.) *Republican*, August 23, 1860; Richmond (Va.) *Enquirer*, August 7, 1860; Asheville (N.C.) *News*, August 9, 1860. For other lengthy reports that were also drawn from Pryor's letters, see Richmond *Daily Dispatch*, September 3, 1860; Charleston (S.C.) *Mercury*, August 13, 1860; Washington (D.C.) *Constitution*, August 3, 1860; Macon (Ga.) *Daily Telegraph*, July 30, August 2, 7, 1860; Milledgeville (Ga.) *Federal Union*, August 7, 1860; Montgomery (Ala.) *Weekly Advertiser*, August 15, 1860; Montgomery (Ala.) *Weekly Mail*, August 3, 24, 31, 1860; Nashville (Tenn.) *Union and American*, August 21, 1860; Natchez (Miss.) *Free Trader*, August 6, September 10, 17, 1860; New Orleans *Daily Delta*, August 15, 1860; Opelousas (La.) *Courier*, August 11, 1860; Paris (Tenn.) *Sentinel*, October 3, 1860; Prattville (Ala.) *Southern Statesman*, September 1, 1860; Tallahassee *East Floridian*, August 16, 1860; Waynesboro (Ga.) *Independent South*, August 24, 1860; Athens (Ga.) *Southern Banner*, August 2, 9, 23, 1860; Atlanta *Daily Intelligencer*, August 18, September 11, 1860; Carrollton *West Alabamian*, August 8, 1860; Centre (Ala.) *Coosa River Argus*, September 8, 1860; Charleston (S.C.) *Daily Courier*, August 8, 16, 1860; Carrollton (Ga.) *Advocate*, August 3, 1860; Tallahassee *Floridian and Journal*, August 11, 1860; Opelika (Ala.) *Southern Era*, September 15, 1860; Spartanburg (S.C.) *Carolina Spartan*, August 2, 1860; Anderson (S.C.) *Intelligencer*, August 14, September 8, 18, 1860; Clarksville (Tenn.) *Jeffersonian*, August 1, 8, 1860; Columbus *Mississippi Democrat*, September 1, 1860; Fayetteville *Arkansian*, August 11, 1860; Fort Smith (Ark.) *Times*, August 16, 1860; Greensboro *Alabama Beacon*, August 10, 24, 1860; Hayneville (Ala.) *Chronicle*, August 23, 1860; Jackson *Weekly Mississippian*, August 3, September 19, 1860; Little Rock *Old-Line Democrat*, September 6, 1860; Alexandria (La.) *Constitutional*, August 13, 1860.

of North Carolina wrote: "I hardly no what more to say for I dont know whether you will ever get this or not for the negros may kill you if they have not all ready done it[.] from what we heare it scares me all most to death[.] report ses that evry town in Texas is burnt[.] write to us an tell us all you no about it."[5]

Many papers that advocated Douglas[6] and Constitutional Unionist John Bell[7] for president, as well as independent sheets,[8] carried the same reports from Texas, although the editors of such journals were, on the whole, less disposed to sensationalize or elaborate on the stories than their fire-eating counterparts. Moreover, when they addressed the issue at all in their editorials, unionists, whatever their political affiliation, frequently took a cautious or even skeptical position, although but few initially were so bold as to assert that there was no truth to the reports.

Alarming new reports of abolitionist activities in at least eight other southern states lent immediacy and urgency to the issue of security raised by the horrifying reports out of Texas. None of these incidents approached in scope or magnitude the Texas "conspiracy," but they were sufficiently alarming to make white southerners everywhere believe that they, too, were in real danger. In view of the sensational and extensive coverage given the Texas Troubles by the southern press, it is not surprising that a shroud of anxiety settled over the whole South. When combined with the Texas panic, the new scares gave the impression that the abolitionist conspiracy extended over all the slave states and made the Union loyalties of the conservatives everywhere even more difficult to defend.

Arkansas, the state through which many of the exiles were passing on their way out of Texas, was particularly nervous in August and September. The Van Buren *Press*, reporting the latest horror stories out of Texas, warned all Arkan-

5. Violet C. Delling, Lincoln County, North Carolina, to B. F. Shelton [no address given], September 4, 1860, "Miscellaneous Letters," James G. Gee Library Archives, Texas A&M University-Commerce, Commerce, Texas.

6. Macon (Miss.) *Beacon*, August 15, 1860; Memphis *Daily Appeal*, August 3, 5, September 5, 1860; Newbern (N.C.) *Weekly Progress*, July 31, September 11, 1860; New Orleans *Bee*, August 6, 1860; Tuscumbia (Ala.) *States Rights Democrat*, August 31, 1860; Van Buren (Ark.) *Press*, August 3, 1860; Prattville (Ala.) *Autauga Citizen*, August 9, 1860.

7. Hamilton (Ga.) *Harris County Enterprise*, August 2, 1860; Hillsborough (N.C.) *Recorder*, August 1, 1860; Lynchburg *Daily Virginian*, August 4, 1860; Nashville (Tenn.) *Republican Banner*, August 4, 1860; Natchez (Miss.) *Daily Courier*, August 14, 1860; Salisbury (N.C.) *Carolina Watchman*, August 28, 1860; Rome (Ga.) *Weekly Courier*, September 7, 1860.

8. Sandersville *Central Georgian*, August 8, 22, September 5, 1860; Greensboro (N.C.) *Times*, August 11, 1860; Richmond (Va.) *Daily Dispatch*, August 6, 1860; Shepherdstown (Va.) *Register*, August 11, September 8, 1860.

sans to be on the lookout for suspicious persons, asking darkly: "Who can tell but what abolition influence may be at work in our midst? It would be well for all suspicious strangers to be watched at least."[9] One woman living on a farm in Richland Township took such warnings seriously. When a traveler stopped and asked to buy some peaches, the woman of the house, after learning that he was from Fannin County in North Texas, said: "They have had some desperate work there, burning houses and the like by the Abolitionists." Saying that the reports were true, the man cautiously added that he had taken "no part on either side." The woman thereupon denounced him for taking a neutral position when there had been "murders of women and children and house burning." She further informed him that a law in that county stipulated "such loafers as you are to be shot if they don't leave the county in ten minutes." The traveler left hurriedly, presumably without his peaches.[10] The Fayetteville *Arkansian* related this incident as an amusing anecdote, but it clearly demonstrated the fear and suspicion felt by the ordinary citizens of Texas's neighboring state.

The frightening news from Texas apparently affected Arkansans of all political persuasions. On August 25, Robert F. Kellan of Camden, who supported John Bell for president, wrote in his diary that he had heard of the awful abolitionist activities in Texas. He seemed to approve of the work of the vigilantes who reportedly had hanged "many of the villains."[11] Two days later, Kellan wrote that the enemies of slavery had apparently struck much closer to home: "Abolition Excitement in our city—the guilty rascal gone." The Camden vigilance committee had sent "runners" in pursuit of the "guilty rascal," whom Kellan identified as "A. W. Marsh [sic], Newspaper Dealer," and an accomplice named Duval.[12]

The Marsh case became something of a *cause célèbre* throughout Arkansas and, though for different reasons, in neighboring Tennessee. Henry A. Marsh was a resident of St. Louis, who had established news depots in Camden and Memphis. Receiving requests for fifty subscriptions to the New York *Tribune,* he had placed the order. The Camden postmaster reported the arrival of the scandalous "abolitionist" newspapers to the local vigilance committee, which immediately acted to retrieve the culprit and bring him to justice. The vigi-

9. Van Buren *Press,* August 10, 1860.

10. Fayetteville *Arkansian,* August 24, 1860.

11. Robert F. Kellan Diary, August 25, 1860, microfilm copy of original, General Microfilm Collection, Arkansas Historical Commission, Little Rock, Arkansas.

12. Ibid., August 27, 1860. Kellan misidentified Henry A. Marsh as A. W. Marsh and, later, the press called him M. A. Marsh. See Des Arc (Ark.) *Weekly Citizen,* September 12, 1860.

lante "runners" found their quarry in Memphis, where he had just boarded the steamer *John Walsh,* headed for St. Louis. The Memphis *Daily Appeal* reported that the vigilantes seized Marsh, "A Supposed Texas Insurrectionary," on September 4.[13]

When the captain of the *John Walsh* protested the kidnapping of his apparently respectable passenger, Marsh's captors answered that their prisoner was "guilty of inciting an insurrection in Texas." But witnesses of the incident, who apparently knew Marsh, indignantly told the Memphis *Avalanche* that they "would sooner suspect the captors of being guilty" than the captured man. The *Avalanche* opined that Marsh, if guilty, should be punished: "But there is a way to dispense justice, and we of Memphis, as a general thing, like to see it administered with order and decency." Witnesses said that the vigilantes had even refused to allow their captive to speak with his wife before returning him to Arkansas, and the *Avalanche* thought that such ungallant treatment indicated "something loose somewhere." The editor concluded, "A very great outrage has been committed."[14]

The chastening by the Memphis press failed to deter the Arkansans, who saw Marsh as the vanguard of an abolitionist train that would soon sweep across the state. The Little Rock *True Democrat* reviled the newspaper agent, calling him an "abolitionist of the most hellish kind." It further charged that the "abolition association" of which he was allegedly a member was statewide in scope and purposed "to excite the negroes to deeds of daring desperation, with the view of gaining their freedom." The *True Democrat* urged all of its readers to "be on the lookout. Let nothing escape which bears the slightest resemblance to abolitionism: We have no doubt but that this association has emissaries in every town in the state."[15]

Meanwhile, four days after his abduction, Marsh and his captors arrived in Camden. Back in St. Louis, according to the St. Louis *Express,* friends of the "well-known citizen" actively worked to gain his release.[16] Apparently their efforts were successful. Robert F. Kellan recorded the swiftly moving events in his diary:

13. Memphis (Tenn.) *Daily Appeal,* September 4, 1860.
14. Memphis (Tenn.) *Avalanche,* September 8, 1860.
15. Little Rock (Ark.) *True Democrat,* September 8, 1860.
16. St. Louis (Mo.) *Express,* n.d., cited in New York *Daily Tribune,* September 12, 1860. The *Tribune* said that it often had been taunted about its miniscule circulation in the South but thought that was easily explainable, since "the penalty of buying it is death by strangulation."

Saturday 8th

Henry & McMahon arrive from Memphis. Bring

Abolition thief Marsh, put him in jail.

The Vigilance Committee arraign Marsh and A. W. Keen,

Theater man of this City. Continued till Monday.

Sunday 9th

Marsh & Keen in jail—

Considerable excitement.

Many say hang them.

Attend Episcopal Church.

Bishop Lay,

Weather cool.

Monday 10th

Marsh & Keen discharged to day by the vigilance & escorted out of town

with penalty of death if they don't immediately leave the State or [are]

ever seen again in it.

Also ordered to leave

Wm Powell & Wm Tully of the Theater Company

Also some Dutch Pedlar.[17]

It is likely that the absence of any proof that Marsh was an abolitionist was also a factor in gaining his release. The newspaper agent's acceptance of orders for a Republican newspaper obviously scandalized those who believed Republicanism was synonymous with abolitionism, but it scarcely amounted to hard evidence of his involvement in a plot like the one allegedly responsible for fires and poisonings in Texas. What may have been an attempt to justify the vigilantes' abduction of Marsh appeared in the form of a mysterious letter, ostensibly addressed to the newspaper agent and reportedly discovered by the same vigilant postmaster who earlier had intercepted the consignment of *Tribunes*. Published by the Little Rock *Old-Line Democrat* five days after Marsh's expulsion, the letter stated:

> *Sir.*—Owing to the recent discoveries in Northern Texas, we will be compelled to send you to some more important post. We want men of back and nerve to heal up for a while the feeling against strangers from the north.

17. Robert F. Kellan Diary, September 8, 9, 10, 1860, microfilm copy of original, General Microfilm Collection, Arkansas Historical Commission, Little Rock, Arkansas.

On receipt of this unless previously notified by A. G. go at once to Dallas, Texas, where you can consult with J. E. Lemons, and get thoroughly posted. Write to me twice a week unless times change. Start without delay, any papers or letters that may come for you at Camden, you must be careful to provide safely for. Do not mention Lemon's name as he is known to be an abolitionist and has been compelled to leave recently.

By and [*sic*] early attention you will confer addition favor on the association.

Yours,

M. M. Duvall

G. will go through your section. M. M. D[18]

This missive no doubt convinced many fearful readers of Marsh's guilt and confirmed the reports in the press that abolitionists were indeed prowling the highways and byways of Arkansas with a network of agents that threatened unspeakable horrors for towns and hamlets throughout the state. An impartial examination of the damning letter, however, should have raised serious questions as to its authenticity. For example, if "recent discoveries in Northern Texas" had so jeopardized the conspirators' work that Marsh would have to be relocated, why would he be sent to Dallas? Not only had much of the town been burned to the ground, but also one can scarcely imagine another community that would have been more suspicious of a newly arrived stranger. Indeed, Dallas would probably have been the last place abolitionist conspirators would choose to send an agent.

The mention of J. E. Lemon in Duvall's letter also raises serious questions. In late July, a vigilante committee in Wood County, about one hundred miles east of Dallas, had found Lemon guilty of publishing abolitionist views and had sentenced him to expulsion from the state.[19] There is no indication that Lemon ever came back to Texas, much less to Dallas, but since his case had been publicized in the press it is not surprising that his name was known to the Arkansas vigilantes; moreover, naming an actual person in the letter would seem to lend credence to the document. The mysterious M. M. Duvall, on the other hand, was never located, even though the Camden vigilantes sent some of its mem-

18. Little Rock *Old-Line Democrat*, September 13, 1860. This letter shows interesting similarities to the Bailey letter, published about three weeks earlier, which was used by promoters of the insurrectionary plot theory to "prove" the existence of the alleged abolitionist conspiracy in Texas. See chapter 6.

19. Lemon's earlier expulsion from Texas is discussed in chapter 4.

bers to search for him in Little Rock. Nor was the "A. G." mentioned by Duvall ever identified.

The Marsh affair faded from the newspapers as quickly as it had appeared.[20] Although the incident turned out to be something of a "tempest in a teapot," the brouhaha over Marsh appears to have accomplished the purpose of its publicists, which was to excite the public about the possibility of abolitionist activity in the state. After publishing the letter that Duvall had allegedly written to Marsh from Little Rock, the *Old-Line Democrat* told of the great excitement in that city, and, apparently referring to possible participants in the "plot," it added: "We noticed a number of individuals who looked remarkably white around the gills."[21]

Incidents elsewhere in the state apparently caused others to squirm as well. The Van Buren *Press* said that it had heard reports "that there is now in this county a Northern Methodist . . . who does not scruple to preach rank abolitionism; we have his name, and when we have undoubted proof against him, will give it in full and show him up."[22] This led a local minister, identified only as Rev. M. Carlisle, to take out an ad in the Fayetteville *Arkansian* announcing to the public that he was a member of the Methodist Church, South, not, as had been rumored, the Northern Methodist Church.[23]

When it was reported that the riverboat *J. J. Cadot,* docked at Jacksonport in northeastern Arkansas, had an abolitionist on board, a delegation of the local vigilance committee boarded the vessel and demanded to "examine" the suspicious man. The captain at first refused to allow his passenger to be interrogated, but the vigilantes drew pistols and got their way. Apparently, nothing came of their investigation, for the newspaper that reported the incident said: "Finally, on the ground that he was insane, the old cloak of such rascals, he was permitted to escape."[24]

20. A month after the conclusion of the Marsh affair, the Little Rock *Old-Line Democrat* said that Governor Isham Harris of Tennessee, possibly reacting to pressure from the Memphis press, had reportedly requested the extradition of Dr. A. S. Huey, leader of the "mission" to Memphis. The newspaper adamantly defended Huey, who it said was only acting under the charge given him by Camden's leaders. The journal sarcastically predicted that Governor Elias N. Conway would probably grant the request, since "he is fond of doing his duty," but it added that the citizens of Camden would fight to prevent Huey's "rendition to a foreign state." In spite of the journal's obvious concern, it is not clear that there was ever a formal request for extradition; nor is there any indication that Huey was ever surrendered (Little Rock (Ark.) *Old-Line Democrat,* October 11, 1860).

21. Ibid., September 13, 1860.

22. Van Buren (Ark.) *Press,* n.d., quoted in Fayetteville *Arkansian,* September 14, 1860.

23. Fayetteville *Arkansian,* September 21, 1860.

24. Little Rock (Ark.) *Old-Line Democrat,* September 27, 1860.

On September 6, Robert Kellan confided to his diary that he had heard of abolitionist emissaries "in many places in the South."[25] Indeed, in the wake of the sensational reports from Texas, abolitionist plots sprang up like toadstools after a hard spring rain in many states of the Lower South. As in Arkansas, these incidents usually were limited to specific locales and none became statewide in scope; nevertheless, the high profile given them by the press served to keep anxiety levels high throughout the Lower South. The local scares were enough to convince white southerners—especially those in the states with large slave populations—that they, no less than the Texans, were imminently threatened with all the horrors of a general slave uprising.

Perhaps no state was more primed for a slave panic than Georgia. A number of mysterious fires occurred in the Macon area during the spring of 1860, and the local citizens determined that arsonists were responsible. Suspicion soon fell upon local slaves, and authorities eventually accused a woman, whose owners subsequently "sent her off into the country," and a male named Bob, who was jailed to await trial. The excitement was waning by late June and might have died away altogether but for the arrival of the horrifying news from Texas.[26] Georgia newspapers, like those of the other southern states, were flooded with reports from the Lone Star State telling of a diabolical plot to murder and wreak havoc on August 6, the day of the state elections. The sheer volume of these accounts, including reprints of Pryor's letters, other private correspondence, and clippings from a wide distribution of Texas newspapers, added to their believability in the eyes of most Georgians. The reaction was almost immediate. Historian Clarence L. Mohr has written: "Within a matter of days it became apparent that racial paranoia was again increasing. The crisis mentality which had shown signs of abating in June gained new life in July and was again at full strength by the middle of August."[27]

Following publication of the frightening news from Texas, the isolated fires and occasional accusations against individual slaves that had predominated in the spring now gave way to sensational allegations of insurrectionary plots. The first reports of an abolitionist conspiracy came from Floyd County in northwestern Georgia. In mid-August, three blacks were reportedly overheard near Rome plotting death and destruction for the slaveholders of the area. Under

25. Robert F. Kellan Diary, September 6, 1860, microfilm copy of original, General Microfilm Collection, Arkansas Historical Commission, Little Rock, Arkansas.

26. Clarence L. Mohr, *On the Threshold of Freedom: Masters and Slaves in Civil War Georgia* (Athens, Ga., 1986), 21–23.

27. Ibid., 26.

the lash, one of them confessed that an insurrection was planned. Although the Rome *Courier* said white abolitionists undoubtedly had inspired the plot, since "there are several suspicious individuals prowling about the county," none was identified.[28] Several weeks later, a Georgia paper, announcing "THE IRREPRESS-IBLE CONFLICT IN GEORGIA," wrote that blacks under interrogation in north-western Georgia had "revealed the existence of a plot to 'murder and burn'" in Floyd County and in the towns of Dalton and Adairsville, "just as has been done in Texas. They all agree that white men are the instigators. . . . We say to all, WATCH!"[29]

According to a mysterious notice that was nailed to the door of the Rome post office, the slaves were to rise up in Adairsville on August 26. Rome's citizens formed a committee that proceeded to Adairsville with the intention of uncovering the guilty abolitionists and punishing them. But all they found was a white man, newly released from prison, passing a counterfeit banknote to a black. They whipped the man and shaved half his head for "instilling wrong notions in the mind of the negro," but presumably returned home disappointed with the meager result of their mission.[30] The Hamilton *Harris County Enterprise* similarly reported that the arrested blacks had left "little doubt" that white men had incited the planned uprising, "but they had made their escape."[31] The Columbus *Sun* provided more specific details of the alleged insurrectionary activity, reporting that certain slaves had planned to burn the town of Dalton and commandeer a train, with which they intended to assault Marietta, about seventy miles away. Exactly what they planned to accomplish by this derring-do was not made clear, but thirty-six slaves were arrested and charged with participating in the aborted plot.[32]

Several isolated incidents illustrate how dangerous it was for any white strangers in Georgia who chanced to arouse suspicions concerning their views on slavery. For example, the Rome *Courier* reported that the local sheriff had arrested one Thomas Cooley, who "was recently heard to utter in the presence of negroes, anti-slavery opinions." Cooley apparently was lucky, however, since the same source said that he had escaped confinement and left the area.[33]

28. Rome (Ga.) *Weekly Courier,* n.d., quoted in Macon (Ga.) *Daily Telegraph,* August 13, 1860.

29. Athens (Ga.) *Southern Banner,* September 6, 1860. See also Mohr, *On the Threshold of Freedom,* 28–30.

30. Barney, *The Road to Secession,* 148–149.

31. Hamilton (Ga.) *Harris County Enterprise,* September 6, 1860.

32. Columbus (Ga.) *Sun,* n.d., cited in Aptheker, *American Negro Slave Revolts,* 254–255. See also Mohr, *On the Threshold of Freedom,* 33.

33. Rome (Ga.) *Weekly Courier,* n.d., quoted in Athens (Ga.) *Southern Banner,* September 6, 1860.

An itinerant well digger named Parker in the southern Georgia community of Georgetown may have been less fortunate. The Hamilton *Harris County Enterprise* reported that he was overheard sympathizing with a slave woman after her master had punished her. He allegedly had assured her that she "was as good as white folks." According to the same report, he had told the woman to set fire to the master's house and had promised to help her escape to a free state. The paper said that whites, aided by bloodhounds, had caught Parker as he tried to escape and added that he "probably" was hanged.[34]

Another report from southeastern Georgia showed how baseless rumors could be magnified, just as they had been in Texas. In Waynesboro, *The Independent South* confidently reported on September 14 that a patrol had discovered a box of dirks, "a lot" of Sharpe's rifles, several swords, and "a good many likenesses of old John Brown" on Parson Peyton L. Wade's plantation in Screven County. Although the owner was absent from the premises, the paper said that his brother-in-law, a native of Massachusetts named Videtto, was living there. Videtto reportedly had taught the blacks on Wade's plantation to read and furnished them with "incendiary documents." The editor indignantly asked why Videtto had not been arrested and warned that the Yankee interloper's case "is but another warning to our people. They will not be convinced that they are slumbering over a volcano, whose smouldering fires may at any quiet, starry midnight blacken the social sky with the smoke of desolation and death." But a week later, after so poetically depicting an insurrectionary apocalypse, the same paper admitted that all those weapons on the Wade plantation had turned out to be two pistols in the possession of slaves, a little ammunition, "and, one swore, a likeness of John Brown."[35]

Other plots were reported in Alabama and Mississippi, and, as in Texas and elsewhere, a liberal application of the lash had elicited from the blacks confessions that whites allegedly had planned violent acts and instigated the slaves to commit them.[36] The editor of the Jacksonville *Republican* returned in late August from a trip to Rome, Georgia, where he had witnessed the recent excitement over alleged insurrectionary activity, only to find a similar agitation in the neighboring community of Talladega.[37] According to the Selma *Issue*, the alarm was sounded in Talladega after a runaway told his captors that a few blacks and whites were concocting insurrectionary plans at a camp outside the town. A

---

34. Hamilton (Ga.) *Harris County Enterprise,* October 4, 1860.
35. Waynesboro (Ga.) *Independent South,* September 14, 26, 1860.
36. Aptheker, *American Negro Slave Revolts,* 355.
37. Jacksonville (Ala.) *Republican,* August 30, 1860.

Sunday in August had been designated as the target date, but, said the captive, rain on the appointed day had washed out the plan. Although this story was vague, the account was alarming enough to cause the community to appoint a vigilance committee to investigate. Subsequently, another slave being whipped by his master "confessed everything," to wit: two white men and a slave named Sam had planned an insurrection that was to culminate in freedom for the blacks after the presidential election. According to the same report, a member of the vigilance committee was able to insinuate himself into the confidence of one of the accused whites. "What he has learned he has not disclosed in full," the paper said, but what he had revealed was enough to warrant the arrest of the two whites and the slave Sam. The suspects were awaiting "their examination" in jail.[38] On August 28, a mob caught the jailer off guard, seized one of the white men, Lem Payne (who was also known as Mahon), and hanged him. "The next morning," said the Montgomery *Mail*, "he was gracefully pendant to a pride-of-China tree."[39]

The anxiety aroused by the events in Talladega spread to other areas in Alabama, conjuring up horrors in the public mind not unlike those that had so terrified the Texans. The Memphis *Daily Appeal* reported that a Tuscaloosa correspondent of one of its editors had described the intense excitement that prevailed there in the wake of the revelations from Talladega. The writer said that the fear was so great in nearby Shelby Springs that the ladies, fearing that they might be assaulted, had all left their homes and crowded into the local hotel for protection.[40] And in Greensboro, rumors—apparently baseless—that black railroad workers had conspired to stage an uprising on September 4 had raised fears throughout the community. One resident of that town wrote that "there were all sorts of reports brought in yesterday respecting plots among Railroad hands & neighboring negroes for a 'rising' tonight,—with very little foundation as it seems, perhaps none at all."[41] The panic in Alabama that began in Talladega lasted about three weeks, and according to one planter "every neighborhood" formed vigilance committees. Nevertheless, in spite of the frenzy that resulted,

38. Selma (Ala.) *Issue*, August 28, 1860, quoted in Hamilton (Ga.) *Harris County Enterprise*, September 6, 1860. A local paper wrote that in addition to the two whites, "eight or ten" blacks were in jail (Talladega *Alabama Reporter*, n.d., quoted in Baton Rouge [La.] *Daily Advocate*, September 6, 1860).

39. Talladega *Alabama Reporter*, n.d., quoted in Baton Rouge (La.) *Daily Advocate*, September 6, 1860; Montgomery (Ala.) *Mail*, n.d., quoted in Richmond (Va.) *Enquirer*, September 11, 1860.

40. Memphis (Tenn.) *Daily Appeal*, September 8, 1860.

41. Serena Watson to Henry Watson, Henry Watson Jr. Papers, Duke University, quoted in Barney, *The Secessionist Impulse*, 173.

it appears that only one person—Payne, or Mahon—actually lost his life.[42]

Apprehension of insurrectionary plots was at least as prevalent in Mississippi as in Georgia and Alabama. Shortly after the Texas plot was publicized, a Georgia newspaper published reports from Mississippi that told of "serious excitement" among the citizens of Clarke, Choctaw, Washington, and Wayne counties over alleged abolitionist activities. Blacks had been congregating under cover of darkness, sometimes as many as fifty at a time, the same source wrote, and even though they had not been caught in one of these clandestine meetings, one of them "confessed this under the lash." White men, including a preacher, were said to be the moving spirits behind the plots. These leaders, said one newspaper, "seem to have been in correspondence with the old Harper's Ferry John Brown."[43]

In Mississippi's Winston County a slave girl's report of a conspiracy led to the arrest of some thirty-five blacks and the reported hanging of a white man identified as G. Harrington.[44] And vigilantes in Leake County, citing the abolitionist activities in Texas as evidence of the need to act forcefully against abolitionist emissaries, arrested five white suspects and forty slaves over a period of several weeks.[45] The excitement over the possibility of insurrectionary activity in their midst kept white Mississippians in a state of high anxiety down to the presidential election in November. Indeed, one alleged plot, uncovered at Aberdeen in October, was supposed to have culminated after the inauguration of Abraham Lincoln.[46]

As in Texas and the other states of the Lower South, northerners continued to be in the greatest danger, even in locales that had not experienced scares. For example, almost on the eve of the presidential election, Sarah Wadley, a young resident of Vicksburg, confided to her diary that she could no longer take music lessons from "Mr. Burr," because it was charged that he was an abolitionist. He had been forced to leave, and his house was up for sale, she wrote. Burr subsequently had sent a young man to teach in his stead, but, said Wadley, no students would enroll, "and the people paid his expenses back to the north as he had no money."[47]

42. Ibid., 172–173.

43. Waynesboro (Ga.) *Independent South,* July 20, 1860.

44. Aptheker, *American Negro Slave Revolts,* 355.

45. Barney, *The Secessionist Impulse,* 174; Ashville (N.C.) *News,* November 1, 1860.

46. Aptheker, *American Negro Slave Revolts,* 355.

47. Sarah L. Wadley Diary, October 26, 1860, microfilm typescript, page 77, Woodruff Library Special Collections, Emory University, Atlanta, Georgia.

William L. Barney, an historian of the secession period in Alabama and Mississippi, has pointed out that despite the frenzied excitement provoked by reports of abolitionist plots in those two states, no terrorist acts had actually materialized: "For all the talk of murder and pillage, none occurred; the plot was always nipped in the bud."[48] The same could be said of similar "plots" exposed in the other slave states. None of the white vigilantes in the affected states caught slaves setting fires to their masters' houses, discovered any poison in the hands of blacks, or found bona fide evidence that white abolitionists had encouraged bondsmen to slaughter their masters and rape their wives and daughters. Ultimately, however, it mattered little that none of the alleged plots had come to fruition. Had slaves, egged on by maniacal northern abolitionists, actually murdered their masters, violated their women, and set fire to their homes and towns, the resulting excitement and consequent damage to unionism in the Lower South could scarcely have been greater. This was largely due to the efforts of secessionist politicians and the southern rights editors, who seized upon these reports of abolitionist plots to fire the fearful imaginations of the whites of the Lower South.

It was no coincidence that the newspapers invariably placed the primary blame for the alleged slave conspiracy upon white men from outside the region. Emulating their Texas counterparts, editors throughout the Lower South admonished their readers to view with suspicion all outsiders whose credentials were not above reproach. At the height of the Texas Troubles, the Sandersville *Central Georgian* charged that the horror inflicted upon the Texans was the handiwork of "itinerant abolitionist emissaries, and encouraged in the free States, for a general servile insurrection . . . even the partially successful issue of which God forbid us from ever witnessing." The same writer warned that this insidious movement could well spread to the other southern states, engulfing them all.[49]

Hamilton, Georgia's *Harris County Enterprise* agreed with the *Central Georgian*. Citing numerous instances of slave insubordination, the editor said people should be on guard, especially scrutinizing "any unknown white man who may be found loafing about through the county."[50] Another paper in the same state echoed these concerns. Although the editor said he did not want to cause any "unnecessary alarm in the country," he said he would be remiss in his duty

48. Barney, *The Secessionist Impulse*, 73.
49. Sandersville *Central Georgian*, August 22, 1860.
50. Hamilton (Ga.) *Harris County Enterprise*, September 6, 1860.

if he failed to warn the people to keep a watchful eye upon "our negro population, and especially upon itinerant peddlers [*sic*], teachers and other stroll-
ing vagabonds." Southern newspapers were obliged to warn the people of the
danger, the same journal wrote, and the editor who failed in that responsibility
"deserves the closest scrutiny himself."[51]

Whether there was evidence of arson or not, anxious southerners automatically assumed any fire to be the handiwork of abolitionists. When fire consumed a store in Alexandria, Louisiana, a local newspaper said, "We have no
doubt that this is a continuation of that damnable plot which was concocted
and has laid in ruins a number of towns in the State of Texas." The same editor
warned every citizen to be "on the alert and every suspicious character who
arrives here should be made to leave forthwith. A strict watch should be kept
every night for there is no telling what a night may bring forth."[52]

Southern rights advocates nodded knowingly when they read that it had
been white men who were supposed to have planned the murderous assaults
upon the communities of North Texas and elsewhere. It was a cherished notion among southern whites that blacks, on their own initiative, were neither
inclined to participate in insurrectionary schemes nor capable of planning and
carrying out such terrible acts. According to this reasoning, nature had en-
dowed African Americans with a mentality and disposition that fitted them for
slavery. Dependency upon their masters, not just for their physical needs but
also for moral guidance, further conditioned slaves toward malleability, subser-
vience, and even gratitude—at least that is what the whites had constantly told
themselves. "A more quiet and orderly peasantry does not exist in the world,
than the slaves of the South," asserted the Charleston *Mercury*, "and the reason
is obvious—no peasantry in the world are better suited, by nature, to the agri-
cultural vocation in which they are employed, and no peasantry are better supplied with all the necessaries of life. Left to the simple control of their masters,
order and peace would continue to reign in the South, as it has done for the last
seventy-five years, with but the most insignificant interruptions."[53] Such journals argued that only outside agitators could disturb this idyllic equilibrium.

Texas southern rights men echoed the *Mercury*'s view at the height of the
panic. The Bellville *Texas Countryman*, for example, said there was a close natural relationship between master and slave, "and when undisturbed by emis-

51. Athens (Ga.) *Southern Banner,* September 13, 1860.

52. Alexandria (La.) *Constitutional,* September 1, 1860.

53. Charleston (S.C.) *Mercury,* August 8, 1860.

saries, this attachment is reciprocal."[54] The Austin *Texas State Gazette* agreed, asserting that a great majority of blacks in the Lone Star State were completely loyal to their masters and rejected any thought of rebellion. Nevertheless, said the same paper, "there are wicked characters in all populations," and white abolitionists could easily lead the "bad apples" within the black population into mischief with their siren call of "freedom."[55] Sounding a similar note, a San Antonio correspondent of the New York *Herald* wrote: "Without being incited to it by white people such an idea as an insurrection would never enter their heads. . . . They are perfectly contented and happy; but . . . white men can make them . . . believe anything they choose to tell them."[56]

Far from attributing any altruistic motives to the abolitionist instigators of slave unrest, southern whites maintained that these wicked northern whites were motivated by base, selfish desires. A Georgia paper undoubtedly spoke the views of many when it declared that the main goal of the abolitionists was not to improve the lives of the slaves, but to secure their help in stealing from southerners and plundering their homes: "We believe this to be their leading object, rather than sympathy and love for the negro," declared the Rome *Weekly Courier*, "for if they cared for the slave's welfare they would not try to dissatisfy him with his normal and proper condition, in which he is doing well, more happy in spirit and more bountifully supplied with the comforts of life than are those villains who are endeavoring to incite him to rebellion against a kind master the result of which will be the negro's own misery and destruction."[57]

Although Charles Pryor, editor of the Dallas *Herald*, had specifically blamed the alleged conspiracy in Dallas upon disgruntled preachers who had sought to exact revenge for being beaten and driven from Dallas the previous year, militant southerners in Texas and other southern states saw more sinister forces behind the Texas Troubles. Some even detected a direct connection with John Brown's famous raid on Harpers Ferry. The San Antonio *Herald*, for example, insinuated such a tie when it asked: "What meant the note alluding to depredations in Texas, found in the camp of the traitorous Brown?"[58] Although there does not appear to have been such a note, it is doubtful that the *Herald*'s readers

54. Belleville *Texas Countryman*, August 25, 1860.

55. Austin *Texas State Gazette*, August 25, 1860.

56. Anonymous letter, San Antonio, to New York *Herald*, August 20, 1860, clipped in Charleston (S.C.) *Mercury*, September 8, 1860.

57. Rome (Ga.) *Weekly Courier*, September 7, 1860.

58. San Antonio *Herald*, n.d., clipped in San Antonio *Alamo Express*, August 26, 1860.

questioned the accuracy of the insinuation. Contending "John Brown's work is yet going on," the Fayetteville *Arkansian* stated that some of the old abolitionist's cohorts had escaped the hangman's noose, "and these are now laying waste the towns of Texas, and others are ready elsewhere to burn other towns." The *Arkansian* apparently forgot that the Texas fires had occurred during the heat of the day when it wrote that Brown's failure had taught his "lieutenants" a lesson; instead of operating boldly in broad daylight like their leader, they now worked at night, using poison and fires to carry out their devilish schemes.[59] The Savannah *News* echoed the view of the *Arkansian* when it wrote: "There can hardly be any doubt that the recent demonstrations [in Texas and other southern states] are parts of the general system of the abolition warfare upon the South inaugurated by old Brown and his associates, and which it is the determination of his survivors to continue."[60]

For most, however, Brown's raid served as a point of comparison, and the publicists of the Texas Troubles clearly thought that the events of the summer transcended in significance the localized attack on Harpers Ferry. For example, Pryor had said in his letter to the Houston *Telegraph* that Brown and "his few followers" were "*fools*," compared with the widespread network of abolitionists at work on North Texas.[61] Similarly, the Tyler *Reporter* considered the Brown raid as "mere child's play," compared to the fiery assault implemented in Dallas and planned for the other targeted towns in Texas. Others made similar invidious comparisons between Brown's actions and the alleged abolitionist plot in the Lone Star State.[62] For the Charleston *Mercury,* the connection between Harpers Ferry and Texas was more symbolic than literal. Brown's raid, said the *Mercury,* "gave expression to the feelings and opinions of millions of people at the North," and "his enterprise was *the inauguration of force* in the policy of the abolitionists, to overthrow the institution of slavery."[63]

It was the assumed anti-slavery attitude of "millions" of northerners that concerned white southerners, and it was hardly surprising that the more radical southern rights editors and politicians trained most of their rhetorical guns upon those entities that they considered most representative of the Yankee ani-

59. Fayetteville *Arkansian,* August 31, 1860.

60. Savannah (Ga.) *News,* n.d., clipped in Tallahassee *Floridian and Journal,* August 11, 1860.

61. Houston *Telegraph,* July 31, 1860.

62. Tyler *Reporter,* n.d., quoted in Marshall *Texas Republican,* August 18, 1860. For similar comments, see: Columbus *Colorado Citizen,* July 28, 1860, clipped in Austin *Texas State Gazette,* August 4, 1860; Washington (D.C.) *Constitution,* August 3, 1860.

63. Charleston (S.C.) *Mercury,* August 29, 1860.

mosity to slavery: the Republican party and its nominee for president, Abraham Lincoln. It was irrelevant to these southern nationalists that the Republicans, in their Chicago platform, had disavowed any desire to abolish slavery where it legally existed in the United States.[64] What did matter was the antipathy toward the South's peculiar institution that had given rise to the Republican party in the first place. It was the same antipathy that in 1846 had spawned the hated Wilmot Proviso that had purposed to prevent slavery's expansion into the West; the same antipathy that in 1854 had caused a massive demonstration in the North against the Kansas-Nebraska Act, which would have given southerners the slim possibility of taking their chattel property into the northern portion of the old Louisiana Purchase territory; the same antipathy that in 1857 had provoked in the North widespread denunciations of the Supreme Court for deciding in the Dred Scott case that southerners could not be denied the right to take their slaves into the common territories of the United States; the same antipathy that had led Senator Charles Sumner, and others like him, to denounce in the most vitriolic terms the "barbaric" South and its pro-slavery leaders.

Southern rights men therefore dismissed as mere political piffle the current assurances that a Lincoln administration would follow a benign policy toward southern slavery, and they pointed to the Texas Troubles as proof that the hated "Black Republicans" had already commenced their bloody mission of destroying the South and its cherished institutions. Shortly after hearing the shocking news from Texas, the Washington *Constitution* declared: "The flag of Lincoln and [Hannibal] Hamlin proclaims everywhere the principles of [Hinton] Helper, and tells to every slave that he has the right to cut his master's throat."[65] The Athens *Southern Banner* warned its readers that if the Republicans were to win the White House, they "would build up an abolition party in the Southern States, who will distribute arms and strychnine among the slaves with which to murder their masters."[66]

The radical southern rights advocates in Texas early emphasized their view of the close connection between the alleged insurrectionists and the national Republican leadership. Such an assumption was implicit in the Bellville *Texas Countryman*'s prediction that "The Lincolnites will no doubt keep their emis-

64. During the election campaign southern newspapers almost never printed the Republican platform, let alone took note of that party's official assurance to the southern people that it would not harm slavery in the states where it was legal. See Donald E. Reynolds, *Editors Make War: Southern Newspapers in the Secession Crisis* (Nashville, Tenn., 1970), 94.

65. Washington (D.C.) *Constitution,* August 3, 1860.

66. Athens (Ga.) *Southern Banner,* November 1, 1860.

saries among us till after the Presidential election and perhaps longer."[67] The answer to the Jacksboro *White Man*'s rhetorical question: "What Will The South Do?" was made clear by the editorialist who said that "a fair and impartial administration" would be impossible under Lincoln, whom he called a "rabbid [*sic*] abolitionist of the deepest dye."[68]

Reminding its readers of Republican senator William H. Seward's famous assertion of 1858 that an "irrepressible conflict" existed between the North and South, the Galveston *News* said it saw evidence that the struggle had already begun "in the flames of Dallas and other towns—in the intended doom of our young women, the slaughter and poisoning of our families. These scenes are the logical results of the teachings of Black Republicans and the doctrines of Douglas." It was high time, said the *News*, for southern "brothers" to join together in the defense of "a common cause, unite for the protection and defence of the Constitution, their homes and their firesides."[69] A citizens' committee in Fort Bend used similar language when it stated: "*Resolved*, that in the disturbances which now prevail in the north eastern counties of our State, we recognize the introduction among us, of that irrepressible conflict, which was first inaugurated in theory by William H. Seward, and in practice by John Brown."[70]

The Galveston *Texas Christian Advocate*, a Methodist journal that supposedly was nonpartisan in politics, sounded as radical as the pro-Breckinridge press when it accepted as true stories of the "plot" in North Texas and tied the events there to the Republican party, which it said sympathized with "such things." Before Brown's raid and the "Texas conspiracies," the *Texas Christian Advocate* said it could understand how an honest man could have been "duped" into supporting the Republican party, "but now, how a man can teach abolition doctrine, or support the Black Republican party, and not be a villain, our casuistry does not enable us to determine. Such a man is, logically, an incendiary and murderer, whatever he may be in purpose." Still, the editor complained, those who opposed compromise with "the insidious monster" were denounced as "fire-eaters and extremists."[71]

67. Bellville *Texas Countryman*, August 11, 1860.

68. Jacksboro *White Man*, September 15, 1860.

69. Galveston *Weekly News*, August 11, 1860.

70. Austin *Texas State Gazette* (weekly ed.), August 18, 1860.

71. Galveston *Texas Christian Advocate*, n.d., clipped in Austin *Texas State Gazette*, October 6, 1860. The same paper earlier had argued that anyone who voted in a way that would result in a Republican victory would, in effect, be placing the government in the hands of an abolitionist. Such an action would amount to giving approval to the insurrectionary war in Texas (Galveston *Texas Christian Advocate*, August 30, 1860).

Such statements demonstrated that the Texas Troubles, combined with the lesser panics elsewhere, gave the radical southern rights advocates a distinct advantage over conservatives in the battle for the hearts and minds of white southerners, particularly in the cotton states, where the alleged insurrectionary activities were most widespread and where slaves were most numerous. Louis T. Wigfall, the leading Texas fire-eater in Congress, early showed that he recognized the value of the panic in pressing the radical cause. In a speech at Tyler on September 3, Wigfall warned his listeners that only Breckinridge and Lane could guarantee "the equality of the States, and the right to protection for our property." The Marshall ultra then pleaded with his audience to "join the only party that can save the Union, or render it worth saving. An enemy is in our midst, not with bayonet and broad sword, but with torch and poison. Is this a time for division?"[72]

Guy M. Bryan, another southern rights Democrat who had served his party in both houses of the Texas legislature and in the U.S. House of Representatives, also saw the value of publicizing the events in North Texas. Writing to his brother, he asked if he had seen the stories about the fires in North Texas. After reiterating many of the reports he had seen in the newspapers, he went on to say that all of the fires were undoubtedly the work of abolitionists and urged his brother to capitalize politically by writing to "the more promenent [sic] men of Northern Texas."[73]

Even John C. Breckinridge, the standard-bearer of the southern rights Democratic party, could not resist referring to the panic, although unionists' allegations that he was a secessionist forced him to be more circumspect than many of his supporters. In a speech at his home in Ashland, Kentucky, on September 5, the Democratic nominee defended himself against charges of disunion, yet he referred to "inroads" made by abolitionists into southern security. He cited Brown's raid and "arson in Texas" as two illustrations of how the South was "environed and beset" by those who meant her harm.[74]

In spite of all the alarmist rhetoric of southern rights radicals, by early September it had become clear that an arsonist's torch had not touched, let alone destroyed, most of the towns that reportedly had burned and that none of the

72. *Speech of Louis T. Wigfall on the pending political issues; delivered at Tyler, Smith County, Texas, September 3, 1860* (Washington, D. C., 1860), 32.

73. Guy M. Bryan to Austin Bryan, July 28, 1860, Guy M. Bryan Papers, Barker Texas History Center Archives, University of Texas, Austin, Texas.

74. Quoted in Richmond (Va.) *Enquirer,* September 21, 1860. See also Charleston (S.C.) *Daily Courier,* September 22, 1860, and St. Louis *Daily Missouri Republican,* September 11, 1860.

"poison" that had figured so prominently in the abolitionist "plots" had materialized. Moreover, it was now apparent that the white "abolitionists" who had paid with their lives were nothing more than poor itinerants—map peddlers, well-diggers, farmers, and the like—who had no discernable connection with one another and, in fact, had little in common other than a recent immigration from the North. They had gone to meet their Maker, along with numerous blacks, on evidence that consisted almost entirely of testimony extracted from terrified slaves through threats and brutal whippings.

The absence of hard evidence proving an abolitionist conspiracy gave the southern unionists heart, and they battled back against the southern rights extremists. If any conspiracy existed, they argued, it was one instigated by the fire-eating press and politicians to elect John C. Breckinridge president, and, failing that, to spark the secession of the slave states. The southern rights men retaliated, accusing their attackers of being traitors to the South. The result was a bitter war of words that would carry over to the post-election period and help determine the fate of the Union.

The Dallas courthouse was one of the few buildings left standing in the business section of town after the fire of July 8. Although the curtains inside its windows were scorched by the intense heat, its masonry construction saved the building from destruction. It was from this building that the three condemned black men were led to their executions on the bank of the Trinity River on July 24. *From the collections of the Texas/Dallas History and Archives Division, Dallas Public Library*

Nathaniel M. ("Nat") Burford, a former law partner of John H. Reagan, was judge of the Sixteenth Judicial District, which included Dallas, at the time of the Dallas fire and ensuing panic. He attended a meeting of the Dallas vigilance committee, and his later reminiscences provide valuable insight into the deliberations of that body. *From the collections of the Texas/Dallas History and Archives Division, Dallas Public Library*

A. B. Norton (1882), editor of the Austin *Southern Intelligencer,* and the most important unionist editor in Texas. His persistence in denying there was an abolitionist conspiracy in 1860 earned him the wrath of southern-rights Democrats. His hirsute appearance was the result of a vow, made as a young man, that he would never shave or cut his hair until Henry Clay was elected president of the United States. He kept the vow until his death in 1893. *Brown (John Henry) Family Papers, 1691-1951 (CN # 00707). The Center for American History, The University of Texas at Austin*

John Marshall moved from Mississippi to Texas in 1852. He entered politics, becoming chairman of the state Democratic party in 1856. That same year he became editor of the Austin *Texas State Gazette,* which he made into the most influential southern-rights journal in Texas. He played a key role in publicizing the allegations that led to the slave insurrection panic of 1860. Marshall joined the Confederate army after the war began and was killed leading a charge in the Battle of Gaines Mill, June 27, 1862. *Austin History Center, Austin Public Library (PICA # PICB05770)*

John H. Reagan, of Palestine, was elected to the U.S. House of Representatives from the Eastern District of Texas in 1857. Although reelected as a committed unionist in 1859, he moved steadily toward a secessionist position after John Brown's raid on Harpers Ferry. He strongly believed that abolitionists were behind the Texas fires in 1860, and during the debate in Congress in December of that year, he argued that the alleged plot justified secession. *Austin History Center, Austin Public Library (PICA # CO9253)*

Louis T. Wigfall, a native of South Carolina, moved to Texas in 1846. He became one of the most vociferous fire eaters in the state during the latter part of the 1850s and was narrowly elected to the U. S. Senate in late 1859, after the John Brown raid in Virginia aroused fears of abolitionism in the Lone Star State. He used his position in the Senate to argue that the Texas slave panic of 1860 was unquestionably the result of an abolition-ist conspiracy, which, together with Lincoln's election, made it imperative for the South to secede. *Author's collection*

Fragment of a letter written by Anthony Bewley. Charles Elliott, editor of the St. Louis *Christian Advocate,* who knew Bewley and defended him from the charge that he was an abolitionist, charged that the vigilantes "invented" William H. Bailey instead of forging a letter from the martyred Bewley, because his distinctive handwriting would have made it difficult to forge a letter with his signature. This fragment provides support for Elliott's view. *Photocopy provided by Bewley's great, great granddaughter, Mrs. Marilyn Irons, of Dallas, Texas.*

DENTON CREEK, July 3d, 1860.

DEAR SIR: A painful abscess on my right thumb is my apology for not writing at Anderson. Our glorious cause is progressing finely as far South as Brenham. There I parted with Bro. Wampler; he went still further South. He will do good wherever he goes. I have traveled up through the frontier counties, part of the time under a fictitious name. I found many friends who had been initiated and understood the mystic red. I met with a good number of our friends at Georgetown. We held a consultation, and were unanimous of opinion that we should be cautious of our new associates: most of them are desperate characters, and may betray us, as there are slave holders among them, and value a poor negro much more than a horse. The only good they will do will be destroying towns, mills, &c., which is our only hope in Texas at present. If we can break Southern merchants and millers, and have their places filled by honest Republicans, Texas will be an easy prey if we will only do our duty. All we want for the time being is control of trade. Trade, assisted by preaching and teaching, will soon control public opinion, (public opinion is mighty and will prevail.) Lincoln will certainly be elected; we will then have the Indian Nation, cost what it will. Squatter sovereignty will prevail there as it has in Kansas. That accomplished, we have but one more step to take, but one more struggle to make, that is, free Texas. We will then have a connected link from the Lakes to the Gulf. Slavery will then be surrounded by land and water, and soon sting itself to death. I repeat, Texas we must have, and our only chance is to break up the PRESENT INHABITANTS in whatever way we can, and it must be done. Some of us will most assuredly suffer in accomplishing our object, but our Heavenly Father will reward us for assisting him in blotting out the greatest curse on earth. It would be impossible for any of us to do an act that is as blasphemous in the sight of God as holding slaves. We must have frequent consultations with our colored friends; (let your meetings be in the night;) impress upon their clouded intellects the blessings of freedom. Induce all to leave you can.— Our arrangements for their accommodation to go north are better than they have been, but not as good as I would like. We will need more agents, both local and traveling. I will send out traveling agents when I get home. You must appoint a local agent in every neighborhood in your district. I will recommend a few [who] I think will do to rely upon, to-wit: Brothers Leake, Wood, Ives, Evans, McDaniel, Vickery, Cole, Nugent, Shaw, White, Gilford, Ashley, Drake, Meeks, Shults and Newman.

Brother Leake, the bearer of this, will take a circuitous route, and see as many of our colored friends as he can. He also recommends a different match to be used about towns, &c. Our friends sent a very inferior article. They emit too much smoke and do not contain enough camphene. They are calculated to get some of our friends hurt. I will send a supply when I get home. I will have to reprove you and your co-workers for your negligence in sending funds for our agents. But few have been compensated for [their] trouble. Correspondent and industrious agent, brother Webber, has received but a trifle — not so much as apprentices' wages. Neither has brother Willet, Mungen, [or Munger,] and others. You must call upon our colored friends for more money. They must not expect us to do all. They certainly will give every cent if they know how soon their shackles will be broken. My hand is very painful and I must close; Yours, truly, Wm. H. BAILEY.

N. B. Brother Leake will give you what few numbers of the Impending Crisis we have; also brother Sumner's speech and brother Beecher's letter, &c. Farewell.

STATE OF TEXAS, TARRANT COUNTY.—Personally appeared before me, the undersigned authority, Paul Isbell, and after being duly sworn, according to law, says—the above and foregoing letter was found by George Grant and himself, near the residence of said Grant, six miles west of Fort Worth, near where a horse had been fed stealthily, as it seemed; and that the said letter has not been out of their possession till now; and that it has not been altered in any respect whatever.

Given under my hand and the seal of the Tarrant County Court, this the 10th day of August, 1860. THOMAS M. MATTHEWS, Dep. Clerk.

BELTON, Bell County, Texas, August 19, 1860.

The above hellish document came into our hands from the most reliable and undoubted source. That it is authentic and true, there is not the shadow of doubt. The events at and near Brenham and in Georgetown, since the date of the letter, and before the finder could possibly have heard of those events, are alone sufficient to prove the truth of the statements in it. To make it public, would destroy all plans to entrap the conspirators. To avoid that and yet profit by its revelations, we print privately sufficient copies to forward one to at least one tried, true and discreet friend in each of the principal counties. To you, as one such, we confide it. Our plan is, to communicate it to a few of the most cool, discreet and unflinching men in our county, and advise the same course to you. There are twenty Abolition names in the letter. Traps may be set for them through true and discreet post masters. Exercise your best judgment—we will do the same. Our advice is, (as a general rule,) whip no abolitionist, drive off no abolitionist — hang them, or let them alone. There may be exceptions — but not many. Yours, in the bonds of country, of patriotism, of home,

E. S. C. Robertson

Dr. A. J. Embree   Jno. Henry Brown

Broadside containing the controversial "Bailey letter" that purportedly outlined the alleged abolitionist insurrection plot in Texas. *Broadside Collection, Center for American History, University of Texas—Austin.*

CHAPTER SIX

A THOUSAND RUMORS

By late August and early September 1860, the withering heat that seared Texas during July had moderated, and with this welcome respite also came a corresponding cooling of the panic, as it became apparent that most of the reports of fires and insurrection were false. But "heat" of another kind developed even as the worst fears began to subside. Unionist newspapers—and even some southern rights sheets—began to assert that the excesses of many vigilance committees had brought shame upon the state by denying the most basic rights of those who had been accused of being abolitionists. Some worried that vigilante extremism had damaged the state's economy, primarily by discouraging immigrants from coming to Texas. Emboldened by the revelations showing that most of the rumors that had fed the panic were false, unionists charged that radical southern rights men had inflated the crisis to serve their secessionist goals. The fire-eaters answered with recriminations of their own, arguing that the abolitionist conspiracy did indeed exist, even though they admitted that its scope had been exaggerated, and they alleged that the Opposition were ignoring the real dangers facing the state and region by promising to support the Union at any price. Editors and politicians, both within and outside the state, joined the debate, and the Texas Troubles became a key issue both during and after the presidential election campaign.

Although most newspapers and their readers initially accepted every rumor that fires had ravaged an astonishing number of towns and dwellings around the state, reports from the supposedly charred communities themselves soon demonstrated the falsity of the stories. For example, on July 18 the Tyler *Reporter* said: "We are in receipt of a rumor that the business portion of the town of Marshall is in ashes, but . . . we are in hopes that it is unfounded." Ten days later, the Marshall *Texas Republican* answered: "His hopes are correct. We are all right so far, and the receipt may be filed with his other receipts for 1860."[1]

A month after the Tyler *Reporter* had printed the false rumor that Marshall had burned, the Tyler *Sentinel* denied widespread reports that its town had been destroyed. Moreover, added the *Sentinel,* "a thorough and most searching investigation, by a number of our leading citizens," had led to the conclusion "that no such thing as an insurrection has been contemplated, or even thought of by our slaves."[2] Reacting to reports in newspaper exchanges indicating that the Titus County towns of Daingerfield and Mount Vernon had fallen victim to the incendiary's torch and that the culprits had paid the supreme penalty, the Mount Pleasant *Union* assured one and all that neither town had burned. "In fact," said the *Union,* "our county has been blessed with order and quiet to an unusual degree, during the reign of terror." Moreover, said the same paper, no one in Titus County had been hanged during "the era of town burnings in Texas."[3] A citizen of Birdville in Tarrant County wrote to A. B. Norton, publisher of the Austin *Southern Intelligencer,* thanking him for correcting a false report that his town had burned. He assured Norton that Birdville "still stands by the mercy of God and is destined to remain a very good little village."[4] The editor of the Weatherford *News* was astonished to receive a letter from Gatesville, commiserating with him over the fiery destruction of his town. The editor said that the report was news to him, since Weatherford was intact. Commenting on this exchange, the Galveston *Civilian and Gazette* wrote: "Rumor has burned almost every town in Northeastern Texas this season."[5]

At the height of the panic, even innocent blazes often became abolitionist conflagrations when they were reported in the press. The La Grange *True Issue,* for example, wrote that "the burning of some trash in the back yard of the Court-house" had led to published reports that incendiaries had struck Brenham. The same journal said that a damaging blaze in Fort Belknap, attributed by many newspapers to incendiaries, had actually resulted from an accidental fire in a government building.[6] In a later edition, the *True Issue* wrote: "That most of the accounts we have received from the Northern part of the State are

1. Marshall *Texas Republican,* July 28, 1860.

2. Tyler *Sentinel,* August 18, 1860.

3. Mount Pleasant *Union,* n.d., quoted in Marshall *Texas Republican,* September 1, 1860.

4. Austin *Southern Intelligencer,* October 10, 1860.

5. Galveston *Civilian and Gazette Weekly,* September 18, 1860.

6. La Grange *True Issue,* August 2, 1860.

falsehoods and sensation tales, is too evident to every well informed man to need contradiction." Even if some of the "occurrences" possessed an element of truth, said the *True Issue*, "as a general thing, the fears of the people have got the better of their judgment, and lead them to give undue importance to accidents."[7] In late September the Marshall *Harrison Flag* went so far as to assert that the only two suspicious fires of the summer had occurred in Dallas and Henderson, and according to that journal, the Henderson fire had been started by one of its own citizens, not by abolitionist incendiaries. The *Harrison Flag* added that other, isolated fires could be explained by a combination of carelessness with matches and the extremely dry weather.[8]

Charles Pryor and other publicists of the abolitionist "plot" had said that in addition to arson, the insurrectionary blacks also had plotted to poison their masters, using strychnine provided by their white sponsors. It was said that vigilantes had discovered large quantities of deadly strychnine in the possession of the slaves, who had even confessed their intention to slip it into wells and cisterns. By late August, however, it was apparent that no one had been poisoned, nor had the investigating whites actually found any strychnine. Clearly, zealous vigilantes had used threats and the lash to intimidate the slaves into making the admissions they wanted to hear. On August 25 the Marshall *Texas Republican*, which earlier had accepted and published the allegations that slaves possessed poison and planned to use it, printed an account by John D. Evans, a local resident who had recently visited Cherokee County. "He . . . informs us that what was supposed to be poison in the hands of the negroes in Cherokee county, when subjected to chemical analysis, turned out to be a harmless preparation." And yet, Evans wrote, "the negroes stated that it was poison and that they had been instructed to place it in the wells and in the food of their masters. Very little reliance can be placed in testimony obtained by coercion or intimidation." The *Texas Republican* saw a parallel between the false confessions in Cherokee County and those of alleged witches in seventeenth-century Salem: "In Massachusetts, during the witch excitement, a great many innocent people were put to death, who confessed their guilt, some of whom acknowledged direct intercourse with the devil. These things should teach caution."[9]

A similar report came from Athens, in Henderson County, the site of the most widely publicized story of abolitionist-inspired plans to poison a community. P. F. Tannehill, "late Secretary of the Vigilance Committee," wrote a letter

7. Ibid., October 18, 1860.
8. Marshall *Harrison Flag*, September 22, 1860.
9. Marshall *Texas Republican*, August 25, 1860.

to the Palestine *Trinity Advocate* in which he said that the report that "over one hundred bottles of strychnine was found in the possession of the negroes in Athens, and one well poisoned, originated in the fact that in one of the boxes of one negro that was implicated, a vial of whisky with a little snake root in it was found." Another vial in the same box contained mainly paregoric and an acid that "the Doctors said might be poison, but it was never tested." Tannehill further explained that the "evidence" that the well in question was poisoned "is that a certain individual saw a 'great-big-nigger track right thar,' close to the well." Secretary Tannehill investigated the allegations and discovered that the blacks had heard of Pryor's version of the alleged abolitionist conspiracy and, if anything, were even more terrified by the rumors of an impending insurrection than their white masters. On one large plantation the slaves were so afraid to stay in their cabins that they begged their master to let them sleep "about the [plantation] house." A disgusted Tannehill said that it made no difference in the eyes of an inflamed public whether an accused slave was innocent, for "the innocent and guilty share the same fate." At the end of the letter, the *Civilian and Gazette*, which had reprinted the *Trinity Advocate*'s account, added: "The Vigilance Committee of Athens dissolved just as soon as they could; and the excitement so far as the fear of 'niggers' is concerned has all died away."[10]

As it became increasingly evident that most of the "burned" towns had experienced no fires at all and that no verified poison had been produced—much less administered to unsuspecting citizens—even the southern rights newspapers that had fanned the flames of fear had to admit that there had been many exaggerations of the extent of the "conspiracy" and called for more restraint. For example, at the end of July, E. H. Cushing's Houston *Telegraph*, the recipient and publisher of one of Charles Pryor's sensational letters, expressed doubt that the plot had ever extended "as far as some think." The same paper further opined that the conspiracy had been "perfected" only in Dallas and Denton, "but had it not been discovered then, it would have been extended to half the counties in the State."[11] In a later edition, the *Telegraph* said that the reported burnings of Palestine, Tyler, McKinney, "and other towns, as well as the reported attempts on half the towns in the interior," had proven false, and concluded that such reports "are not to be believed until they are confirmed."[12]

Even the Austin *Texas State Gazette*, the publisher of Pryor's first letter and

10. Palestine *Trinity Advocate*, n.d., clipped in Galveston *Civilian and Gazette Weekly*, September 4, 1860.

11. Houston *Telegraph*, July 31, 1860.

12. Ibid., n.d., quoted in the Bellville *Texas Countryman*, August 25, 1860.

the leading publicist of the "abolitionist plot" in the state, urged caution when it was alleged that the white conspirators and their black allies had targeted the capitol city itself. Apparently trying to calm the fears of Austin's residents, the *Texas State Gazette* wrote: "There is much excitement in the community arising chiefly from the existence of startling rumors, often greatly exaggerated." Austin's mayor had ordered a search of the "quarters," the *Texas State Gazette* wrote, and it had turned up some pistols, muskets, bullets, a half keg of powder, and knives. However, since blacks customarily had been allowed to possess arms, the *Texas State Gazette* professed to be unconcerned about most of the discoveries, concluding: "The powder is the only ominous sign, and it may yet be explained."[13] An Austin businessman, writing to a friend in early August, confirmed the *Texas State Gazette*'s conclusion that early reports of large stockpiles of arms had been false, saying that the investigation had turned up "nothing significant."[14]

Thomas J. Crooks, editor of the Paris *Press,* a staunch Breckinridge paper that had done its share in publicizing the early reports, later said that many of the accounts of abolitionist arson had proven false, including one that supposedly had occurred in Paris. In the *Press*'s edition of August 18 Crooks wrote: "We have heard so many reports of 'attempted insurrections,' 'well poisoning,' 'diabolical plans of abolitionists,' &c., within the past few weeks, the majority of which, when fully investigated turn out to be totally false, that we are tempted to disbelieve all reports of the kind." Crooks had just read in the Jefferson *Herald and Gazette* "that a 'party of negroes and several white men were found assembled together at or near Paris, that fifteen were arrested and the rest fled towards Tarrant.' This must be news to the citizens of Paris as it certainly is to us." Paris had maintained "a most vigilant patrol every night," the editor continued, and it had discovered nothing to indicate "that any plot has been made known to the negroes of Paris, either insurrectionary or incendiary."[15] And in another column, Crooks showed his disgust with the vigilante system. Many innocents had died as a result of irresponsible accusations, Crooks believed. He

13. Austin *Texas State Gazette,* August 4, 1860. The Austin *Southern Intelligencer,* on August 15, 1860, denounced the printing of unsubstantiated reports that arsonists had destroyed many towns, including Austin. It blamed those whose extremist political agenda led them to exploit "the weaknesses of men and the fears of women and children." Specifically it singled out such southern rights journals as the Galveston *News,* Houston *Telegraph,* Dallas *Herald,* and Belton *Democrat* for their irresponsible reporting.

14. John T. Allen to D. C. Osborn, August 2, 1860, quoted in Lack, "Slavery and Vigilantism in Austin, Texas," 17.

15. Paris *Press,* August 18, 1860, clipped in Marshall *Texas Republican,* August 25, 1860.

was especially horrified by the bloodthirstiness of some: "One valiant defender of southern rights, not content with the idea of hanging *suspected* persons, desires to drink the blood of an abolitionist, whilst another, not quite as ferocious, will be content if he can kill one before he dies. . . . A thousand rumors are in circulation every day in the week and the public seems to demand something horrible."[16]

Editor Crooks was not alone in feeling revulsion at the excesses of the vigilance committees. The growing realization that many Texas communities had overreacted to the stories of abolitionism and arson led many Texans of all political persuasions to question the continued use of vigilance committees. Since such committees in their haste clearly had taken the lives of many innocents, the conviction grew that it was perhaps time to rely once again upon the regularly constituted legal processes. P. F. Tannehill, the former vigilante who had expressed his disillusionment over the false accusations of poisonings in his letter to the Palestine *Trinity Advocate*, concluded that "under any and all emergencies the laws of the land if enforced, are superior in efficacy to the action of any self-constituted bodies—that it will not do to trust 'life liberty and property' to the exercise of arbitrary power in a land of law and stable government— that it is eminently the duty of every citizen to see that the 'majesty of the law' be vindicated."[17]

By early September a number of journals began to echo Tannehill's rejection of vigilantism as a means of effecting justice. The Centerville *Times*, of Anderson County, said that it opposed "everything in the shape of a Vigilance Committee," because such bodies endangered the community and did more harm than good: "They set law at defiance, and inaugurate a system of mob law approaching a despotism, which in the hands of bad men, may be used to defeat the very purposes for which they were intended." The regularly constituted legal system was perfectly adequate to deal with most crises, including the current one, said the *Times*.[18] The Indianola *Bulletin* agreed. After alleged abolitionist activity had led townsmen to expel a young stranger, who was told a "change of location might be better for his health," the community had hastily formed a vigilance committee. The *Bulletin* sharply disagreed with this action, stating that while the times necessitated vigilance, "they do not require a

16. Paris *Press*, n.d., clipped in Austin *Southern Intelligencer*, September 5, 1860.

17. Palestine *Trinity Advocate*, n.d., clipped in the Galveston *Civilian and Gazette Weekly*, September 4, 1860.

18. Centerville *Times*, n.d., quoted in Galveston *Civilian and Gazette Weekly*, September 11, 1860.

regular banded organization to usurp the powers and exercise the functions of established legal authority."[19]

The Galveston *News* showed that some extreme southern rights journals also had begun to have qualms about vigilante justice, even in cases where guilt was presumed. On August 14 the *News* reported the case of a "negro boy" suspected of setting fire to the stable and kitchen of a Georgetown resident. A white music teacher "hailing from higher latitude" allegedly had induced the black to commit arson. Upon being implicated, the accused white instigator "made it convenient to decamp." The African American was not so lucky; a report that he had been "seen near the premises" was enough to convince local vigilantes of his guilt, and they promptly hanged him. Even though it had supported the formation of vigilance committees, the *News* criticized this hasty action, stating: "He may have been, and no doubt was, guilty, and richly merited the extreme penalty of the law; yet, would it not have been better to have waited four weeks, and tried him according to law?"[20]

Still another Breckinridge supporter, the Galveston *Civilian and Gazette*, conceded that the detection and punishment of the accused conspirators "without their own compulsory confessions" would have been very difficult. Even so, the editor wrote, there could be no excuse for violating the constitutional right of the accused to be presumed innocent until proven guilty by the evidence. Unfortunately, said the *Civilian and Gazette*, this cherished constitutional protection had been turned on its head, and some had "been assumed to be guilty, and either required to prove their innocence, where there was no evidence to the contrary, or denied the privilege of defence altogether."[21]

Especially troubling to the critics of the vigilance movement were reports indicating that participants in some instances had exceeded their mandate in their zeal to root out abolitionists. For example, the *Civilian and Gazette* cited reports of punishment that had been inflicted "by men disguised and unknown either to the parties punished or the people at large." The journal probably was referring to a letter it had received from Dallas, signed "*Soit et Avant.*" Written on September 2, the letter stated that a mob of ten disguised men had gone to the house of "a Mr. Barnett" in the middle of the night, seized him from his bed and had taken him away. Nothing was known of the fate or whereabouts of the victim, nor of the reason he might have been kidnapped, even though "the community at large" had no complaints against him. The correspondent

19. Indianola *Bulletin*, n.d., quoted in Austin *Texas State Gazette*, September 1, 1860.

20. Galveston *News*, August 14, 1860, clipped in Austin *Texas State Gazette*, August 25, 1860.

21. Galveston *Civilian and Gazette Weekly*, September 18, 1860.

deplored the use of "midnight assassins" to avenge "public wrongs," because they "thrust terror and a sense of danger into the bosom of every good family." Law-abiding citizens could never feel secure while such lawlessness was rampant, the editor said, "and more especially when the mob is composed of topers and grocery loafers."[22]

Calling for a greater restraint in the use of vigilance committees, the Weatherford *News* said the tendency of such bodies to act in secrecy naturally gave rise to doubts about the "justice" they meted out. The editor concluded: "Whenever the facts upon which an individual has been punished by a Vigilance Committee will not bear publication and the parties who inflict the punishment are not willing to be known, doubt naturally arise[s] as to the justice and necessity of the transaction." The use of vigilance committees, except in extreme circumstances, should be avoided, and in most cases the alleged malefactors should be tried in regular courts of law, for, warned the *News,* "a Government which has not the power to enforce its laws, can afford no security to life or property and cannot long sustain itself."[23]

Although many newspapers had touted the respectability of the vigilance committees' members at the time they were formed, by late summer there was a growing concern that less desirable types were responsible for vigilante excesses in some locales. In his letter to the *Civilian and Gazette, Soit et Avant* had charged that "topers" and "grocery loafers"[24] had been involved in the Dallas abduction. An anonymous letter to the Marshall *Texas Republican* expressed a similar concern. Asserting the need for a greater reliance on courts of law, the letter writer said that there was a tendency for the more respectable members of the vigilance committees to tire of their duties and resign, and "other men of a more violent disposition" too often replaced them. Thus, said the correspondent, there was real danger "the very body to which we at first looked for assistance may in time become a terror to us all."[25] The *Texas Republican* seemed to agree with the letter writer, although it had generally supported the vigilance movement. After a mob had demanded custody of a young man in Gilmer and had promptly hanged him, that journal had said that anyone guilty of inciting slaves to insurrection—as the young man was accused of doing—"merits death," but the editor now thought the law should be allowed to run its course in such cases.[26]

22. Ibid., September 11, 1860.
23. Weatherford *News,* n.d., clipped in Galveston *Civilian and Gazette,* September 18, 1860.
24. "Grocery" was a term often used for saloons in the nineteenth century.
25. Marshall *Texas Republican,* August 25, 1860.
26. Ibid., September 1, 1860.

The younger, less disciplined vigilantes sometimes irritated the local populace by their noisy conduct while on night patrol duty. For example, the Matagorda *Gazette* reported that it had heard complaints about "the rowdy and indiscreet conduct" of some who were on night watch duty. The editor feared that such behavior, which apparently had disturbed sleeping citizens, might reflect discredit upon the organization that had worked so hard to protect "the security of life and property." The committee should tolerate no "levity or boisterous conduct," the *Gazette* said, and young men ought to wait until they were off duty to engage in "fun and frolic."[27]

A growing realization throughout the state that the danger from fire and poison had been greatly exaggerated seems to have led to a decline in zeal on the part of many vigilance committee members, a least in some parts of the state. The Bellville *Texas Countryman* reported on September 1 that the local vigilante committee meeting several days earlier had been poorly attended. It chided the members who failed to show up, arguing, "There is as much cause for vigilance now as ever."[28]

The *Texas Countryman*'s warning notwithstanding, the growing realization that vigilance committees had gone too far clearly contributed to the demise of the panic and the restoration of the legal processes. In mid-September, a resident of Central Texas who had previously been much alarmed by the stories of abolitionist activity admitted to a northern correspondent that "we have been too much engaged in hanging and cutting those reckless simpletons" who had been sent by "northern fanatics."[29] He later wrote friends in Texas that "our Negro insurrection has quietly subsided." Although a number of blacks had been "severely punished, . . . no facts of importance have been ellicited by it," and this had led him to conclude, much as the Houston *Telegraph* had, that the only "real abolition movement" had been confined to the northern part of the state.[30]

There were other indications in late summer that the tide of fear was ebbing, even in the area that had been most affected. On September 14 the New Orleans *Picayune* said that the counties in North Texas that had so recently been agitated by reports of insurrection and fires "are becoming confident and quiet."[31] As early as August 5, Charles Pryor, the editor whose letters had given rise to

27. Matagorda *Gazette,* September 5, 1860.

28. Bellville *Texas Countryman,* September 1, 1860.

29. Gideon Lincecum, Long Point, to C. S. Cook, Mason City, Ill., September 16, 1860, Lincecum, Phillips, and Redshaw, eds., *Gideon Lincecum's Sword,* 64.

30. Gideon Lincecum, Long Point, to D. B. and Emily Moore, Castroville, October 12, 1860, in ibid., 65.

31. New Orleans (La.) *Daily Picayune,* September 14, 1860.

the panic, reported to the Austin *Texas State Gazette* that the excitement in Dallas was "somewhat subsiding," and he theorized that the executions in Dallas and other counties had "struck terror" in the abolitionists, thus thwarting their plans for a general insurrection.[32] Another Dallasite, in a letter written later that month to the Galveston *Civilian and Gazette,* confirmed Pryor's report that there had been a subsidence of anxiety and said the town was making a rapid recovery from both the drought and recent fires. He closed his letter with the trenchant comment: "We have no more excitement about abolitionists."[33]

After the Dallas *Herald* had resumed publication in October, editor Pryor elaborated on the town's return to normality. Although some blacks had been executed for their roles, he said, "the vast majority of them have confessed, repented, been punished, continued at work, [and] will yet live to become as faithful as if the Northern fanatics had never poisoned their minds with the foolish notion of liberty, and the awful design of murder and arson." The small number of abolitionists responsible for the seduction of faithful slaves had left the state, Pryor said, and confidence and harmony had been restored to the community.[34] So confident had Dallas become by early September that the Democrats made plans to hold a "grand State Barbecue" in the town that, only two months before, had been leveled by fire. Notable among those who were to attend were such prominent political figures as Senator Louis T. Wigfall, Representative John H. Reagan, and John Marshall, secretary of the state Democratic party and editor of the Austin *Texas State Gazette.*[35]

The revelations that most rumors of fires and all of the instances of reported poisonings had proven false, coupled with the growing disillusionment with vigilance committees, led to a movement to restore to the courts the responsibility for enforcing the law. By October this movement appears to have been in full swing, as judges began to reassert their authority. For example, the Austin *Southern Intelligencer* wrote on October 10: "Let the Judges of the different Districts take the same bold stand that Chief Justice Wheeler and Judges Terrill and Devine have taken against this mobocratic feeling."[36]

32. Austin *Texas State Gazette,* August 18, 1860.

33. "*Droit et Avant,*" August 28, 1860, Galveston *Civilian and Gazette,* September 11, 1860.

34. Dallas *Herald,* n.d., clipped in New Orleans (La.) *Daily Picayune,* October 23, 1860.

35. Austin *Texas State Gazette,* September 8, 1860.

36. Austin *Southern Intelligencer,* October 10, 1860. Royal T. Wheeler was chief justice of the Texas Supreme Court. Although he was an old Whig and embraced that party's conservative political philosophy, he supported secession in 1861 as the best course of action for the South. He was given to fits of melancholy, and as the fortunes of the Confederacy declined in 1864, he committed suicide (*Handbook of Texas Online,* s.v., www.tsha.utexas.edu/handbook/online/articles/WW/

Perhaps the most publicized instance of a district judge taking control occurred in Sherman. The Sherman *North Texian* reported that District Judge Waddill had delivered a scathing denunciation of vigilante justice in his charge to the grand jury in Sherman. The judge asserted that criminal statutes were quite adequate to deal with all manner of crimes, including those of slave tampering, abolitionism, and insurrectionary activity. The *North Texian* said that the judge "deplored the mistaken policy which has been resorted to by some of our citizens in various parts of the country, prompted, as they think by extreme necessity, of usurping to themselves the right of making, administering and executing laws." Waddill concluded his indictment of the vigilance movement by warning that no one person, or committee of one hundred for that matter, had the right to take the life of "the lowest and meanest person in our State, and that those who engage in it are guilty of murder." The *North Texian* obviously approved of the judge's admonition, saying that "every law-abiding citizen of Grayson [County]" had applauded him. The Austin *Southern Intelligencer* also praised the Sherman judge for refusing to allow "the reign of terror" or vigilance committee "bullyism" to keep him from doing his duty.[37]

On a more mundane level, some openly expressed concern over the detrimental effect that vigilante law might be having on the economy of the state, particularly by frightening off prospective immigrants. A correspondent of the Paris *Press,* writing about a recent trip to Arkansas, said that, while there, he had learned that hundreds of prospective settlers on their way to look at sites in the Lone Star State were deterred by the frightening news from Texas and had turned back. The writer worried that the discouragement of immigrants— so necessary for the state's growth and economic development—meant that it would take the Lone Star State "years to recover" from the effects of the panic. The pro-Breckinridge Galveston *Civilian and Gazette* reprinted the letter under the heading: "THE EFFECTS OF UNDUE EXCITEMENT AND LYNCH LAW."[38]

---

fwh9.html [accessed August 3, 2006]). Alexander W. Terrell, of Austin, was judge of the Second District. He was a friend of Sam Houston and an ardent unionist, but after his judicial term expired in 1863, he joined the Confederate Army (*Handbook of Texas Online,* s.v., www.tsha.utexas.edu/handbook/online/articles/TT/fte16.html [accessed August 3, 2006]). Thomas J. Devine was district judge in San Antonio. He served as a member of the secession convention in 1861 and helped supervise the surrender of federal forts, troops, and property (*Handbook of Texas,* s.v., www.tsha.utexas.edu/handbook/online/articles/DD/fde50.html [accessed August 3, 2006]).

37. Sherman *North Texian,* n.d., quoted in Austin *Southern Intelligencer,* October 10, 1860. See also Galveston *Civilian and Gazette,* October 16, 1860; New Orleans (La.) *Daily Picayune,* October 19, 1860.

38. Paris *Press,* n.d., quoted in Galveston *Civilian and Gazette,* September 18, 1860.

The Fayetteville *Arkansian,* another Breckinridge supporter that had done its share of publicizing the abolitionist danger in Arkansas, added credibility to this alarming report in late September when it wrote: "The late raids in Texas have driven out thousands of good, true, decent men; and now deter good, true, decent men from entering her borders." The *Arkansian* cited a specific example of an editor from Illinois, who had planned to take his wife to Texas for her health. He had changed his mind, however, when he was advised "not to visit Texas at present."[39] In another case, the Austin *Southern Intelligencer* told about a man from "one of the wealthiest families of Virginia" who came to Austin with the intention of purchasing land and moving his family to Texas in the fall. But he had received letters from his family begging him not to buy "on account of magnified reports" of alleged abolitionist incendiarism; consequently, he had abandoned his plan to resettle in Texas and returned to Virginia.[40]

A. B. Norton, editor of the *Southern Intelligencer,* blamed radical southern rights newspapers for spreading the stories that he believed were damaging the economy: "If the [Galveston] *News,* the [Houston] *Telegraph,* the [Austin] *Gazette,* the editor of the Dallas *Herald,* and the Belton *Democrat* can succeed in convincing the people that our negroes, inflamed with lust, stand with the torch and the knife ready at a favorable moment to cut our throats, burn our houses and ravish our women, then we ask them how much they have added to the value of slave property in the State? How much will such things increase the already low prices of our lands? How many slave holders from other States will immigrate to Texas with their property?"[41]

A resident of Kaufman, a town southeast of Dallas, wrote to the Marshall *Texas Republican* on September 8 about his concerns that the panic was having a detrimental effect on the Texas economy. Signing himself "Warsaw," the writer said that he had been traveling out of state during the panic; therefore, "I have but little personal knowledge of what has been taking place at home, but I do know that the exaggerated accounts published, are having a very injurious effect in preventing emigrants from even the Southern States settling among us, and also in the withholding of foreign capital so greatly needed to help forward our internal improvement enterprise."[42]

A few critics of the frightful rumormongering that had swept the state in the wake of the fires in North Texas were able to find humor in the scare sto-

39. Fayetteville *Arkansian,* September 28, 1860.
40. Austin *Southern Intelligencer,* n.d., quoted in San Antonio *Alamo Express,* September 10, 1860.
41. Austin *Southern Intelligencer,* n.d., quoted in McKinney *Messenger,* September 14, 1860.
42. Marshall *Texas Republican,* September 22, 1860.

ries. Oscar M. Addison wrote a letter to his brother, J. H. Addison of Fairfield, poking fun at him for overreacting to the reports of insurrectionary activity. Although the letter is no longer extant, we may surmise its content by the recipient's petulant reply. His brother was not amused and answered that the "horrors" were real, "at least in the main, and though such valor as yours may attempt to turn it into ridicule, yet such conduct only displays the ignorance, or weakness of mind of the person who affects to despise the rumors." Oscar had apparently offered to ride to his brother's rescue, to which J. H. replied: "Please don't distress yourself about bringing an 'army' to help me, as I have gotten over my fears somewhat, and I hope that I will not get badly scared until you come over, when the sight of you will at once dispel all my fears." And should the situation take a turn for the worse, J. H. said that he would welcome his brother's assistance, "for it is rather dull work 'watching cisterns' by myself, but if you are present, all fear will vanish, and *watching* will be a pleasure."[43]

Lucadia Pease of Austin, wife of former governor E. M. Pease, was able to see humor in grim newspaper accounts of supposed abolitionist actions. In a chatty letter to her sister, Lucadia said: "We read in Northern papers accounts of the most awful insurrections in Texas and are quite amused at the additions which stories gain by so long a journey." The former First Lady of Texas shrugged off the possibility of real danger, saying, "There was a little excitement got up by the newspapers before the election for political effect—but the stories of fires and murders are all exaggerated."[44]

Most unionist editors and political figures, both within and outside the state, saw nothing humorous in the panic, which they increasingly viewed as an extravagant, orchestrated ploy to enhance the chances of John C. Breckinridge to gain the presidency, and, failing that, to prepare the state and the South for secession. The San Antonio *Alamo Express,* in its very first edition published on August 18, called the fire-eaters' efforts to blame the Republican party for the alleged insurrectionary activity "a silly attempt to mislead the thinking people of Texas." James P. Newcomb, a prominent unionist and the editor-publisher of that new journal, said that if any party was responsible, "reason would point

43. J. H. Addison, Fairfield, to Oscar M. Addison, August 29, 1860, Oscar M. Addison Papers, Barker Texas History Center Archives, University of Texas, Austin, Texas.

44. Lucadia Pease to "Dear Sister" [Juliet Niles], Austin, September 20, 1860, Pease-Graham-Niles Family Papers, Austin Public Library, Austin, Texas. Lucadia's husband, Elisha M. Pease, served two terms as governor between 1853 and 1857. He aligned himself with the unionists in 1859 and "quietly maintained his loyalty to the Union" to the end of the war (*Handbook of Texas Online,* s.v., www.tsha.utexas.edu/handbook/online/articles/PP/fpe8.html [accessed July 18, 2006]).

to the Yancey men, who seem to leave no stone unturned to create fire-eating excitement." In its next edition, the *Alamo Express* attacked its local Democratic rivals, the *Ledger and Texan* and the *Herald,* for alleging that the Republican party had conspired with abolitionists to wreak havoc on Texas as a means of advancing their presidential candidate's chances of victory in November. Newcomb asked: "How could the burning of the entire State of Texas effect the election of Lincoln?" On the other hand, he asserted, the fires and accompanying excitement accorded perfectly with the goals of the secessionists, "for it does seem their extreme desire to get up a rabid Southern feeling just at the full tide of the Presidential contest."[45]

Taking a similar tack, A. B. Norton's Austin *Southern Intelligencer* pointed out that it was much easier to control public opinion by appealing to passion than to reason, "and the secessionist crew have used this weakness to great advantage—By misrepresenting facts [and] distorting them, people have been led to believe they are in imminent danger of the torch, the knife and the lust of an infuriated servile insurrection." Norton expressed the hope that right-thinking Texans would resist "the mobocratic feeling" that had endangered the liberties of all Texans: "And above all, we call upon every conservative, Union loving man in the State to set his face against these Breckinridge and Lane Clubs [the vigilance committees], for they are nothing else, and let us show the agrarian leaders of the secession party that they have not yet succeeded in indoctrinating the people of Texas with their disloyalty to the Government of our common country."[46]

Unionist office-holders commended newspapers and politicians that had refused to accept the stories of abolitionist depredations in Texas. For example, E. W. Cave, the Texas secretary of state, wrote to Alexander H. Stephens, the Georgia unionist who would later become vice president of the Confederacy, commending him for a speech he had made defending the Union and

45. San Antonio *Alamo Express,* August 18, 26, 1860. Born in Nova Scotia, Newcomb had immigrated to Texas with his family in 1839. He worked for various newspapers in the state before establishing the *Alamo Express* in 1860, at the height of the insurrectionist scare. As in the case of Norton, his denial of the plot allegations and outspoken denunciation of the secessionists earned him the ire of southern rights men. When he continued his criticism after the state had joined the Confederacy, his paper was burned to the ground by the Knights of the Golden Circle and Confederate Rangers. Following the war he returned to Texas, where he reentered the newspaper business and supported the Reconstruction administration of Governor E. J. Davis (*Handbook of Texas Online,* s.v., www.tsha.utexas.edu/handbook/online/articles/NN/fne19.html [accessed July 18, 2006]).

46. Austin *Southern Intelligencer,* October 10, 1860.

especially for his "declarations in reference to the pretended insurrections in Texas." Noting that he and his brother, Georgia Supreme Court justice Linton Stephens, had taken much abuse because of their opposition to the fire-eaters, Cave assured Stephens that no one appreciated his comments more than Governor Sam Houston, "the gallant old Chief with whose Administration I have the honor to be associated." Cave said that he had taken the liberty to send Stephens some back copies of the Austin *Southern Intelligencer*, "a journal which has done much to combat and expose the ridiculous stories which have so inflamed the public mind in Texas and elsewhere." Although the disunionists had used the issue to good advantage, said Cave, "a reaction is now taking place."[47]

The "gallant old Chief" himself weighed in on the issue of the alleged abolitionist conspiracy at a mass meeting of unionists held in Austin on September 22. Governor Houston was ailing but arose from his sickbed to plead eloquently for the Union, and in the process he delivered a scathing attack upon those who had exploited the Texas Troubles to arouse anti-Union feelings among the citizens. In addressing the issue, he confessed: "My weak condition warns me against giving vent to my feelings, which will come up when I behold the efforts of whipsters and demagogues to mislead the people" to gain political capital. Houston admitted that some property had burned, and there had been "here and there a case of insubordination . . . among the negroes." There had even been a few cases in which "a scoundrel has attempted to run a negro off to sell him; and all these things are charged to abolitionism." The governor then summed up the alleged insurrectionary activities: "Terrible stories are put afloat of arms discovered, your capitol in flames, kegs of powder found under houses, thousands of negroes engaged in insurrectionary plots, wells poisoned, and hundreds of bottles of strychnine found. Town after town has been reported in ashes and by the time the report has been found to be false, some new story to keep up the public excitement has been invented."[48]

The governor next addressed the economic damage that he believed was being done by these rumors: "The people of the South have been filled with horror by these accounts and, instead of Texas being looked upon as the most inviting spot on earth, they turn from it as from a land accursed. Who will buy land here, so long as these continue? What Southern planter will emigrate with his slaves to such a country?" Still, said the governor, if there were a basis in

47. E. W. Cave, Austin, to Alexander H. Stephens, September 20, 1860, Alexander H. Stephens Papers, microfilm copy, vol. 11, reel 6, Library of Congress, Washington, D.C.

48. Amelia W. Williams and Eugene C. Barker, eds., *The Writings of Sam Houston, 1813–1863*, 8 vols. (Austin, 1938–1943), 8:155–156.

fact for the insurrectionary stories, "we could bear it without a murmur; but there has been no cause for the present state of feeling. We all know how every occurrence has been magnified by the disunion press and leaders and scattered abroad, and for no other purpose than to arouse the passions of the people and drive them into the Southern disunion movement; for if you can make the people believe that the terrible accounts of abolition plots here are true, they will be ready for anything, sooner than suffer their continuance."[49]

And, asked Governor Houston, who were the men circulating the rumors and using them to fan the flames of disunion?

Are they the strong slaveholders of the country? No; examine the matter and it will be found that by far the large majority of them never owned a negro, and never will own one. I know some of them who are making the most fuss, who would not make good negroes if they were blacked. And these are the men who are carrying on practical abolitionism, by taking up planters' negroes and hanging them. They are the gentlemen who belong to the dueling family that don't fight with knives, but choose something that can be dodged. Some of them deserve a worse fate than Senator Wigfall would visit upon me [tar and feathers]; and, sooner or later, when the people find out their schemes, they will get it.[50]

Unionist journals in the other southern states generally kept an eye on the reports out of Texas. Some "smelled a rat" early on. For example, on July 28 the Lynchburg *Virginian,* which in its edition of the previous day had run reports of the alleged plot, expressed skepticism. There might be some factual basis for the stories, said the *Virginian,* "but we shall be somewhat surprised if it does not turn out to have been greatly exaggerated; agitating the country and inflaming the popular mind to no good purpose whatever."[51]

On August 3, after the fire-eating Montgomery *Mail* had devoted prominent, ominous headlines to the alleged abolitionist plot in the Lone Star State, the Hayneville *Watchman,* a pro-Bell paper, answered with parody and sarcasm. Mocking the *Mail's* frightful headlines, the *Watchman* wrote:

Blood, Thunder, Destruction!
DESTRUCTION, THUNDER, BLOOD!
Blood, Destruction, Thunder!

49. Ibid., 8:156.
50. Ibid.
51. Lynchburg *Virginian,* July 28, 1860.

Houses Burnt, Niggers Abolished,
Things in Confusion!

Under these satirical headlines the *Watchman* gave a tongue-in-cheek version of the *Mail's* account and concluded: "For this startling news we are indebted to that unequalled paper the Montgomery *Mail,* which has made a collection of abolition news a *specialty,* and has it by telegraph very frequently days in advance of its transpiring."[52]

Upon receiving the reports of the fires in Dallas and the "plot" to devastate North Texas, the Wadesborough *North Carolina Argus,* another unionist journal, said that the reports were "very indefinite, and look like attempts either to hoax or to get up an anti-abolition excitement in the South." The same paper reminded its readers that "We are just on the eve of the Presidential election, it will be remembered, and it is the wish of certain parties . . . to intensify sectional feeling."[53]

Like the *North Carolina Argus,* other unionist journals increasingly saw political motivations behind the Texas Troubles. Specifically, these papers asserted that secessionists within the Democratic party were using the fears inspired by the Texas Troubles and subsequent copycat panics in the other southern states to advance Breckinridge's chances of election and, if they were unsuccessful, to bring about a dissolution of the Union. The Richmond *Whig* succinctly summed up this view: "We have no doubt that the Breckinridge Disunionists would readily aid the impression that invaders and insurrectionists abound in the Southern States. Their object is to increase the enmity between the sections, in order to bring about a dissolution of the Union. Let the people receive with caution insurrection stories."[54] On September 25, North Carolina's pro-Douglas Newbern *Weekly Progress* expressed its belief that both the Texas rumors and the allegations of incendiary plots in other southern states had been greatly exaggerated and said: "We beseech the fire-eating journals not to get up any more slave panics until after the election is over." In another passage, however, the *Weekly Progress* clearly showed that it did not expect its plea to be honored, gloomily predicting more frightful headlines in the southern rights press: "'Mass Meetings,' 'Abolition Raids,' and 'Servile Plots' will be all the rage now until after the election. We wish it was over."[55]

52. Hayneville (Ala.) *Watchman,* August 3, 1860.

53. Wadesborough *North Carolina Argus,* August 2, 1860.

54. Richmond (Va.) *Whig,* September 13, 1860.

55. Newbern (N.C.) *Weekly Progress,* September 25, October 23, 1860. For similar opinions, see: Wheeling (Va.) *Daily Intelligencer,* August 27, 1860; Wellsburg (Va.) *Herald,* September 21, 1860;

Other southern unionist journals took a more ambivalent position. The pro-Bell Montgomery *Weekly Post,* for example, printed the allegations of incendiary activities on August 1 but withheld judgment, suggesting that they might have been fabricated. A week later, the *Weekly Post* published other reports of abolitionism in Texas and appeared to accept their validity, but on September 5 the paper carried new articles from its exchanges that were critical of the earlier reports and said: "These accounts show that the reports have been greatly exaggerated, and it is proper that we should arrive as near to the exact truth as possible." People should not be frightened by the stories of abolitionist activity, said the *Weekly Post*; nevertheless, it advised its readers to be vigilant.[56]

The unionist New Orleans *Picayune,* like the *Post,* cautiously gave credence to the early reports of the alleged plot in Texas, saying that the fires, "occurring simultaneously in different and distant towns and farm houses have created a well-grounded suspicion of concert and design among some white desperadoes, who are actuated by revenge or some other more villainous motive." Those "desperadoes" might be abolitionists, the *Picayune* suggested, but they should be dealt with "in a spirit of justice" and punished, but only after a "thorough and impartial inquiry."[57] Less than three weeks later, the same paper said that a careful examination of the many reports coming out of Texas showed that they had been exaggerated, "and that many of the reported incidents did not in fact happen." Enough mischief had been done to justify continued vigilance on the part of the citizens of North Texas, the *Picayune* stated, but it saw "no evidence of any concerted plot among the negroes for . . . insurrection against the authority of the whites."[58] On September 8 the *Picayune* reiterated this opinion and said that further investigation had shown there was no plot supported by outside abolitionists. In a few cases, said the *Picayune,* "demoralized" blacks—egged on by unscrupulous white men—had set some fires: "But not half of what has been confessed seems to be borne out by later facts." The "strychnine" turned out to be "very harmless," and the "poisoned" wells were found "to be untainted with any deleterious substance." The *Picayune* said that their fears had caused Texans to view "the slightest circumstantial evidence as strong as proof from holy writ"; nevertheless, it still thought a heightened level

---

Vicksburg (Miss.) *Daily Whig,* October 18, 1860; Raymond (Miss.) *Hinds County Gazette,* November 7, 1860; Nashville (Tenn.) *Republican Banner,* August 4, 1860; Savannah (Ga.) *Republican,* n.d., quoted in Milledgeville (Ga.) *Federal Union,* October 9, 1860.

56. Montgomery (Ala.) *Weekly Post,* August 1, 8, September 5, 1860.

57. New Orleans (La.) *Daily Picayune,* August 2, 1860.

58. Ibid., August 19, 1860.

of vigilance was justified in the Lone Star State—and in all the South, for that matter—for lax treatment had given the slaves too much "freedom."[59]

The reaction of northern journals to the reports of abolitionist activities in Texas largely depended upon their political orientation. Although unaffiliated with a political party, James Gordon Bennett's New York *Herald* was staunchly anti-Lincoln and decidedly pro-southern. Reacting to Senator William H. Seward's criticism of the Texans' actions, the *Herald* blamed the New York Republican leader for helping to provoke sectional conflict by his assertion that free and slave societies were incompatible. "It is Mr. Seward's 'irrepressible conflict,' which is now going on in the Lone Star State," said Bennett, who asked: "Will the conservative masses of the Central States permit the conflict to extend all over the South? They can arrest it by defeating Lincoln. Will they do it?"[60] The pro-southern St. Louis *Missouri Republican,* which reprinted the *Herald's* editorial, agreed with Bennett and suggested that the Texas Troubles were but a foretaste of what awaited the country if the abolitionist movement were not checked.[61] Connecticut's Hartford *Times,* which supported Breckinridge, accepted the accounts it had received of depredations in Texas and, like many southern counterparts, linked the alleged insurrectionary activity to John Brown.[62]

Predictably, Republican journals had a far different take on the alarming reports from Texas. Some reprinted the stories with little editorial comment. For example, the Cincinnati *Daily Commercial* published a long list of reports from Texas papers without elaborating but clearly conveyed its opinion in the heading: "The Tragedy and Farce of a Rumored Slave Insurrection."[63] The Boston *Journal,* another Lincoln supporter, scoffed at the plot stories, arguing that the comparative lack of valuable property and slaves made the lightly populated communities of North Texas unlikely targets for conspirators hoping to strike a blow against slavery.[64]

59. Ibid., September 8, 1860.

60. New York *Herald,* n.d., quoted in St. Louis *Daily Missouri Republican,* September 9, 1860. Although the *Herald* clearly accepted the reports of an insurrectionary plot, on July 28 it printed a letter from a Washington correspondent, who wrote: "The telegraphic report of an abolition conspiracy in Northern Texas, is viewed here by Southern men as a humbug gotten up for political effect." The Austin *Southern Intelligencer* gleefully quoted the letter on August 15, saying that the "late excitement about negro insurrections and incendiarism . . . seems as well understood in Washington as here."

61. St. Louis *Daily Missouri Republican,* September 8, 9, 1860.

62. Hartford (Conn.) *Weekly Times,* September 8, 1860.

63. Cincinnati (Ohio) *Daily Commercial,* August 20, 1860.

64. Boston (Mass.) *Journal,* n.d., clipped in Washington (D.C.) *Constitution,* August 3, 1860.

The New York *Times* gave considerable space to the Texas Troubles, and it was skeptical from the beginning. Noting that there were close parallels between the current panic and that experienced in Colorado County, Texas, during the presidential election campaign of 1856, the *Times* said: "One of the worst features of these Slavery panics is their close proximity to the Presidential election. We now hear of one every day in some of the Slave States." The "coincidence" was unfortunate, said the *Times*: "We should be sorry to accuse any party of conducting a canvass in blood, of slaughtering hecatombs of deluded negroes and peddlers and preachers on the altar of political Victory, but we wish sincerely there was a longer interval between the conflagrations and strychnine stories, and confessions, and executions, and the Presidential election."[65]

Like the Boston *Journal*, the *Times* thought an abolitionist plot in Dallas, Ellis, and Denton counties, where there were comparatively few slaves, made no sense. The distance from these counties to free territory meant that an insurrection in that locality "could promise no desirable result for the slave," argued the *Times*, which could not resist tweaking the southern alarmists with a bit of sarcasm: "A Spanish American revolution . . . in Tierra del Fuego, or a parliamentary crisis in Kamtchatka, would be hardly less amazing."[66]

The *Times* said it was horrified by the cruel excesses of vigilante law and even asserted, "A more absolute and fearful reign of terror perhaps never existed than that which, for the moment, seems to be supreme in Texas." Men had been hanged on no other evidence than the testimony extorted from hapless blacks who had been "driven to the verge of madness" by "the liberal use of the lash and cord."[67] Indeed, said the *Times*, the cruelest "minion of the Austrian Kaiser that ever sat in judgment upon an Italian Carbonaro, is humane, reasonable, enlightened, merciful and religious, compared with a drunken, excited Pro-Slavery Texan mob." Nor, asserted the same editorialist, had any Turkish Pasha ever exulted over "a heap of infidel skulls" more than Texas newspapers were doing over the "daily murders" carried out by drunken vigilantes in the Lone Star State.[68]

Horace Greeley's New York *Tribune*, like the *Times* and other pro-Lincoln journals, early refuted the notion that there was an abolitionist conspiracy in

65. New York *Times*, July 28, September 7, 1860.
66. Ibid., July 28, 1860. Tierra del Fuego is an archipelago off the southernmost tip of South America, separated from the continent by the Strait of Magellan. Kamtchatka is the remote peninsula in extreme eastern Russia, located between the Pacific and Sea of Osahk.
67. New York *Times*, August 10, 1860.
68. Ibid., September 7, 1860.

Texas. On July 30, Greeley said the idea of a plot had its roots "a year or two back," when "itinerating preachers of the Gospel" had been accused of abolitionist activities and run out of the state, even though the only "proof" against them was their affiliation with the Northern Methodist church.[69] In an editorial published six weeks later, the *Tribune* observed that Texans had then been in the throes of the panic for two months, "although not one particle of evidence has yet been made public that there is any ground for their apprehension." Even Texas newspapers, try as they might, could not cite any viable evidence to prove that any blacks had conspired to murder whites by fire and poison, said the *Tribune,* which added: "The conductors of those sheets, and their informants, exhaust their powers of invention in the stories of conflagration."[70]

Referring to the report that vigilantes had discovered in the possession of slaves one hundred bottles of strychnine at Athens, Texas, the *Tribune* said that story alone should have been enough to destroy the credibility of the alarmists. "A hundred bottles of this deadly poison," stated the *Tribune,* "a grain of which any man however trustworthy and respectable he may seem to be, would find it difficult to purchase of any druggist in this city! A hundred bottles in the hands of negroes in a small and obscure frontier village in Texas, all of whose inhabitants, no doubt, could be disposed of by a vial full!"[71]

Anti-slavery papers saw in what they perceived to be the irrational behavior of the Texans an opportunity to moralize about slavery. The Boston *Journal* contended that the slaveholders, in spite of their efforts to defend the peculiar institution, knew that slavery was "unnatural," and this knowledge made them susceptible to alarms like the one sweeping over Texas and the South. The *Journal* believed that the Texas Troubles clearly showed that the slave society was "false and unstable."[72]

The New York *Times* thought that the immediate cause of the panic might have been the makeup of the Texas population, which it said was largely composed of "the more restless and lawless of Southern adventurers" and fugitives of justice from all over the United States. Habitual drunkenness and the routine

---

69. New York *Daily Tribune,* July 30, 1860. Greeley clearly referred to William Blunt and Solomon McKinney, who had been expelled from Dallas in 1859. The reports, originating in Texas, that Blunt and McKinney were Northern Methodists may have been inaccurate. For reports that identified both men as "Campbellites, " see Madison *State Journal,* n.d., quoted in William Lloyd Garrison, *The New "Reign of Terror" in the Slaveholding States, for 1859–1860* (New York, 1860; reprint, New York, 1969), 30; see also Grimsted, *American Mobbing,* 175.

70. Ibid., September 7, 1860.

71. Ibid.

72. Boston (Mass.) *Journal,* n.d., clipped in Washington (D.C.) *Constitution,* August 3, 1860.

wearing of concealed weapons, asserted the *Times,* had disposed the Texans to act with "a ferocity of manners [and] and reckless disregard of human life," and these characteristics had made them quick to commit violence against all strangers. More fundamental, however, was the slave system itself. "As long as Slavery exists, and wherever it exists," opined the *Times,* "there will be design-ing and indefatigable Abolitionists and suspicious and excitable masters, and a social organization which can only be saved by fits of anarchy and bloodshed and mob-law every four years, is not worth saving."[73]

But even if there were nothing to the allegations of an abolitionist conspir-acy in the Lone Star State, some thought that the Texans and publicists of the plot stories in other states were playing a dangerous game that amounted to a two-edged sword. Greeley's *Tribune* warned: "A popular frenzy, founded in the fear and distrust of a class who, if they did not know it before, will learn now that there is reason to fear and distrust them—such a frenzy, created for selfish purposes, may be turned to torment its inventors."[74]

William Lloyd Garrison, publisher of *The Liberator,* the Boston journal that was the best-known and most radical abolitionist newspaper in the country, clearly agreed with Greeley and seized the opportunity afforded by the Texas Troubles to mount his anti-slavery "soapbox." Garrison said he did not know whether there was any truth to the allegations of a plot to devastate North Texas, although he expressed a measure of doubt, saying, "Even if some parts are true, others are absurdly improbable." Yet, regardless of whether there was any truth to the fearful accounts, said Garrison, "Slaveholders, like other ty-rants, are always in danger. Men who are robbed at once of liberty and all other rights, and who are familiarized with violence by the example of their oppres-sors, *may,* at any moment, resort to violence; men who are constantly treated like brutes will be likely, when rendered desperate, to show themselves brutal in revenge." Consequently, even if there had been no uprising of the slaves in Texas, said Garrison, the oppressed bondsmen might well rise up against their oppressors in the future. The only sure preventive would be for slaveholders to free their chattel property "immediately and unconditionally."[75]

Stung by allegations that they had vastly exaggerated the scope of the Texas Troubles and had fabricated the stories of abolitionist involvement to serve their political goals, southern rights editors fought back. Although they had

73. New York *Times,* September 7, 1860.
74. New York *Tribune,* September 7, 1860.
75. Boston (Mass.) *Liberator,* August 3, 1860.

been forced to admit that many rumors of fires and poisonings were false and that journals had published them without testing their validity, most of them still insisted that the basic elements of the stories were factual: Certain abolitionists had carefully planned to devastate North Texas, using misguided blacks to accomplish their purpose. Moreover, they bristled at the charges that they had treated both accused whites and suspected black slaves cruelly or that they had hanged many on no evidence other than the testimony extorted from terrified blacks by means of whippings and other torture.

Apparently operating on the premise that the best way to defend themselves was to attack their opponents, the southern rights editors mounted a fierce counterattack. Leading the attack was John Marshall, editor of the Austin *Texas State Gazette,* chairman of the state Democratic party, and staunch supporter of John C. Breckinridge for president. Marshall rejected the accusations that his party had invented and circulated rumors of an abolitionist plot as a means of furthering their political goals, arguing that no party was "mad and vile enough" to stoop to such a strategy.[76] He pointed out that members of the Opposition as well as Democrats had served on the vigilance committees and argued that this bi-partisan participation showed that no one party was using the panic for its benefit. Although the *Texas State Gazette* admitted that some innocent persons may have "come under suspicion" because an overexcited public may have overreacted in a few cases, it insisted that the plot was real. As proof, Marshall pointed to the near simultaneous origins of the July 8 fires. Also, he said, many suspected whites and blacks in different areas of the state had told the same general story of a plot, thus raising "that reasonable presumption [of a conspiracy] to a degree of certainty."[77]

While the Marshall *Texas Republican* also admitted that "a thousand" baseless reports had been circulated and that normally prudent men had been carried away by the alarm that swept the country, it, like the *Texas State Gazette,* still insisted that there had been an abolitionist plot, at least "in the burnt district." Strongly denying that the plot story had been invented by Democrats to serve their political purposes, the same journal said: "It would be very strange for men to burn their own towns, stores, mills and dwellings, and to hang their slaves for such a cause." Ironically, in the same edition that had compared the confessions of blacks in Cherokee County to those who had confessed to consorting with the Devil during the Salem witch trials, the *Texas Republican* argued

76. Austin *Texas State Gazette,* September 4, 1860.
77. Ibid., September 1, 1860.

that there had been a "deep laid, well matured, mysterious plot, to compass the destruction of a portion [of Texas] if not the entire State."[78]

Addressing itself to the Austin *Southern Intelligencer*'s assertion that the so-called abolitionist plot was "humbug," invented by the Democrats, the Corsicana *Navarro Express* asked: "Does the editor of that paper believe in the doctrine of concerted and concurrent accidents?"[79] Although most of the Opposition journals agreed with the *Southern Intelligencer*'s position, at least one such paper, the Cameron *Sentinel,* broke with its party leaders on the issue of whether a plot existed. The *Sentinel* echoed the view of the *Navarro Express* when it asserted that it was incredible to assume "our citizens should fire their dwellings and business houses—reducing themselves to a state of want and beggary; furnish their negroes with poison to be administered back to them in their food, and then hang them for having it in their possession—all for political affect [*sic*]. How supremely ridiculous such an idea!"[80]

In the immediate aftermath of the July 8 fires, and before Charles Pryor wrote his letters, North Texans had attributed the "concurrent accidents" to a combination of the unprecedented heat and the presence of the new, unstable prairie matches. Although witnesses had seen the matches combust spontaneously, the Democratic journals now dismissed this possibility out of hand. The Marshall *Texas Republican* reported that a committee in Paris had investigated the matter and reported that no "thermometer heat will ignite matches." Said the *Texas Republican,* "This proves that the late burnings in the northern portion of the State were produced by incendiaries."[81] Perhaps the Galveston *News* had the Paris committee's conclusion in mind when it answered the *Southern Intelligencer*'s argument that the fires had "sprung from the ignition of matches" by saying: "Facts have overwhelmed all such subterfuges."[82]

Proponents of the abolitionist conspiracy theory concentrated their fire upon the Opposition leaders that had denied that a plot existed. Their prime target was A. B. Norton, editor of the Austin *Southern Intelligencer.* Norton, a Henry Clay Whig, turned Know-Nothing, turned Oppositionist, had come to Texas from Ohio in the mid-1850s. He had supported Sam Houston's successful bid for the governorship in 1859 and received as his reward an appointment

78. Marshall *Texas Republican,* August 25, 1860.

79. Corsicana *Navarro Express,* August 25, 1860.

80. Cameron *Sentinel,* n.d., quoted in Austin *Texas State Gazette,* September 8, 1860. See also Jacksboro *White Man,* September 15, 1860.

81. Marshall *Texas Republican,* August 4, 1860.

82. Galveston *News,* n.d., clipped in Jacksboro *White Man,* September 15, 1860.

as state adjutant general. Norton became editor of the *Southern Intelligencer* in 1860 and turned it into the primary journalistic organ of the Opposition party and the best-known unionist paper in the state.[83] As such, the journal and Norton himself became lightening rods for the fire-eaters' assault.

The Houston *Telegraph* said that the *Southern Intelligencer* "and some other papers of that class" should be condemned for denying the veracity of the plot stories and charging the Democrats with creating a hoax for political purposes. The *Telegraph* then posed the question that became the mantra of southern rights journals whenever unionists questioned their motives: "We now ask: Are these men sound on the slavery question?" The *Telegraph* left no doubt about the answer to its rhetorical question, concluding that "all types" of abolitionism—which obviously included Oppositionists like A. B. Norton—"must be rooted out."[84] Other Democratic journals made similar charges. The Jacksboro *White Man* said that in charging that the Democrats had invented the plot stories for their political effect, the Opposition papers had done "an incalculable amount of mischief, by giving aid and comfort to the enemy."[85] In the same vein, the Galveston *News* sharply criticized the *Southern Intelligencer* and its editor: "We think such things come with ill grace from A. B. Norton, who has been in this State comparatively, a short time from Ohio."[86]

Various citizens' groups also expressed disapproval of the Opposition papers, especially the *Southern Intelligencer,* for denying the existence of an abolitionist plot. For example, a citizens' meeting in the Austin County community of Pine Grove, after commending the Houston *Telegraph* for publishing many alarming reports from all over Texas, expressed regret that "other prints" had "not thought it proper to pursue the same course," but instead had published editorials "diminishing the danger in which we stand." The committee thereupon resolved that such journals "are not entitled to the patronage of the public."[87]

Other citizens' groups used stronger language. On August 30 an anti-Norton "indignation meeting" convened in Dallas and resolved that because of

83. As a young man in Ohio, Norton became an ardent Whig and supporter of Henry Clay. In 1844 he vowed never to shave or cut his hair until Clay had become president. He kept the vow, and even in an age when beards and long hair were common, Norton's unusually hirsute appearance turned heads and excited comment. Sibley, *Lone Stars and State Gazettes,* 280. See also *Handbook of Texas Online,* s.v., www.tsha.utexas.edu/handbook/online/articles/NN/fno9.html (accessed July 18, 2006).

84. Houston *Telegraph,* n.d., clipped in Galveston *The Crisis,* September 3, 1860. This editorial was also reprinted in the Marshall *Texas Republican,* September 8, 1860.

85. Jacksboro *White Man,* September 15, 1860.

86. Galveston *News,* quoted in Jacksboro *White Man,* September 15, 1860.

87. Bellville *Texas Countryman,* August 25, 1860.

his criticism of the citizens who had acted in defense of their communities, the Austin editor "deserves the detestation of every honest man in the State."[88] A citizens' meeting in Fort Worth went even further, leveling a thinly veiled threat. It resolved: "That we look upon the course of the Austin Intelligencer, and other papers and persons who attribute the late fires to accident, and who assert that the hue and cry about Abolition incendiarism has been raised for political effect, as insulting to the intelligence of Texas, and is justly subjecting the editor of the Austin Intelligencer, or any other papers or persons guilty of the like offense, to be placed at once on the list of persons whose future course is to be carefully watched by the proper committee."[89] The animosity of Fort Worth's citizens was so great that it forced Norton to sell his newspaper there, the Fort Worth *Chief*.[90]

John Marshall's Austin *Texas State Gazette* published the Fort Worth resolution condemning the *Southern Intelligencer*, and it was Marshall who led the attack on Norton. Turning on its head the Opposition's argument that the Democrats had invented the "plot" out of whole cloth for political purposes, Marshall charged that it was Norton and the "opposition clique" who aimed to achieve their own political goals by denying the existence of an abolitionist plan to devastate Texas. The Opposition was determined to preserve the Union at any cost—even if it meant the sacrifice of the peace and safety of Texas homes and firesides. Marshall charged that Norton and his friends in the press and state house advocated submitting to Lincoln and the "Black Republicans" and their anti-slavery policies, which allegedly included support for incendiary plots like those that the Lone Star State was experiencing. Although the *Texas State Gazette* said that it hoped that the Opposition "may yet recover from the madness of party prejudice," it clearly did not think it would. The paper closed with a stern warning: "We call upon the people to look to their homes and their firesides—to the formidable enemy who is at their door—to the torch of the incendiary—to the poison and dagger of the assassin—and to the demagogues who would sacrifice their existence as a people, the safety of their dwellings, the lives and honors of their families, to the lust of power or the fury of party rage."[91]

The feud between the editors of the *Texas State Gazette* and the *Southern Intelligencer* became so acrimonious and personal that, on August 9, Marshall

88. Austin *Texas State Gazette*, September 15, 1860.
89. Ibid., September 22, 1860.
90. Ferdinand B. Baillio, *A History of the Texas Press Association* (Dallas, 1916), 352.
91. Austin *Texas State Gazette*, September 8, 1860.

challenged Norton to a duel.[92] Marshall's attempt to settle differences with Norton on the field of honor probably surprised no one in Austin, since his caustic pen had often caused trouble. Years later, W. S. Oldham, a contemporary of Marshall and a fellow Democrat, recalled that the editor's "ridicule was terrible" and his "sarcasm . . . was withering." Although he stood only five feet, seven inches tall, he was fearless and combative, and his hair-trigger temper led to his involvement in frequent physical confrontations with opponents.[93] Norton could give as good as he took—as long as words were the weapons—but there is no evidence that he was inclined to resolve issues by physical action, or, for that matter, that he would have been adept at doing so. Nevertheless, he would have lost face had he refused Marshall's challenge, so the match was made.[94]

The impending confrontation between the most important secessionist and unionist editors in the state attracted a good deal of attention from the beginning. On August 23, local resident John Campbell wrote to his brother, "Politics run pretty high with us. Our Editors have gone of [sic] to try to kill each other I suppose." They had left the week before for the Indian Territory "to settle their dispute by the code of honor," said Campbell, who added: "Some reflections of Marshalls upon the private character of Nortons is the cause—immediate of the troubles and politics the cause—remote."[95] The two editors had headed north, reported the San Augustine Red Land Express, to try to "kill themselves a man."[96] The Galveston Civilian and Gazette observed that Marshall and Norton had gone "to the Indian Nation to take a crack at each other with something heavier and harder than [the] paper pellets with which they have been pelting each other heretofore."[97]

92. Marshall's version of the events surrounding the "affair of honor" appeared in the *Texas State Gazette* on September 15, 1860. Norton may have given his own account, but, if so, the editions in which they appeared no longer exist.

93. W. S. Oldham, "Colonel John Marshall," *Southwestern Historical Quarterly* 20 (October 1916): 132–138; Sibley, *Lone Stars and State Gazettes*, 280. Oldham was Marshall's associate and friend. He edited the Austin *Texas State Gazette* from 1854 to 1857, after which Marshall assumed that position (*Handbook of Texas Online*, s.v., www.tsha.utexas.edu/handbook/online/articles/OO/fol2.html [accessed July 18, 2006]). For a brief account of Marshall's life and career, see *Handbook of Texas Online*, s.v., www.tsha.utexas.edu/handbook/online/articles/MM/fma55.html (accessed July 29, 2006).

94. Reynolds, *Editors Make War*, 113.

95. John E. Campbell to his brother, August 23, 1860, Campbell Papers, Barker Texas History Center Archives, University of Texas, Austin, Texas.

96. San Augustine *Red Land Express*, September 15, 29, 1860.

97. Galveston *Civilian and Gazette*, September 11, 1860.

The two editors settled upon the Indian Territory because dueling was against the law in Texas. Given his choice of a site, Norton chose Tahlequah, which was located in the northeastern corner of the territory, some 450 miles from Austin. Norton never explained why he chose a site almost 200 miles north of the Red River, instead of a more accessible location. An historian of Texas newspapers during this period has suggested that the unionist editor may not have wanted to fight and hoped that the long distance from Austin would cool Marshall's temper.[98] Possibly showing a touch of paranoia, Marshall later asserted that Norton chose Tahlequah, located in a remote wilderness area, because he had planned to set an ambush there for his editorial rival.[99]

There followed a series of misadventures that, a generation later, might have provided Gilbert and Sullivan a scenario for one of their comic operas. When the two would-be combatants separately arrived in Sherman, they were arrested on grounds that it was not only against the law to stage a duel within the state, but it was also unlawful in Texas to *challenge* anyone to a duel. Marshall escaped custody on September 5 and crossed the Red River into the Indian Territory. An exchange of communications between the editors' seconds apparently confused the principals. Marshall maintained that he was still willing to fight and would wait for Norton to join him across the river. But the Sherman *Patriot* reported that after Norton's release from jail on September 6, he had crossed into the Indian Territory to meet his adversary, only to find that Marshall had already returned to the Texas side. Norton sent a message via his second, inviting his opponent to return north of the river to settle the matter. Marshall refused the oral invitation, stating that he must receive it in writing. According to the *Patriot,* Norton complied with this demand, but Marshall had already started home before it was received and refused to turn back.[100] Marshall's version blamed the mix-up on Norton, whom he accused of cowardice.[101] Both men returned to Austin, where they resumed pelting each other with "paper pellets." The amused Galveston *Civilian and Gazette,* reporting on the muddled denouement of the fiasco, said that henceforth the two adversaries should subscribe to the old adage that "the pen is mightier than the sword."[102]

Although the Marshall-Norton affair gave a bit of comic relief to some edi-

98. Sibley, *Lone Stars and State Gazettes,* 287.

99. Austin *Texas State Gazette,* September 15, 1860.

100. Sherman *Patriot,* September 8, 1860, quoted in Galveston *Civilian and Gazette,* September 25, 1860.

101. Austin *Texas State Gazette,* September 15, 1860.

102. Galveston *Civilian and Gazette,* September 25, 1860.

tors, it did not dispel the tension created by the charges and countercharges of the unionists and their fire-eating opponents. The Breckinridge supporters flailed away at the southern loyalty of those who dared to question the authenticity of the plot stories, but their blustering attacks could not obscure the fact that most of the reports of arson, and all of the stories of poisonings, had proven false. The Opposition leaders repeatedly stressed the multiplicity of false reports and pointed out that the only evidence adduced to prove the conspiracy theory was that which had been extorted from blacks by threats and the lash.

Determined to validate their contention that there was an abolitionist plot, the Democrats, in late August, claimed to have found the hard evidence that had been missing. Their "proof" consisted of a mysterious letter that purportedly revealed the abolitionist plans to wreak devastation on the state—plans that allegedly had been put into effect on July 8. The letter ultimately was linked to an elderly Methodist minister, who became the last recorded victim of the Texas Troubles. The heated controversy that erupted over the hanging of this reluctant martyr provided a dramatic coda to the most extensive, and arguably the most significant, panic of antebellum history.

CHAPTER SEVEN

WHO IS WILLIAM H. BAILEY?

Late in the evening of September 13, four men accompanied a stagecoach into the town of Fort Worth, Texas. The gray-haired, fifty-six-year-old man they removed in chains was none other than the notorious Anthony Bewley, a minister of the Methodist Episcopal Church accused of complicity in the plot to devastate Texas by fire and poison. Although he was a native southerner, Bewley's affiliation with the Northern Methodist denomination automatically made him suspect in the eyes of most Texans. Publication of Charles Pryor's sensational allegations that an abolitionist conspiracy was the cause of the fires in Dallas and Denton counties inevitably meant that Bewley—one of the last Northern Methodist ministers still active in Texas—would become a prime suspect.[1]

Anthony Bewley had become a Methodist minister in his home state of Tennessee in 1829. He moved to Missouri in 1837, and when the national church divided over slavery, Bewley, unlike most of his southern co-religionists, refused to join the M.E.C., South. Instead, he helped organize the Missouri Conference of the northern church in the late 1840s. That organization planned to revitalize the church in the Southwest and to that end sought to build churches

1. Elliott, *South-Western Methodism,* 21. Elliot was the editor of the St. Louis *Central Christian Advocate,* which feuded bitterly with journals of the Methodist Episcopal Church, South over the treatment of Northern Methodist churchmen in the southern states. Although Elliott's bias is obvious, his work is valuable, partly because it is the most detailed account of the events that it narrates, but also because he includes many letters that are no longer available elsewhere. Elliott was meticulous with the documents he used, and although he interpreted them from the Northern Methodist perspective, the details of his narrative on Bewley closely accord with other accounts found in letters and newspapers. For a detailed modern account of the Bewley Affair, see Wesley Norton, "The Methodist Episcopal Church and the Civil Disturbances in North Texas," 317–341.

in Arkansas and Texas. Bewley first headed up a mission near Fayetteville, Arkansas, and after the Missouri Conference determined to extend its work to Texas, he moved to the Lone Star State. As chief minister of the work in Texas, Bewley presided over churches in a half dozen counties of North Texas. In 1858 he established and personally pastored a mission in Johnson County, about sixteen miles south of Fort Worth. But the response of North Texans to the missionary's message was disappointing, to say the least. By 1859, four years after Bewley had begun his work in the Lone Star State, total membership in the several churches in Texas amounted to no more than 232 souls.[2]

Most citizens not only resisted the preaching of men whose church believed that slavery was evil, but they also resented their very presence in the state. No matter that neither Bewley nor his church advocated eradicating the peculiar institution by force. As the secession crisis loomed ever nearer, Texans saw any critic of slavery, no matter how mild, as a potential threat to the social order and therefore branded him persona non grata.

A full year before the panic broke out, North Texans had demonstrated their intolerance of Northern Methodists when, in March 1859, they had forced the adjournment of the Timber Creek conference.[3] Bewley was in attendance at that meeting; consequently, he must have well understood the precarious position in which he and others of his denomination would find themselves if they were to continue their ministry in Texas. Virtually the entire Northern Methodist missionary program in Texas collapsed in the wake of the Timber Creek debacle. Only Bewley and one other minister, William Butts, continued to labor in the Lone Star State. Ministering in Johnson County, Bewley managed to avoid open confrontations with local citizens by preaching only in the homes of the faithful few who supported his work. His inability to make new converts and continual harassment by pro-slavery whites finally convinced him that his efforts in North Texas were a waste of time, and he left the state at the end of 1859. Bishop Edward A. Ames nevertheless urged the discouraged missionary to continue the work in the Lone Star State and promised to increase his financial support. The bishop's powers of persuasion must have been considerable, for Bewley and a co-worker, Thomas M. Willet, agreed to return to Texas in the spring of 1860, this time to work among the South Texas German communities, whose citizens might be more receptive to the Northern Methodist doctrines.[4]

2. Elliott, *South-Western Methodism,* 45; Norton, "The Methodist Episcopal Church and the Civil Disturbances in North Texas," 321.

3. See chapter 1 for a full account of the confrontation at Timber Creek.

4. Elliott, *South-Western Methodism,* 21; Norton, "The Methodist Episcopal Church and the Civil Disturbances in North Texas," 328–331.

Bewley never made it to his new mission field. He had been back in Texas only one month, pausing on his way south to visit friends and former parishioners in Johnson County, when he learned of Pryor's allegations of an abolitionist conspiracy. Bewley instantly recognized that both his life and the safety of his family were in jeopardy. On July 17, five days after Pryor wrote his first letter to the *Texas State Gazette,* Bewley loaded his belongings on a wagon and with his wife and eleven-year-old son George headed northeastward, intending eventually to make it to Kansas and safety. The rest of his family, including two grown daughters and their husbands, three other sons, and a blind teenage daughter followed in other wagons. Tom Willet left Texas at about the same time, although it is unclear whether he accompanied the Bewleys.[5]

Traveling north through Arkansas, Bewley stopped to visit friends he had made during his earlier ministry at Fayetteville. But most Arkansans were no more disposed to welcome Northern Methodists than were the Texans, especially in the wake of the fearful stories coming out of Texas. Upon learning of Bewley's presence, the local vigilance committee ordered the family "to leave Arkansas and not stop 'til they reach a free State." The Fayetteville *Arkansian* offered some gratuitous advice to its northern neighbor: "Our fellow citizens of Missouri are advised to keep them moving north, unless they would see trouble."[6]

Finally, six weeks after beginning their flight, the Bewleys arrived in southern Missouri. Bewley probably believed that he was now out of danger. He had no way of knowing that a posse of determined Texans, spurred by the offer of a $1,000 reward for Bewley's capture and return to Fort Worth, was in hot pursuit.[7]

5. Norton mistakenly identified Willet as Bewley's son-in-law (see Norton, "The Methodist Episcopal Church and the Civil Disturbances in North Texas," 331, 334), possibly because he was so identified in a few contemporary Texas sources. For examples, see Dallas *Herald,* December 26, 1860, and the letter of a Southern Methodist minister, H. W. South, to the *Southern Methodist Itinerant,* October 31, 1860 (reprinted in Elliott, *South-Western Methodism,* 191). Elliott, however, calls Bewley's two married daughters "Mrs. Roper" and "Mrs. Garoot," and although he refers several times to Mr. Garoot as Bewley's son-in-law, he never attributes the same relationship to Willet. Elliott does not mention Mrs. Roper's husband, but the Fayetteville *Arkansian* specifically reported in late August that Bewley's "son in law, David Roper," was in the family party when it left Fayetteville for Missouri (Fayetteville *Arkansian,* August 31, 1860). Family genealogical records supplied by Bewley's great, great granddaughter, Mrs. Marilyn Irons, also give no indication that Willet was a son-in-law. The married names of the two daughters in question are revealed in these records as "Garout" (a variation of Elliott's spelling) and "Baker." The apparent discrepancy in the latter name may indicate simply that Mrs. Roper later remarried.

6. Fayetteville *Arkansian,* August 31, 1860.

7. The reward was offered jointly by the Fort Worth and Sherman vigilance committees, but

Knowing Bewley's route would take him through northwestern Arkansas, vigilance committee members had written to their Fayetteville counterparts, notifying them that they had dispatched riders to capture and return Bewley to Texas and requesting that he and Tom Willet be held until the posse could arrive. Since the Bewleys had already left town by the time the letter arrived, the local vigilance committee sent some of its members to apprehend and return him to Fayetteville to await the Texans' arrival.[8] Having gotten as far as southwestern Missouri, Bewley apparently believed he could afford to slow the pace of travel. It was a fatal miscalculation. His pursuers caught their man near Cassville, Missouri, on the morning of September 3, as he gathered forage for his horses.[9]

Bewley's captors returned him to Fayetteville, where he was kept for a few days, while a search party scoured the countryside for Tom Willet, who had not left Fayetteville with the Bewley party. Willet barely escaped his pursuers by hiding in the Ozark woods and living on nuts—his only food. Eventually he made it to safety in southern Kansas.[10] Still, the vigilantes had bagged their primary quarry. On September 8, the Texans placed Bewley on an Overland stagecoach for the return trip to Fort Worth. According to the Fayetteville *Arkansian,* "The Reverend proclaimed his innocence to the last yet said that the Texans would certainly hang him upon his arrival." Bewley's many friends in the Fayetteville area evidently shared Bewley's fateful premonition. Before his departure, said the Fayetteville *Arkansian,* "A petition was drawn up and signed by numerous citizens of this county, requesting the people of Texas to hear Buley's story, give him ample defence, do him justice and not deal with him rashly." Curiously, in view of its negative reporting on Bewley, the *Arkansian* endorsed this request, saying, "We sincerely hope the counsel will be followed."[11]

After entering Texas, the hapless preacher and his escorts stopped overnight in Sherman on September 10. According to the editor of the Sherman *Patriot,* who saw him at the hotel, "he is just such a man as one would suppose would engage in the scheme of desolation and rapine; vulgar features, low thick-set, flat head, thick neck and small gray eyes."[12]

---

the five men who retrieved Bewley reportedly received only a total of $250, or fifty dollars each, for their efforts. See Elliott, *South-Western Methodism,* 157–161.

8. Fayetteville *Arkansian,* August 31, 1860.

9. Elliott, *South-Western Methodism,* 157–161.

10. New York *Tribune,* n.d., quoted in Dallas *Herald,* December 26, 1860.

11. Fayetteville *Arkansian,* September 14, 1860.

12. Sherman *Patriot,* September 15, 1860, quoted in Galveston *Civilian and Gazette,* October 9, 1860. See also Elliott, *South-Western Methodism,* 160.

Arriving in Fort Worth late in the evening of September 13, the captive was taken to a hotel, fed, and placed under guard in an upstairs room. He seems to have dozed off quickly, probably because he was exhausted—after all, he had been on the road more or less constantly since mid-July, covering over eleven hundred miles in less than two months. But he was given little time to slumber. At about 11:00 P.M. a delegation of vigilantes awakened him and took him outside, where a mob had gathered. They led him to a large pecan tree about three hundred yards west of the intersection of White Settlement and Jacksboro Roads, and there they hanged him from the same limb that had suspended William Crawford on July 17—the day Bewley had begun his futile flight. He was left hanging all night and much of the next day, after which he was cut down and hastily buried "without shroud or coffin." But to say "buried" is to exaggerate, for he was placed in such a short, shallow grave that his body could not assume a prone position; consequently, the dead man's knees poked through the earth. About three weeks later, unnamed individuals unearthed the corpse, stripped its bones of their remaining flesh, and placed the skeleton upon the roof of Ephraim Daggett's storehouse.[13] According to one source, the bones were "in the care" of Dr. Carroll M. Peak, who occasionally went up and "turned them about." Young boys made Daggett's roof a favorite place to play. They would "set up the bones in a variety of attitudes by bending the joints of the arms and legs, and . . . mocked [the skeleton] by crying, 'old Bewley,' 'old abolitionist,' etc."[14]

Area believers in the conspiracy theory welcomed, even took delight in, Bewley's demise. One such individual, Jesse Hitson, wrote that he had seen the body of a man hanging from a tree in Fort Worth "who was no less a person than the Rev. Parson Buley of this county. *Good lick.*"[15] The Jacksboro *White*

13. Elliott, *South-Western Methodism,* 166–170. Ephraim Daggett was an influential citizen and former legislator who owned considerable property in and around Fort Worth. He also owned and operated a mercantile store (*Handbook of Texas Online,* s.v., www.tsha.utexas.edu/handbook/on-line/articles/DD/fda3.html [accessed July 18, 2006]).

14. G. Evans, Rolla, Missouri, to St. Louis (Mo.) *Central Christian Advocate,* September 7, 1867, quoted in Elliott, *South-Western Methodism,* 170. Apparently, the bones stayed on Daggett's roof until at least sometime after the Civil War had ended. One old-timer, during the 1930s, told how he and his family had moved away from Fort Worth during the Civil War, but when they returned at war's end, the bones were still on top of Daggett's storehouse. "People forgot about them during the war . . . but after we got back—you know how kids will do—Eph Daggett and I crawled up . . . and saw [Bewley's] bones, right on top of the roof and bleached white" (Charles Ellis Mitchell, "Reminiscences of Charles Ellis Mitchell," in Texas Writers' Project, Research Data, Fort Worth and Tarrant County Texas, vol. 6 [1941], page 2002, typescript, Fort Worth Public Library).

15. Jacksboro *White Man,* September 15, 1860.

Man could not resist indulging in a bit of gallows humor in its report of the hanging:

> The Rev. Wm. Buley.—This distinguished parson, one of Sam Houston's 'Vicegerents of God,' met with a sad accident at Fort Worth not long ago. By some means he got on the Abe-Lincoln-Sam-Houston platform, and somehow, or somehow else, got a string entangled about his neck, and just as he stept on the Squatter Sovereignty plank of the platform, some of the screws gave way, and down came this 'Vicegerent,' and broke his pious neck. Gov. Houston, of course, will rejoice with us, to think that so good a man has at last got his just deserts. May these worthy 'Vicegerents' all stand on the same platform sooner or later, and share the same fate.[16]

Predictably, a sharp controversy soon broke out among members of the two Methodist denominations over the treatment given to Bewley, whose long years of service had made him widely known and well respected in Northern Methodist circles. The New York *Christian Advocate and Journal* thought that it was inconceivable that Bewley could have been involved in a murderous abolitionist plot, not only because he was "a devoutly pious and inoffensive" man, but also because he was not even an abolitionist. In fact, said the same journal, Bewley's anti-slavery views were of "the mildest type," and he had always taken a conservative position whenever the issue had been raised in church conferences. Recollecting such a debate at the 1856 Indianapolis general conference of the M.E.C., the *Christian Advocate and Journal* wrote: "All through that session he stood shoulder to shoulder with the Border [slave state] delegates." Considering Bewley's history of opposing strong anti-slavery platforms in such conferences, the editor concluded that anyone who accused him of harboring abolitionist principles, much less participating in an abolitionist plot, was guilty of slandering his good name.[17]

Southern Methodist editors scorned the testimony asserting the mildness of Bewley's anti-slavery opinions; that his views were critical of slavery at all was enough to brand him as a miscreant in their eyes. The Raleigh *North Carolina*

16. Ibid.

17. New York *Christian Advocate and Journal,* September 27, October 25, 1860. The most controversial issue before the general conference of 1856 was a proposal by anti-slavery delegates that the M.E.C. ban slaveholders from church membership. Conservatives and moderates, led by delegates from Maryland, West Virginia, and Missouri, opposed such a move.

Christian Advocate reacted sharply to the *Christian Advocate and Journal*'s depiction of Bewley as an innocent victim. Reiterating the frightening reports of the alleged plot in Texas, the North Carolina paper said that the Texans had been right in hanging "the traitor" Bewley. Moreover, its editor professed to be scandalized by the New York paper's characterization of the dead man as "a devoutly pious and inoffensive man." "If he was pious, who is wicked?" asked the editor: "And if such is the judgment a religious journal gives upon the worst of criminals, what sort of laudation by the northern secular press will reward the traitor who quenches the light of southern civilization in blood?"[18]

Parson William G. Brownlow likewise bristled at the New York paper's allegation that Bewley suffered hanging for no other reason than that he was a minister of the Northern Methodist church. Brownlow angrily denied the charge. In any case, he said, Texas rightfully "belonged" to the southern church after the schism of 1844; thus, Bewley, a Northern Methodist, had no business proselytizing there. Brownlow said that he believed that the people of Texas had "served him right" and added that he would have said so even if "he had been my brother." On a more humorous note, reminiscent of the Jacksboro *White Man*'s satiric eulogy, Brownlow reacted to the New York *Christian Advocate and Journal*'s assertion that Bewley was a "devoutly pious and inoffensive" man, saying: "If this be the case, hanging was 'a short cut' to the Kingdom of God, and the crossing of a 'River, the streams whereof shall make glad the City of God.' And ere this time the Reverend Abolitionist has realized the truth of the declaration of the modern poet:

'Celestial fruit from earthly ground,
From faith and hope may grow.'"[19]

On a more serious note, the Galveston *Texas Christian Advocate* argued that even if the charges against Bewley were untrue and he was innocent of the specific crime with which he had been charged, still, "the worst that can be said is that he fell victim to a reign of lawlessness which he and others of his kind have for some time been laboring to inaugurate and promote in Texas." More-

18. Raleigh *North Carolina Christian Advocate*, October 11, 1860.

19. Knoxville (Tenn.) *Whig*, September 29, 1860. Six weeks later, Brownlow changed his opinion about the alleged conspiracy. Having received information from a Tennessean "of high standing," who was in Texas, Brownlow wrote, "they have not been able to learn of a single case in which abolitionist emissaries participated. . . . The report of poison being found in wells, is also contradicted, and is without foundation in truth. These tales were originated by scheming politicians and were a part of their vile plan to . . . fire the Southern mind" (Knoxville [Tenn.] *Whig*, November 17, 1860).

over, said the same journal, since Bewley and his co-religionists had refused to leave the state after being warned to do so the previous year at the Timber Creek conference, his blood was on his own head, not on the vigilantes who had hanged him.[20]

Although Bewley's affiliation with a church that held anti-slavery views was sufficient to condemn him in the eyes of the Southern Methodists, his good reputation among most of those who knew him well seemed to require more concrete evidence to justify the mob's summary and grisly treatment of the elderly minister. This need to confirm Bewley's abolitionist credentials coincided with pressure from the increasingly vocal attacks by the Oppositionists upon the fire-eaters to produce concrete evidence that the plot existed. Well before the ill-fated Methodist preacher's capture, there were hints from some North Texans that such proof would be forthcoming. Smarting from allegations that the vigilance committee in Dallas was guilty of acting in a "mobocratic" manner, Charles Pryor, in a letter written to John Marshall on August 5, indignantly denied that charge, which he characterized as "political twaddle." He promised that "the facts" would soon be published, and the whole country would see the horrors that the abolitionists had planned to inflict upon unsuspecting Texans.[21]

Similarly, a citizen of Fort Worth, who signed his name only as "S," wrote to Marshall insisting that "the danger is real and not imaginary" and informing the editor, "We have in our possession the evidence conclusively showing that there is an organization in this State having for its object the destruction of the property of the present inhabitants." The anonymous correspondent further assured Marshall, "at the proper time this evidence will be made public."[22] Three days after S's letter appeared in the *Texas State Gazette*, the same journal published the promised "evidence" in the form of the so-called Bailey letter.[23]

In a remarkable stroke of luck, or so it seemed, the incriminating letter's recipient had carelessly dropped it on the prairie, six miles west of Fort Worth, where two members of the local vigilance committee had happened upon it. Although the letter is lengthy and rambling, its critical place in the controversy over the alleged abolitionist plot and Bewley's alleged role in it make a detailed examination imperative. Dated July 3, the letter listed Denton Creek as its point

20. Galveston *Texas Christian Advocate*, September 13, 1860. The editor said that the hanging of Bewley had not been confirmed. In fact, this editorial appeared on the day of his death, and thus was premature and apparently based on speculation.

21. Pryor to Marshall, August 5, 1860, Austin *Texas State Gazette*, August 18, 1860.

22. Austin *Texas State Gazette*, September 22, 1860.

23. Ibid., September 25, 1860.

of origin. It began: "Dear Sir,—A painful abscess in my right thumb is my apology for not writing to you from Anderson." [One of the newspaper references later would say that the writing, which was presumably shaky, showed evidence that the writer suffered from a hand injury.] There followed a disorganized account of the writer's travels, which apparently covered a sizeable portion of the Lone Star State. Specifically, he noted, "Our glorious cause is prospering finely as far south as Brenham," where he said he had parted with his fellow-traveler, a "Bro. Wampler," who was to go still farther south. The writer sprinkled the narrative with numerous references to other co-workers and spoke at length about the activities of a clandestine organization, which he referred to as "the mystic red." The immediate goal, he reminded his unnamed reader, was to cripple the economy by "destroying towns, mills etc. . . . If we can break Southern merchants and millers, and have their places filled by honest Republicans, Texas will be all easy prey. . . . Lincoln will certainly be elected; we will then have the Indian nation, cost what it will. Squatter sovereignty will prevail there as it has in Kansas. That accomplished, we have at least one more step to take, but one more struggle to make; that is, free Texas. We will then have a connected link from the Lakes to the Gulf. Slavery will then be surrounded by land and water, and soon sting itself to death." He further urged his correspondent to meet frequently with "our colored friends. (Let our meetings be at night). Impress upon their clouded intellects the blessings of freedom; induce all to leave you can. . . . Brother Leake, the bearer of this, will take a circuitous route, and see as many of our colored friends as he can."[24]

Acknowledging that additional agents were necessary for the task at hand, the author promised to send more "when I get home." Meanwhile, the author admonished his correspondent to appoint a local agent "in every neighborhood in your district," and he listed the names of sixteen men who would be reliable to act in that capacity. The writer said that "Brother Leake" wanted to recommend a different kind of match for use in firing the towns, because "Our friends sent a very inferior article. They emit too much smoke and do not contain enough camphene." Finally, he took his reader to task for having sent insufficient funds to support the work: "Our faithful correspondent, Brother Webber, has received but a trifle—not so much as an apprentice's wages; neither have brothers Willet, Mangum and others. . . . My hand is very painful, and I close. Yours truly, Wm. H. Bailey." The writer then added a postscript: "N. B. Brother Leake will give you what few numbers of the Impending Crisis we have,

24. Ibid., August 25, 1860.

and brother Sumner's speech and brother Beecher's letter, &c. Farewell."[25]

The finders of the letter, recognizing that the fortuitous circumstance of stumbling upon the sensational document on the open prairie might cause raised eyebrows, took the unusual step of swearing out an affidavit in the county clerk's office at Fort Worth, attesting to the genuineness of their discovery. According to the affidavit, Paul Isbell and George Grant found the document near the latter's residence, some six miles from Fort Worth, "near where a horse had been fed, stealthily as it seemed." T. M. Matthews, the deputy county clerk who affixed the county seal to the affidavit, added his own addendum stating that the copy he had made of the letter "is a true and correct copy of the original . . . excepting that some of the spelling has been corrected."[26]

According to the Galveston *News,* John Henry Brown, editor of the Belton *Democrat,* had received a copy of the letter—probably from the Fort Worth vigilance committee—and he, together with two other prominent Democrats, E. S. C. Robertson and A. J. Embree, had decided to use it to warn the counties that seemed to be in the greatest danger. On August 19 they printed the missive in the form of a broadside and sent copies to "reliable men" in eighteen counties. The letter was supposed to go unpublished, at least for the time being, so that the twenty alleged abolitionists mentioned in it would not be forewarned and thus allowed to escape. In a paragraph of their own that they added to the broadside, the three men warned: "To make it public would destroy all plans to entrap the conspirators." Hence, they were forwarding the letter only to "a few of the most cool, discreet and unflinching men in our county, and [we] advise you to do the same." These precautions would enable vigilantes to take the named abolitionists unaware.[27]

Despite the admonition to keep the document secret, the Austin *Texas State Gazette* published the Bailey letter within a week of its being printed. The premature revelation of the missive provoked a minor protest from those Democratic journals that believed the contents should have been kept confidential. One of these was E. H. Cushing's Houston *Telegraph,* which demanded to know who had forwarded the letter to the *Texas State Gazette.* Interestingly, Cushing did not criticize Marshall for publishing it, but said that the sender, if identified, should be watched: "If not a knave he is too indiscreet to be permitted to remain [in North Texas]." The Jacksboro *White Man,* which printed the *Telegraph*'s rebuke, sought to soothe the ruffled feathers by explaining that it had

25. Ibid.
26. Ibid.
27. Galveston *News,* n.d., clipped in Charleston (S.C.) *Mercury,* September 29, 1860.

been the local vigilance committee that had forwarded the copy to the *Texas State Gazette*. According to the *White Man,* the issue had been discussed "in all its bearings" by the committee, and many members favored publication so that people all over the state could be made aware of "the damnable plot."[28]

Publication of the Bailey letter caused a sensation. A few Democratic papers reacted cautiously at first. For example, after running the letter on September 4, the Galveston *Civilian and Gazette* said: "We have no means of judging whether it is a genuine document over a real signature, or not."[29] Said the San Augustine *Red Land Express,* "We publish it for what it is worth, not knowing what it is worth."[30] The most skeptical such journal was the Marshall *Texas Republican,* a staunch southern rights paper, which reprinted the letter on September 15 but wrote: "We should like to know something of the character of the men who found, or pretend to have found the foregoing letter. While all the evidences elicited in the State point to the existence of an abolition plot such as is here detailed, it is not very probable that a man engaged in such business would be so careless as to drop a letter revealing it with such minuteness. The affair looks suspicious."[31]

As if in response to the *Texas Republican*'s desire to know more about the character of the finders of the letter, the *Texas State Gazette* on September 22 declared that Paul Isbell, one of the vigilantes who had discovered the missive, was "a gentleman of unimpeachable integrity and veracity."[32] The *Texas Republican* later recanted its doubts, admitting that additional information showed that its first impression that the document had been "manufactured" was incorrect.[33]

Few, if any, other Breckinridge Democrats questioned the authenticity of the Bailey letter. Democratic papers both within and outside Texas saw the missive as the incontrovertible proof of a conspiracy that, until now, had been missing.[34] The Belton *Democrat* triumphantly declared that most of the names mentioned as conspirators in the letter were "known to be of the stripe indicated";

28. Houston *Telegraph,* n.d., quoted in Jacksboro *White Man,* September 15, 1860.

29. Galveston *Civilian and Gazette,* September 4, 1860.

30. San Augustine *Red Land Express,* September 15, 1860.

31. Marshall *Texas Republican,* September 15, 1860.

32. Austin *Texas State Gazette,* September 22, 1860.

33. Marshall *Texas Republican,* November 10, 1860.

34. For some examples, see Galveston *News,* September 24, 1860; Corpus Christi *Ranchero,* September 8, 1860; Indianola *Courier,* October 27, 1860; Des Arc (Ark.) *Weekly Citizen,* September 26, 1860; Fayetteville *Arkansian,* September 21, 1860; Nashville (Tenn.) *Union and American,* September 26, 1860; Jackson *Semi-Weekly Mississippian,* September 14, 1860; Jacksonville (Ala.) *Republican,* October 25, 1860.

moreover, Bailey's mention of his visits to Anderson, Brenham, and George-town was "confirmed by subsequent events at those places." Those "events," by which the *Democrat* apparently meant fires or attempted acts of arson, "could not possibly have been known in Tarrant county when the letter was found," and this in turn—at least as far as the *Democrat* was concerned—meant that the letter could not have been forged.[35]

Although most Democrats accepted the Bailey letter as genuine, others who refused to believe that there was an abolitionist conspiracy in Texas did not. The New York *Times,* which closely followed the reports coming out of Texas, denounced the new "evidence" as a fraud. The *Times* published the letter in full under the heading: "A CURIOUS DOCUMENT—AN EVIDENT FORGERY." It pref-aced the letter with the statement: "It needs no explanation. Its bogus character is sufficiently apparent. . . . Every line of it contained clear evidence that it was the composition of a stupid and ignorant defender of the 'peculiar institution,' [and] that the writer was not only a forger, but a blockhead."[36] The *Times* obvi-ously thought the missive was so transparently fraudulent that it was unneces-sary to explain the reasons for its conclusion. Charles Elliott in his book *South-Western Methodism,* written eight years later, reprinted the letter and called it a "clumsy forgery."[37] But other than pointing to the suspicious circumstances of its discovery, Elliott, like the *Times,* did not bother to explain why he thought it was forged.

Nor, until recently, has any modern historian supplied more specific reasons for discrediting the Bailey letter. In fact, those who have done the most detailed examination have tended to accept the letter's authenticity.[38] But it is not diffi-cult to see why some contemporaries branded it as fraudulent. The writer would have been "a blockhead" indeed to have detailed names and places of the Mystic Red's members and activities in a letter that was to be carried on a "circuitous route" by a white man who was to stop along the way and visit with "as many of our colored friends as he can." But even supposing that an abolitionist could have been so foolish, internal criticism alone is sufficient to support the *Times*'s charge that the letter must have been written by a southern sympathizer, and almost certainly not by an abolitionist. For example, an abolitionist would not

35. Belton *Democrat,* n.d., quoted in Galveston *Civilian and Gazette,* September 25, 1860.

36. New York *Times,* September 7, 1860.

37. Elliott, *South-Western Methodism,* 184.

38. For examples, see Marcus Phelan, *A History of Early Methodism in Texas, 1817–1866* (Dallas, 1924), 453–456; William W. White, "The Texas Slave Insurrection of 1860," *Southwestern Histori-cal Quarterly* 52 (January 1949): 265–267; Wendell G. Addington, "Slave Insurrections in Texas," *Journal of Negro History* 35 (October 1950), 408–434.

have exulted at the prospect of having the broken "Southern millers and merchants" replaced by "honest Republicans." Republicans were free-soilers, whose
national platform, both in 1856 and 1860, vowed to leave slavery alone in the
southern states, although it opposed its extension into the territories. This position was unacceptable to the militant abolitionist—the kind who might be willing to risk his life in the manner of John Brown for the cause of black freedom.

For the same reason, the dedicated abolitionist would not have spoken so fa-
vorably of Lincoln's prospective election. And certainly no self-respecting anti-
slavery zealot would have exulted over the possibility that "Squatter Sovereignty
will prevail [in the Indian Nation] as it has in Kansas." The true abolitionist
abhorred popular sovereignty, which would have permitted the citizens to decide whether slavery should be legalized in a particular territory. On the other
hand, the southern fire-eater believed that there was no difference whatsoever
between Republican free-soilism, "squatter sovereignty" (the southern term for
popular sovereignty), and abolitionism. He believed that all three would result
in the destruction of slavery, and he often used these terms interchangeably.
Thus, although the Bailey letter purportedly revealed abolitionist goals, they
were abolitionist goals as seen from the unique perspective of a pro-slavery
southerner, just as the New York *Times* asserted.

Given the doubts that had arisen when some of the more sensational plot
stories proved to be false, it is hardly surprising that the Oppositionists regarded the new exposé with great suspicion. Neither the affidavit of the Tarrant
County vigilantes nor the added warning by Brown, Robertson, and Embree
impressed those who were disposed to see in the panic not an abolitionist plot
to devastate Texas, but a fire-eaters' plot to further the cause of secession. Not
surprisingly, A. B. Norton led the charge. He ended a sarcastic piece on the
Bailey letter by asking: "But let us know who [sent the letter to the *Gazette*]:
and *who* is William H. Bailey?"[39] The Jacksboro *White Man* had answered the
first question, but the second was especially pertinent, and, significantly, no one
ever answered it. Nor, with a single exception, were any of the "abolitionists"
listed in the letter identifiable.[40] The one exception—indeed, the one undeniably

39. Austin *Southern Intelligencer*, September 5, 1860.

40. Despite the Belton *Democrat*'s claim that most of those named in the letter were known
to harbor abolitionist views, the failure of the author to include given names proved to be problematical. Since most of the last names of those listed were common ones, a large number of Texas
citizens were at least theoretically in jeopardy of being identified as one of the named conspirators.
Nevertheless, a diligent search of available sources turned up only one such accusation. On September 7 the Huntsville *Item* charged that "Richard Leake," an agent of the Galveston *News*, was
the "Bro. Leake" who was the letter's courier. The *News* quickly came to the defense of its employee,

real name in the letter—was that of Willet. Tom Willet, of course, was Anthony Bewley's coworker. This must have been the Willet, then, who had eluded the vigilantes for eight days in the forests around Fayetteville and eventually made his way to Kansas. This raises the question unasked either by contemporary critics or modern historians: where was Anthony Bewley's name? Why was this most notorious of alleged abolitionists missing from the lengthy list of W. H. Bailey?

Those who had publicized the letter soon provided an explanation for the glaring omission of the Methodist parson's name from the text. In late September, Democratic newspapers began reporting that Bewley had, in fact, been the *addressee* of the Bailey letter. Writing to the Galveston *News* on October 3, A. G. Fowler, a leader of the Fort Worth vigilance committee, said:

> None of the published copies of this letter have ever contained the address upon the back, which is thus:
>
> Rev. W. Buley
> Politeness of C. E. Leake[41]

The belated allegation that Bewley was the recipient of the letter and had carelessly dropped the damning evidence on the open prairie seemed incredible to the friends and coworkers of the slain preacher. But for the publicists of the Bailey letter and the conspiracy theory, it provided some needed answers to questions that had arisen since the discovery of that document. For one thing, the revelation that Bewley was the letter's recipient added an actual person to Bailey's list of "phantom" abolitionists and thus lent a measure of credibility to the whole document. Moreover, it explained why Bewley had been omitted from such a long list of operatives, whereas Tom Willet, his junior partner in missionary work, had not. Also, in focusing the spotlight upon Bewley,

---

pointing out that he spelled his name "Leeke," not "Leake," and averring that he was present in the newspaper office on July 6, making it physically impossible for him to have been the bearer of the Bailey letter, which was dated three days earlier and was written several hundred miles away, at Denton Creek. This tempest soon died down, and it does not appear that agent Leeke suffered any serious consequences for having been confused with abolitionist Leake. For a detailed account of this contretemps, with quotes from the *Item* and the *News,* see the Galveston *Civilian and Gazette,* September 21, 25, 1860.

41. Galveston *Weekly News,* n.d., quoted in Austin *Texas State Gazette,* November 3, 1860. This new information was published in a number of other Democratic journals. For examples, see Jacksboro *White Man,* September 28, 1860; Austin *Texas State Gazette,* October 13, 1860; Dallas *Herald,* n.d., clipped in Indianola *Courier,* October 27, 1860; San Augustine *Red Land Express,* October 20, 1860.

defenders of the letter's genuineness were able to divert attention from the mysterious William H. Bailey, who, despite his own account of extensive travels throughout much of North and Central Texas, had managed to remain unseen and unheard of—a remarkable achievement indeed, especially in light of the heightened vigilance of Texans and the increased scrutiny that they gave to strangers in the wake of the fires and the alarms raised by Charles Pryor. That Bailey was also totally unknown in the North added pertinence to the question previously posed by A. B. Norton: "*Who* is William H. Bailey?" Shifting attention to Bewley's connection with the conspiracy might make finding an answer to that question less urgent.

On the other hand, a belated allegation that Bewley had acknowledged being the addressee before his death raised new questions. First, if the notorious preacher had been Bailey's correspondent, how could this possibly have been overlooked, first by those who had found the letter and had been so careful to swear out an affidavit as to its contents, and then by those who publicized it for the expressed purpose of entrapping the conspirators named in the document? The Galveston *News,* writing about the letter shortly after its publication by the *Texas State Gazette,* had specifically referred to Bailey's "unknown correspondent."[42] Even allowing that the first published reports somehow could have inadvertently omitted this key information, how could an entire month pass before Bewley's complicity was suddenly—and posthumously—remembered?

Subsequently, stories were published alleging that Bewley had confessed to receiving—and losing—the Bailey letter. But these, too, are problematical. It is true that at least two editors who saw Bewley when he was en route to Fort Worth in the custody of the vigilante posse reported that he had admitted complicity in the "plot." But each of these journalists contradicted themselves. For example, the Fayetteville *Arkansian* on September 28 repeated the assertion that before he was hanged, Bewley had confessed that he was the man who had lost the letter from Bailey and added that he did not want to die "with a lie in his mouth." Yet elsewhere in the same edition it repeated its report of September 8: "The Reverend proclaimed his innocence to the last."[43] After the posse had stopped over at Sherman, Texas, on the last leg of its journey to Fort Worth, the editor of the Sherman *Patriot* wrote, "He told us he was an Abolitionist," yet later in the same article said, "He remarked that he did not preach such [abolitionist] doctrine."[44]

42. Galveston *News,* n.d., clipped in Charleston (S.C.) *Mercury,* September 29, 1860.

43. Fayetteville *Arkansian,* September 28, 1860.

44. Sherman *Patriot,* September 15, 1860, quoted in Galveston *Civilian and Gazette,* October 9, 1860.

The most convincing evidence that Bewley never confessed to having been involved with either the alleged plot or the Bailey letter came from the doomed preacher himself. While Bewley awaited the arrival of the Fort Worth vigilantes, his Fayetteville captors allowed him to write a farewell letter to his wife, Jane. He asked her to inquire whether an acquaintance of some standing, Henry McCary, would write an intercessory letter to "Capt. Daget [*sic*],"[45] but the tone and substance of his own missive showed that he held out little hope that such a document would save his life. In addition to expressing love for his family, predicting his death, and advising his wife on how to raise the children alone, he proclaimed his innocence:

> But, dear wife and children, who are big enough to know about these things, know that, so far as I am concerned, all these things are *false*. You have been with me, and you know as well as I do that none of these things have ever been countenanced about our home, but that we have repudiated such to the last. So you see that I am innocent, and you, my love, will have the lasting satisfaction to know that your husband was innocent, for you have been with me for some twenty-six years, and your constitution is emaciated and gone down to feebleness. . . . Tell George and baby, when they get old enough, they must seek religion and be good boys, and meet pa in heaven. I want William and John, as they are the oldest, to be good to their mother and their blind sister.
>
> Do with your scant means as you think best. I have feelings—I can not tell you *how* I feel for you. . . . But I can only leave you in the hands of Him in whom I put my trust. I know you will not forget me in your prayers; you have mine—shall have while I have breath. I believe much in prayer. I feel no guilt, from the fact that I have done nothing to cause that feeling.[46]

One story asserted that Bewley had stood trial before "civil authorities" and that the original Bailey letter was presented during the proceedings as the principal evidence against the prisoner. The same account said that Bewley had acknowledged receiving and subsequently losing the letter.[47] This wild newspaper story may have originated from a letter that Otis G. Welch, of Denton, had

45. Ironically, this was the same Ephraim Daggett upon whose storehouse roof Bewley's bones would soon lie bleaching in the Texas sun and serving as toys for Fort Worth's children. Elliott, *South-Western Methodism,* 165.

46. Elliott, *South-Western Methodism,* 164–165.

47. St. Louis (Mo.) *Central Christian Advocate,* n.d., quoted in Elliott, *South-Western Methodism,* 170.

written to the Houston *Telegraph,* alleging that "Wm. Buley," on being shown the Bailey letter when he arrived in Fort Worth, had "confessed that he was the man who lost it, and that it was lost while getting some oats from a stack near where it was found."[48] Both of these versions were clearly false; a mob had unceremoniously hanged the reluctant martyr within a few hours of his arrival in Fort Worth, and this, together with his several unequivocal declarations of his innocence, made a gallows confession most unlikely.

Then there is the problem of Bewley's name. Otis Welch referred to the hanged man as "Wm. Buley." A. G. Fowler said that the addressee given on the back of the letter was: "Rev. W. Buley." These letters were remarkable indeed, not only for what they belatedly added to the Bailey letter, but also because of their spelling of the alleged recipient's name. Although those in the North who had known him always spelled Bewley's last name correctly, it was generally spelled "Buley" in Texas and Arkansas newspapers. Yet William H. Bailey, supposedly a close associate in crime, had also spelled his name "Buley" and, worse than that, had erred additionally in writing Bewley's initial as "W." For some reason, Anthony Bewley was sometimes mentioned in the regional press with the initial "W.," or the first name "William," or "Wm.," as Welch had written it.

The different versions of Bewley's name seem to have created some confusion in the press. At least one journal even got the alleged letter writer mixed up with the alleged recipient. After Bewley had passed through Fort Smith, Arkansas, on his way to Fort Worth, the Fort Smith *Herald* said that it was the *writer* of the letter who had been captured: "On Sunday last," wrote the *Herald,* "Rev. W. H. Bailey arrived here on the Overland, under charge of Mr. Johnson, an officer from Texas."[49] And the Fayetteville *Arkansian,* which had contradicted itself in first saying that Bewley had protested his innocence, then stating that he had admitted his complicity in the plot, gave an even more confusing version when it declared: "Mr. Bewley confessed that he wrote the famous letter *addressed to one Bailey* [author's italics], which was picked up near Denton Creek, Texas, and published generally in the Southern papers."[50]

Northern friends of Bewley were quick to point out the inconsistencies and contradictions. In November, Bishop Thomas A. Morris of Springfield, Ohio, took note of the misspelling of Bewley's name in the Fowler letter to the Galveston *News* and, referring to the statement by the author that the original Bailey

48. Otis G. Welch, Denton, to the Houston *Telegraph,* n.d., quoted in Austin *Texas State Gazette,* October 13, 1860.

49. Fort Smith (Ark.) *Herald,* n.d., quoted in Richmond (Va.) *Enquirer,* October 5, 1860.

50. Fayetteville *Arkansian,* n.d., quoted in Elliott, *South-Western Methodism,* 184–185.

letter was still in the hands of the Fort Worth vigilance committee, said: "I am glad it is. There is some difference between Buley and Bewley, and still more between William and Anthony. . . . Now, if A. Bewley had united with others to raise an insurrection, his associates in crime would have known his name, and so directed the letter as to prevent it falling into other hands." In fact, argued Morris, the Bailey letter was nothing but "a humbug," designed to snare an innocent man.[51] Charles Elliott approvingly quoted Morris's analysis in his book, and in his conclusion to the chapter on Bewley, he raised an interesting question. If the object of the vigilantes was to incriminate the Methodist minister, "Why did they not forge a letter and sign Anthony Bewley's name to it?" His answer was that they had not dared to do so, because Bewley's handwriting was distinctive, and it would have been easy to prove the forgery; hence, they had chosen to invent William H. Bailey. Since he did not exist, argued Elliott, there could be no other samples of the mysterious abolitionist's writing for comparison with the infamous letter.[52]

Elliott's theory is intriguing, but there may be a better explanation. What if the vigilantes *did* forge a letter from Bewley and *thought* they had signed his proper name? After all, the parson had lived and worked in Johnson not Tarrant County, thus he probably was not personally well known to those who conspired to kill him. It is reasonable to assume, therefore, that the Fort Worth vigilantes had only a pronouncing knowledge of his name. For some unknown reason, his first name was thought by those close to the investigation to be William; this is evident from the several references to him by that name in the press and in the letters of Welch to the Houston *Telegraph* and Fowler to the Galveston *News.* It may well be that some in nearby Fort Worth had heard him referred to by his actual given name, Anthony, as well. Living in a rural area sixteen miles south of Fort Worth, he almost certainly had made trips into town to buy supplies—perhaps at the store of Ephraim Daggett, the influential businessman whose intercession Bewley had sought and upon whose rooftop his bones found their resting place. In conversations that local vigilantes must have had concerning the notorious "abolitionist" preacher in the adjacent county, it is entirely possible that the surname "Bewley" metamorphosed into the far more common name of "Bailey" and that William and A. (for Anthony) similarly changed to "William H." If one speaks the names with a Texas drawl, William A. Bewley and William H. Bailey sound remarkably similar.

51. Elliott, *South-Western Methodism,* 186.
52. Ibid., 198–199.

This hypothesis not only explains Bewley's absence from the text of the letter, it also accounts for the letter writer's apparent effort to disguise the handwriting, which he explained by complaining of a sore thumb. If he had been writing the words of a fictional William H. Bailey, as Elliott suggested, there would have been no need to alter the handwriting. This theory could explain as well the lapse of one month between publication of the letter and the first public mention of Bewley as the addressee. It probably took a while for the vigilantes to realize their mistake and figure out a way to correct it. Finally, it would explain the curious report in the Fort Smith *Herald* that it was "W. H. Bailey," not Anthony Bewley, whom the vigilantes had just escorted through their town on his way to meet his fate. The Fort Worth vigilantes would have known the real origin and purpose of the Bailey letter and may well have told the local paper that it was indeed the famous letter *writer* whom they had in tow. This would explain that journal's confused report.

Whether or not this scenario is correct, it is clear that Anthony Bewley was indeed a martyr, though a reluctant one. His death for a cause that he did not support and for crimes he had not committed angered many northerners and added to their conviction that the southern slaveocracy would stop at nothing, not even the murder of a blameless servant of God, to protect their peculiar institution. The Boston *Zion's Herald* undoubtedly spoke for many when it said: "It is such acts [as the hanging of Bewley] that make all truly religious papers, and all truly religious men at the North, to a certain extent political."[53]

But the Bailey letter and Bewley's hanging had an even more provocative effect upon white southerners. Many in the South already believed that the North's slavery critics sought the South's destruction and would stop at nothing to achieve their goal. Bewley's church had broken with the southerners over the issue of slavery, and even though neither the M.E.C. nor Bewley advocated stirring up dissatisfaction among the slaves or the criminal violation of state laws, their dislike of the peculiar institution was enough to identify them with the likes of John Brown in the minds of southerners. Charles Elliott accurately observed, "The term abolitionist at this time was very equivocal." Elliott noted that when the pro-slavery Cherokees had banished the Northern Methodist missionaries from the Indian Territory in 1854, they had defined an abolitionist as "one who teaches a negro or slave to read, write, or sing or who sits at meat with him." In short, said Elliott, the slaveholders had reached such a state of fanaticism concerning their peculiar institution that "every one who could

53. Boston (Mass.) *Zion's Herald*, n.d., quoted in Galveston *Texas Christian Advocate*, November 8, 1860.

not actually plead and act for slavery and against freedom was considered an enemy to the South, and fit only to be banished from the entire South-West."[54]

In a letter to the editor of the New York *Day Book*, written at the height of the panic, a Fort Worth citizen identified only as "J. W. S." wrote: "Our citizens look upon a Free-soiler alone, as a murderer and incendiary—as one who advocates principles which must necessarily lead to every species of iniquity known in the catalogue of crime."[55] Such a viewpoint made Bewley's martyrdom all but inevitable. It also motivated those who used the Texas Troubles to push the South toward secession. Given the growing likelihood that Lincoln would be the next president, the fire-eaters argued that only the creation of a separate southern nation could protect the South from the horrors of a race war.

54. Elliott, *South-Western Methodism*, 44.
55. New York *Day Book*, September 8, 1860.

CHAPTER EIGHT

THE MORTAL ENEMY OF THE SOUTH

Southern rights editors and politicians largely ignored the mounting evidence that the Texas Troubles had been greatly exaggerated by false rumors of arson and poisonings, which had been enhanced and made more believable by the fraudulent Bailey letter. As the presidential election loomed nearer, those who refused even to consider accepting a Republican president stepped up the intensity of their attacks on Abraham Lincoln. They reiterated the stories of arson and poisonings and repeated the charges made earlier by Breckinridge supporters that Lincoln's party had been responsible.

The attacks directed at Lincoln became increasingly personal and vicious. Secessionists not only depicted the Illinois Republican as the enemy of slavery, but also as a man who would not hesitate to encourage the slaughter of innocent whites. As proof, they cited the alleged Republican support of the Mystic Red's depredations in the Lone Star State. This tactic forced the friends of the Union in the South to assume a defensiveness that they were never able to overcome. When unionists tried to minimize the danger that a Republican administration would pose to slavery, the secessionists accused them of disloyalty to the South, alleging that by advocating "submission" to a "Black Republican" administration they were, in effect, expressing a willingness to subject their families, and the families of all southerners, to all the horrors of the Texas Troubles.

The slave panic could not have come at a worse time for those who loved the Union, or at a better time for those who wished to destroy it. The secessionists' skillful use of the Texas Troubles in effect robbed the Unionists of their most effective argument and helped them seize the initiative in the battle for the hearts and minds of southerners. Most southerners had long equated Republican free-soilism with abolitionism; nevertheless, the northern party's opposition to slavery's expansion and its supposed ambition to abolish the peculiar institution in the southern states hardly posed an immediate threat to the average white person in the South. Unionist papers repeatedly pointed out that the Republicans almost certainly would fail to win control of both houses of Congress; moreover, the Supreme Court, which likely would have a decidedly Democratic majority for years to come, would block any efforts to strike a blow at slavery. Since Lincoln, as president, would be unable to abolish slavery, even if he so desired, the South should be willing to accept his election and give him a chance to show that he would treat the slaveholding states fairly. If he were to commit an "overt act" against the South's constitutional rights, there would be plenty of time for the slave states to join together and secede cooperatively, as a unit.[1]

The fire-eaters knew that the "cooperationist" approach was a sure formula for defeating their dream of a southern confederacy. They had traveled that road in 1849–1850, only to see their hopes dashed when the Nashville Convention failed to create southern solidarity. It was essential from the secessionists' point of view that one or more of the more radical slave states of the Lower South act unilaterally to leave the Union. Such a bold step would undoubtedly lead to a confrontation with the federal government, which in turn would force the more timid slave states to support the state (or states) that had seceded. William Lowndes Yancey, Robert Barnwell Rhett, and other like-minded radicals worked out this strategy at the Southern Commercial Convention that convened at Montgomery, Alabama, on May 10, 1858. Although they admitted that the southern people as a whole were unready for secession, the Montgomery radicals were hardly discouraged, for they recognized that revolutions are instigated by small groups of dedicated men, not by the masses.[2]

A few weeks after the convention finished its work, Yancey summed up the new strategy in a letter to James S. Slaughter of Atlanta. Secessionists should emulate their revolutionary forefathers, he said, by forming "committees of public safety" all over the Deep South. Yancey was convinced that through the activities of such small cadres "we shall fire the Southern heart—instruct the Southern mind—give courage to each other, and at the proper moment, by organized concerted action, we can precipitate the Cotton States into a revolution."[3]

1. Avery O. Craven, *The Growth of Southern Nationalism, 1848–1861* (Baton Rouge, La., 1953), 350–351.

2. Laura A. White, *Robert Barnwell Rhett: Father of Secession* (New York, 1931), 144–145.

3. Quoted in Allan Nevins, *The Emergence of Lincoln*, vol. 2, *Ordeal of the Union* (New York, 1950), 406.

The "proper moment," the secessionists had long proclaimed, would be the election of a "Black Republican" as president. Before the Texas Troubles of 1860, most southern whites probably agreed with the fire-eaters that the fledgling northern party posed a threat to slavery, but it is far from certain that, outside South Carolina, a majority in any state had thought that the election of a Republican president would warrant such a drastic step as secession. Given the checks and balances provided by the other branches of government, even a hostile chief executive would be limited in the damage he could do to southern interests.

Southern revolutionaries clearly needed an emotional issue to drive their secession engine. They believed they had found one in the person of John Brown, the bearded fanatic, whose abortive raid on Harpers Ferry in October 1859 sent a shiver of horror throughout the South. Shortly after hearing of the incursion, Edmund Ruffin recorded in his diary the "news of remarkable events." Having heard that northern abolitionists had planned the raid with the expectation of initiating a general slave insurrection, the Virginia secessionist wrote, "I earnestly hope that such may be the truth of the case. Such a practical exercise of abolition principles is needed to stir the sluggish blood of the South."[4]

Ruffin and all the secessionists were soon disappointed, however, for the excitement quickly subsided after the old abolitionist's execution. After all, Brown's mission had fizzled, and conservative southerners could point to his failure to enlist the local slaves in his cause as proof of their contention that their chattels were generally a loyal and docile folk. Although Brown was hardly forgotten—as can be seen by the newspaper reports that sought to link his followers to the events in Texas—the press soon found other issues to discuss. By early 1860 southern newspapers were giving relatively little space to Brown or to the possibility of a new slave insurrection.[5]

The Montgomery *Mail*, Charleston *Mercury*, and other secessionist journals and politicians denounced the drift toward apathy, but in the first several months of the year they were unable to reverse the trend. As early as January 18, a Georgia paper proclaimed the demise of the John Brown panic, saying it had "died a natural death."[6] But if this were so, the Texas Troubles "resurrected" insurrectionary fears in the minds of white southerners. The panic also revi-

4. William K. Scarborough, ed., *The Diary of Edmund Ruffin* (Baton Rouge, 1972–1989), entry of October 19, 1860, 1:349.

5. Crenshaw, *The Slave States in the Presidential Election of 1860*, 91–92.

6. Savannah *Republican*, January 18, 1860, quoted in Clarence L. Mohr, *On The Threshold of Freedom*, 20.

talized the Breckinridge camp and gave the secessionists a formidable weapon with which to attack those conservatives who argued that a Republican victory in the presidential election would have a minimal impact upon the South.

The press was the secessionists' primary instrument for demonizing Lincoln and building support for separation from the Union. Southern rights journals in Texas had alleged a connection between the "John Brownites" and the Republican party from the beginning of the panic, and they continued to hammer away in September and October, undeterred by the Opposition's exposure of false reports, exaggerations, and even apparent fraud. As the presidential election grew nearer, the Austin *Texas State Gazette,* the leading publicist of the alleged insurrectionary plot, could scarcely contain itself when it considered the prospect of the Illinois Republican's elevation to the presidency. On November 3, it said that the election would determine whether Lincoln, "the deadly enemy of the institution of slavery, the wicked sympathizer of John Brown, the apostle of murder, arson and servile war, the chosen chief of associated traitors, shall wield the high powers of the executive branch of the federal Government, shall control its vast patronage, and command the Army and Navy of this Confederacy."[7]

Many of the more radical southern rights newspapers in the other southern states expressed sentiments similar to those of the *Texas State Gazette.* Ignoring the fact that the Republican party had set forth an ambitious, multi-faceted domestic program in its platform, the Washington *Constitution* asserted that the *idée fixe* of that party was its hatred of the South. That party had progressed, said the *Constitution,* "from a sickly and false philanthropy to the murder and arson of John Brown and his imitators in Texas" to a point where its anti-slavery, anti-southern philosophy was the "sole basis upon which the black republican party rests its claims to obtain control of the nation and inaugurate its policy into the Government of the United States."[8]

In the same edition that carried a lengthy story on the events in Texas, the Natchez *Free Trader* predicted that Lincoln and other leaders of the Republican party "would hail a servile insurrection as the 'dawn of a political millennium.'" Indeed, said the *Free Trader,* the "Black Republican" leaders "pant for the hour to arrive when the black man . . . will wage a war of extermination against the white man."[9] The Montgomery *Mail,* Yancey's organ in Alabama, obviously agreed with this sentiment when it opined that the Texas fires constituted the "begin-

7. Austin *Texas State Gazette,* November 3, 1860. For similar statements, see: Marshall *Texas Republican,* August 25, 1860; San Antonio *Daily Herald,* July 25, 1860.

8. Washington (D.C.) *Constitution,* August 29, 1860.

9. Natchez (Miss.) *Free Trader,* August 13, 1860.

ning of Black Republican operations in the South! This is *practical Lincoln-ism*! This is what we must 'acquiesce in,' if we 'acquiesce in' Black Republican government! If LINCOLN is elected, let the people see, by the light of the Texas flames, that we will be forced to fight or go out."[10]

Acquiescence in a Republican victory and waiting to see if the new president would commit an "overt act" against the South before taking action would be fatal, the secessionists argued. A Louisiana journal warned, "Delay may mean death," but Sam Dixon of Alabama's Wetumpka *Enquirer* expressed the issue more dramatically: "If I find a coiled rattlesnake in my path, do I wait for 'his' 'overt act,' or do I smite him in his coil?"[11]

After recounting the reports of the alleged abolitionist depredations in Texas, the Fayetteville *Arkansian* warned that if Breckinridge should fail to be elected, "we believe from the bottom of our soul that events will immediately take place so dark and terrible that the imagination now refuses to picture them." Lincoln and other "Black Republicans" might not have lit the fires in Texas themselves, said the *Arkansian,* but "these excesses are the legitimate results of their doctrines," for there were numerous "devils incarnate" in the party who would see Lincoln's election as "the signal to work out their fanatic mission, viz: to burn slaveholders' houses and towns, massacre their families and 'set niggers free.' That is the only creed, faith and hope of hundreds and hundreds who will vote for Lincoln. Treason they worship as higher than either Law or God."[12] Shortly after learning that Lincoln had been elected, a North Carolina paper echoed the *Arkansian's* prediction but prophesied with even greater urgency: "*We proclaim it now and mark us if it is true—If we submit to Lincoln's election, before his term of office expires, your home will be visited by one of the most fearful and horrible butcheries that has cursed the face of the globe.*"[13]

10. Montgomery (Ala.) *Weekly Mail,* August 3, 1860.

11. Opelousas (La.) *Courier,* November 17, 1860; Wetumpka (Ala.) *Enquirer,* n.d., quoted in Florence (Ala.) *Gazette,* November 14, 1860.

12. Fayetteville *Arkansian,* August 17, 31, 1860.

13. Fayetteville *North Carolinian,* November 17, 1860 (italics in the original). For other such dire post-election forecasts, see Sulphur Springs *Independent Monitor,* December 1, 1860; Dallas *Herald,* December 5, 1860; Corsicana *Navarro Express,* November 16, 1860; Carrollton *West Alabamian,* December 12, 1860; Montgomery (Ala.) *Weekly Advertiser,* November 14, 1860; Grove Hill (Ala.) *Clarke County Democrat,* November 29, 1860; Jackson *Weekly Mississippian,* November 14, 23, 1860; Florence (Ala.) *Gazette,* November 21, 1860; Athens (Ga.) *Southern Banner,* November 29, December 3, 1860; Hayneville (Ala.) *Chronicle,* November 8, 22, 1860; Paulding (Miss.) *Eastern Clarion,* n.d., quoted in Jackson *Weekly Mississippian,* November 21, 1860; Wilmington (N.C.) *Daily Journal,* November 13, 1860; Norfolk (Va.) *Southern Argus,* November 8, 1860; New Orleans

Thus, in the view of the fire-eating press the election of Lincoln portended nothing short of the systematic destruction of the South and the murder and rape of its white citizens. Moreover, such journals frequently pointed out that the Brown raid and Texas fires had occurred under a pro-southern Democratic administration. The Charleston *Mercury* gave voice to the question that must have vexed many whose fears had been raised by the slave insurrection panic. In a prominent editorial titled "The Terrors of Submission," the *Mercury* proclaimed: "If, in our present position [under Democratic control] we have the raid of JOHN BROWN—and twenty towns burned down in Texas in one year, by Abolitionists—what will be the measures of insurrection and incendiarism, which must follow our notorious and abject prostration to Abolition rule at Washington, with all the patronage of the Federal Government, and a Union organization in the South to support it?"[14]

Asserting that the alleged plots in Texas and elsewhere were "the logical and inevitable consequences of Black Republican teachings," the New Orleans *Delta* asked: "If Southern States are invaded, Southern citizens murdered, Southern property destroyed, Southern towns delivered over to the merciless torch of the incendiary while the Government is still administered by a party friendly to the South, what are we to expect in case an avowedly hostile party, a party whose teachings have stimulated these outrages, a party which avowedly aspires to subjugate the South—what are we to expect in case such a party should gain control of the Federal Administration?"[15]

James Gordon Bennett's New York *Herald,* which was as anti-Lincoln as any southern journal, thought it knew the answer to the *Delta's* question. The *Herald* predicted that Lincoln's election would signal the incendiaries that they could pursue their hellish activities in the full knowledge that, if caught and tried, they would assuredly face friendly judges and juries. As a consequence of a Lincoln victory, warned the *Herald,* "the abolition promptings to incendiarism now seen in Texas will be witnessed in every slave State from the Delaware to the Rio Grande, and from the Ohio to the Gulf of Mexico."[16]

(La.) *Daily Delta,* November 23, 1860; Troy (Ala.) *Advertiser,* n.d., quoted in Florence (Ala.) *Gazette,* November 21, 1860; Spartanburg (S.C.) *Carolina Spartan,* December 6, 1860; Barbour (Va.) *Jeffersonian Democrat,* n.d., quoted in Richmond (Va.) *Examiner,* November 13, 1860.

14. Charleston (S.C.) *Mercury,* October 11, 1860.

15. New Orleans *Daily Delta,* July 31, 1860. For other examples of this reasoning, see Athens (Ga.) *Southern Banner,* September 6, 1860; Clayton (Ala.) *Banner,* August 9, 1860, quoted in Barney, *The Secessionist Impulse,* 179.

16. New York *Herald,* n.d., clipped in Charleston (S.C.) *Mercury,* September 8, 1860.

It is difficult to see how the readers of such twisted characterizations of Lincoln and his party, together with the dire predictions of the awful consequences of a Republican victory in November, could have been unaffected by them. Indeed, there are indications that such fearmongering tactics were successful. A Texas correspondent of the New York *Herald* exaggerated only in degree when he said that the "excitement growing out of these matters has killed off all conservative feeling in Texas. You may now note down every Texan as a disunionist." Moreover, said the same writer, the Texans had come to believe that abolitionist incursions would continue, regardless of the outcome of the election; "therefore the great majority of us do not care how soon the crisis comes. We believe that it is bound to come, and it had as well come now as any other time."[17] An Alabama woman wrote in her diary: "The country is getting in a deplorable state owing to the depredations committed by the Abolitionist[s] especially in Texas; and the safety of the country depends on who is elected to the presidency."[18]

Sarah Lois Wadley of Vicksburg, the sixteen-year-old who had lost her piano teacher to abolitionist concerns, in late October wrote that she prayed for the Union but feared that it now existed in name only, for "there is no concord, no real heart[felt] Union any longer." Her father was born in New England and many of her ancestors were buried there, "yet dear as is its soil to me never can I claim Friendship with those who have contemplated my country's ruin," she wrote. In an anguished passage that contained clear allusions to the Texas Troubles, Miss Wadley revealed both her fears and despair over a likely breakup of the Union and the possibility of armed conflict between the sections:

> The Abolitionists have sowed the seeds of dissension and insurrection among us, those seeds are fast ripening and a bloody harvest seems impending; they have burnt our homesteads, killed our citizens, and incited our servants to poison us, think they that we will submit to continue disturbances oft repeated wrongs, much longer, no! They shout Freedom and Union, but they would take away our freedom and give it to the negro, they would sap the foundations of that Union which our ancestors labored amid bloodshed and tyranny to found.

"I shudder to contemplate a civil war," Wadley wrote; nevertheless: "Better far

17. Anonymous letter to the New York *Herald,* August 20, 1860, clipped in Charleston (S.C.) *Mercury,* September 8, 1860.

18. Sarah R. Espry Diary, August 11, 1860, quoted in Barney, *The Secessionist Impulse,* 167.

for us would be civil war than this dreadful incubus which hangs over us now, this continual wrangling and bitter malediction with which we are persecuted."[19]

Even political conservatives were affected. On September 20, Robert F. Kellan, the Camden, Arkansas, diarist who supported Bell for president, clearly equated Lincoln with abolitionism when he wrote: "All the Idle men Talk Politics. The Nation seems to be in Trouble. Great fears are talked about in the event Lincoln the Abolition Candidate for the Presidency is elected in November."[20] Another conservative, who identified himself as a "Henry Clay Whig," in a letter to the Baton Rouge *Daily Advocate* professed that he still loved the Union but had come to believe that it would be folly to submit to this "vile Black Republican party. . . . Is it that we are to live under the presidency of a man who will permit his Abolition hordes to incite our slaves to the work of applying the midnight torch to our homes and murdering our parents, our wives, our children and ourselves, in cold blood? O Power Supreme, forbid!"[21]

Shortly after the election, R. S. Holt, a wealthy planter of Yazoo City, Mississippi, wrote of his despair to his brother, Joseph Holt, who was the U.S. postmaster general. The "planting states," he wrote, had experienced "a foretaste of what Northern brother-hood means, in almost daily conflagrations & in discovery of poison, knives & pistols distributed among our slaves by emissaries sent out for the purpose by openly organized associations." Holt said that the abolitionists had been so numerous that one could not find as much as ten square miles where they had not been active. He added that northern pharmaceutical factories must have had to work overtime to supply the large quantities of poison that had been discovered.[22]

But it was not only those of wealth and position that worried about the future under a Republican administration. Those without a direct economic stake in the slave system were as concerned about the reported abolitionist assaults as large slaveholders. One historian of the secession movement wrote: "No issue so galvanized white fears or engendered such blind hatred of the North as did the rumors of slave uprisings that swept over the South in 1860." The same scholar pointed out that this fear of slave insurrections obscured class lines and

19. Sarah L. Wadley Diary, October 26, 1860, microfilm typescript, page 77, Woodruff Library Special Collections, Emory University, Atlanta, Georgia.

20. Robert F. Kellan Diary, September 20, 1860, microfilm copy of original, General Microfilm Collection, Arkansas Historical Commission, Little Rock, Arkansas.

21. Baton Rouge (La.) *Daily Advocate,* November 14, 1860.

22. R. S. Holt to Joseph Holt, November 9, 1860, manuscript, Joseph Holt Papers, Library of Congress, quoted in Crenshaw, *The Slave States in the Presidential Election of 1860,* 105–106.

drove all southerners, regardless of status, together to defend against the common enemy—the abolitionists.[23]

Southern ultras recognized that the specter of a horrible race war, such as that which had devastated Santo Domingo before the turn of the nineteenth century, was as much a cause of dread among the poorest whites as it was among planters. Senator Albert Gallatin Brown, of Mississippi, played on this fear when he suggested that nonslaveholders would suffer the most in the event of a general uprising of bondsmen. Planters could use their wealth to protect themselves and even leave the country, if necessary, leaving poorer whites to bear the brunt of the slaves' rage. "The Negro will intrude into his preserve," Gallatin warned, demand that he be "treated as an equal," that he be allowed in the "white man's bed," and that "his son shall marry the white man's daughter. . . . In short that they shall live on terms of perfect equality." Of course, the senator added, "The non-slaveholder will . . . reject the terms. Then will commence a war of the races such as has marked the history of Santo Domingo."[24]

Such blatant exploitation of the deep-seated apprehensions of ordinary whites unquestionably had the desired effect in many cases. At the height of the secession crisis a nonslaveholding farmer in Tennessee expressed his anger and anxiety in a letter to Senator Andrew Johnson. The Constitution and the law were on the side of slavery and the South, the letter writer said, but "Higher Law Republicans" had resorted to "John Brown spikes and murder in the first degree" to override legalities. By instigating "murder in Virginue and in Texas stricnine[,] fire and blood," the Republicans apparently meant "God's law" when they used the phrase "higher law." But, asked the farmer, "Does God require them to use stricnine[,] powder[,] lead[,] fire[,] and every means of destruction [to take] the life of innocent Women and children to fulfill his Law[?] God forbid such hypocracy[.]"[25]

In Texas, where the panic had begun, fire-eaters played upon the fear of ordinary white citizens by arguing that the only way to avoid further insurrections was through the creation of a southern nation that would protect slavery. Historians Robin Baker and Dale Baum analyzed voting patterns in the Lone Star State for the period leading to secession and concluded that the switch of various conservative blocs on the issue of secession could only be explained by

23. Barney, *The Road to Secession*, 146.

24. Quoted in Avery O. Craven, "Coming of the War Between the States, An Interpretation," *Journal of Southern History* (August 1936): 321–322.

25. J. H. C. Basham, Union City, Tennessee, to Andrew Johnson, December 1, 1860, in *The Papers of Andrew Johnson*, ed. LeRoy P. Graf and Ralph W. Haskins (Knoxville, 1972), 3:676.

the emotionalism that swept the state and skewed traditional political loyalties. Most white Texans believed that Lincoln's election threatened them with "an imminent revolutionary assault," and they came to believe that only by joining a confederacy of slave states would they be able "to seal off their region from the contagion of 'Black Republicanism.'" According to Baker and Baum, the fire-eaters successfully presented secession "to non-slaveholding farmers, towns-people, and frontiersmen as the best way to preserve law and order, prosperity and social stability. Protection from abolitionist violence, maintenance of the subordination of black Africans, and fear of further division among white men were rational concerns of Texas voters when they went to the polling places in 1861."[26]

The leaders of the secession movement throughout the slave states early recognized that the fearful reactions of southerners of all classes to the confla-gration in Texas, and to the brushfires it had spawned in other states, could be used effectively in the cause of southern nationalism. Like the southern rights press, they often emphasized the alleged horrors to dramatize their contention that the South could ill afford to remain in the Union under a "Black Repub-lican" president who personified the evils of abolitionism.[27] The panic, they argued, was the "fire bell" that clearly signaled a coming national political up-heaval, for which all southerners should prepare themselves. After admonish-ing a correspondent in Texas to "fight all invaders in your state, and hang all you can catch," Henry A. Wise, the Virginia governor who had signed John Brown's death warrant, wrote: "It is time that the slave States were ready for the revolution which is coming inevitably."[28]

Lawrence M. Keitt, a South Carolina secessionist whose own brother had been murdered by slaves the previous February, was clearly referring to the Texas Troubles when he wrote to James H. Hammond: "Our Negroes are be-ing enlisted in politics. I confess this new feature alarms me, more even, than everything in the past. If Northern men get access to our Negroes to advise poison and the torch, we must prevent it at every hazard."[29] In a letter to an-other South Carolina correspondent, Keitt made clear his belief that it was the

26. Robin E. Baker and Dale Baum, "The Texas Voter and the Crisis of the Union, 1859–1861," *Journal of Southern History* 53, no. 3 (August 1987): 419.

27. For a good summary of key secessionists' views on a prospective Lincoln victory, see Cren-shaw, *The Slave States in the Presidential Election of 1860*, 89–111.

28. Henry A. Wise, Richmond, Va., to T. D. Murray, Paris, Texas, August 16, 1860, quoted in Richmond (Va.) *Enquirer*, September 7, 1860.

29. Lawrence M. Keitt to James H. Hammond, September 10, 1860, quoted in Walther, *The Fire-Eaters*, 185.

Republicans who were "enlisting" the blacks in politics and who thus constituted the chief threat to the South. Keitt cited Lincoln's "house divided" speech as proof that the South either must sacrifice its peculiar institution or expect more John Brown raids, "more torches to her dwellings, and more poison in her fountains." Lincoln intended "that the South must be abolitionized, or she must be lighted with the blaze of the incendiary, and harried with the steel of the assassin."[30] As the election neared, Keitt predicted that a Lincoln victory would usher in the "wildest democracy" since the Reign of Terror during the French Revolution. "What of conservatism? What of order? What of social security or financial prosperity can withstand Northern Republican license? A drunken and licentious soldier would hardly be as bad."[31]

Edmund Ruffin of Virginia first heard details of the events in the Lone Star State on September 5, while traveling in Tennessee. Although he confided to his diary his suspicion that the reports probably were exaggerated and that many innocent persons would suffer along with the guilty, he nevertheless was convinced that there was an abolitionist conspiracy at work in Texas. Even if only one-tenth of the reports were true, he said, when added to the Brown raid, "it would be alone sufficient for a separation of the Union to exclude northern emissaries & incendiaries from southern territories." Until secession was accomplished, Ruffin wrote, such Republican-sponsored incursions were bound to continue, "while, after separation, we may more securely defy the whole power of northern abolitionism."[32]

The secessionist who made the most extensive use of the slave insurrection panic during the presidential campaign was Alabama fire-eater William

30. Lawrence M. Keitt to William Murray, Orangeburg Court House, South Carolina, September 22, 1860, quoted in Charleston (S.C.) *Mercury,* September 27, 1860.

31. Lawrence M. Keitt to William Porcher Miles, October 3, 1860, William Porcher Miles Papers, Southern Historical Collection, University of North Carolina at Chapel Hill, Chapel Hill, North Carolina.

32. Scarborough, ed., *The Diary of Edmund Ruffin,* 1:455–456, 470. After the Brown raid, Ruffin became obsessed with the idea that secession was the only way to prevent slave tampering by abolitionists. In the spring of 1860 he published a strange, futuristic novel, set in the years 1864–1870, in which the new Republican president William H. Seward (Lincoln having served only one term) sponsored a massive abolitionist crusade against a separate southern nation (the South had previously seceded), with the intention of raising a Santo Domingo–like insurrection. In Ruffin's apocalyptic vision, the brave South, with the help of loyal slaves, crushed the invasion, thus maintaining its independence. Ruffin's argument was that the South was able to repel the northern army and maintain the institution of slavery only because it had seceded and created a unified government that could successfully resist such an invasion. See Edmund Ruffin, *Anticipations of the Future, To Serve as Lessons for the Present Time* (Richmond, 1860).

Lowndes Yancey, whom historian Clement Eaton has aptly called "the orator of secession."[33] Yancey made a much-publicized speaking tour of the South and portions of the North during late September and October. In what his biographer called "the most remarkable oratorical tour in American history," Yancey made twenty speeches in seven weeks. Beginning in Georgia on September 17, the famous fire-eater worked his way through the South Atlantic states and made it as far north as Boston.[34]

In a widely reported speech in New York City, the Alabama ultra began moderately enough, telling his audience that the South wanted only to maintain its social system, which had been ordained both by geography and the Constitution. Before long, however, he reverted to his usual harangue about the northern anti-slavery men who, he said, were determined to destroy the South. Asserting the orthodox southern view that the Republicans "are the same as the abolitionists," Yancey alleged that if the government were to come under the control of a Republican president, "the emissaries of the Abolitionists would be found everywhere through the South with strychnia to put in their wells as they are now found in Texas." The New York *Times,* which printed the speech in its entirety, reported that this statement was greeted with a mixture of applause, hisses, and "cries of 'Put him out!'"[35] Undaunted by the catcalls, Yancey forged on:

> In Texas it was proven beyond all doubt, men calling themselves Reverend had been arrested with strychnia upon their persons, and arms had been found stored away. How came they there? They were there for the purpose of carrying on the "irrepressible conflict." The emissaries of the Abolitionists there crawled about at midnight with their incendiary torches, poison and incitements to insurrection. Those things were there and they were traced to the Abolitionists. Now, if the Black Republicans were in power, would not the institution be in danger of being blown up at any time by some insignificant being—capable of little good but able to do a great deal of mischief? With the emissaries of the North among them, with the offices of the Government in the hands of their enemies, their property would be deteriorated; there would be general desolation and the North would share in the universal ruin.[36]

33. Clement Eaton, *The Freedom-of-Thought Struggle in the Old South* (New York, 1964), 51.

34. John W. Du Bose, *The Life and Times of William Lowndes Yancey: A History of Political Parties in the United States, from 1834 to 1864,* 2 vols. (Birmingham, Ala., 1892; reprint, New York, 1942), 2:494.

35. New York *Times,* October 11, 1860.

36. Ibid.

The *Times* predictably observed that Yancey was out-of-bounds in equating abolitionism with Republicanism. So did the New York *World,* which said: "The designs he imputed to the republican party are not the thoughts of the majority of that party. If they were, and it was so understood, that party could not stand a day." Thus, in the view of the *World,* secession in the event of Lincoln's election would be unjustified.[37]

The intrepid Alabamian delivered another speech in Cincinnati and provoked criticism similar to that which he received in New York. The Cincinnati *Daily Commercial* complained that the southern orator seemed to be under the impression that his audience was made up of "New Englanders and Abolitionists." Moreover, said the editor, "He did not in any sentence recognize the possibility that Republicans are not Abolitionist," nor did he seem to comprehend that a party could gain majority status in one section of the country "without an assault being made upon the constitutional rights of the minority."[38]

The mixed reception accorded Yancy by his northern audiences and the incredulous reaction of the Republican newspapers contrasted dramatically with the welcome given him in southern cities, where he played to enthusiastic audiences and a much more receptive press. In the nation's capital, much of his address centered upon the dangers of submitting to Lincoln's election. He dwelled heavily upon the familiar theme that other fire-eaters had stressed: Given that the assaults of Brown and the Texas conspirators had occurred under a friendly administration, southerners must expect even worse under Lincoln. "Why, gentlemen, if Texas is now in flames, and the peace of Virginia is invaded under this administration . . . tell me what it will be when a higher law government reigns in the city of Washington?" When Yancey asked whether "any brave and heroic people" could sacrifice their constitutional principles and betray their "families and firesides" by submitting to a Republican president, his southern audience shouted, "Never, never."[39]

Yancey's grand tour ended on a triumphant note in New Orleans, where, on October 29, an estimated twenty thousand people crowded Canal Street to hear the celebrated orator. Yancey did not disappoint them. He eloquently painted a scenario depicting what might happen after the Republicans had taken control of the government and abolitionists had overrun the South:

> When you call on one of them [Republican authorities] to arrest an incendiary who is prowling about in your neighborhood, he will tell

37. New York *World,* October 11, 1860.
38. Cincinnati (Ohio) *Daily Commercial,* October 27, 1860.
39. Richmond (Va.) *Enquirer,* September 25, 1860.

you that he is sleepy; that he will attend to it in the morning; and by that time your house will have been burned, and the incendiary will be at a safe distance. You call one of them in the daytime, and he will tell you it will take him some time to find his horse, and some time to get ready, and a long time to find the offender; and when he starts, he will find a cold track; for you know how easy it is for a man to appear to do something, even when he is doing nothing.[40]

The Texas Troubles and their satellite panics in the other states had subsided well before the presidential election, but the issue did not die. Secessionists vigorously continued to stir the cauldron in their effort to play upon the fears of southerners. Indeed, the Texas Troubles proved to be their most powerful weapon in the battle against those conservatives who argued that the South had little to lose by adopting a wait-and-see policy with respect to a Republican administration.

After Lincoln's election, the battle shifted to the state houses, where legislators debated whether a "Black Republican's" elevation to the presidency required the convocation of secession conventions. The cotton states all decided this question in the affirmative, and a key factor in this decision was the specter of race violence that the secessionists raised time and again.

Georgia was the pivotal state in the Deep South. Its geographical location and role as the transportation hub of the Lower South, connecting the states of the Southwest to those of the South Atlantic region, made its participation in the proposed southern government essential. But Georgia was home to a sizeable contingent of powerful anti-secessionists, led by Alexander H. Stephens, Benjamin Harvey Hill, and Herschel Johnson, among others. These opponents of secession were not unconditionally committed to remaining in the Union, but they believed that Lincoln should be given a chance to show that he would respect southern rights. If, as president, he were to violate those rights, the Georgia cooperationists believed that the state should secede, but only in concert with the other slave states.

The Georgia secessionists knew from the outset that they faced a difficult task in overcoming their formidable opponents. Shortly before the election a Georgia correspondent of the Charleston *Mercury* wrote that the secessionists would make a great effort to take his state out of the Union if Lincoln were elected, but he feared that they would fail, since there were many Georgians who were "shutting their eyes to JOHN BROWN's raid in Virginia—to the incendiarisms

---

40. New Orleans (La.) *Daily Delta*, October 30. See also Walther, *The Fire-Eaters*, 77.

and insurrections in our sister States—to the murder and poisoning of our un-offending people."[41]

Edmund Ruffin, who later at Charleston delighted in firing one of the first shots of the Civil War, harbored a similar concern about Georgia. Although he deplored the "horrors" that the Texans had been forced to undergo, Ruffin on September 11 confided to his diary that if another such plot should exist, "I earnestly hope that it may be in Georgia," for if the "dull spirit and lethargic" attitude of that state could be overcome, then every adjoining state, except possibly North Carolina, would join her, and, ultimately, the border states would be forced to follow.[42] Secessionists had reason to worry about Georgia, at least before the Texas Troubles erupted. Historian Clarence L. Mohr has observed that radical southern rights men "were waging an uphill fight" during the summer of 1860. "It was scarcely surprising," wrote Mohr, "that Breckinridge agitators in Georgia seized upon a rash of mysterious fires in the distant state of Texas to rekindle the flames of racial fear and hostility at home."[43]

The Georgia legislature set January 2 as the date for a statewide election to select delegates to a convention that would decide the issue of secession. In advance of the election a series of debates was held at the state capital of Milledgeville. Governor Joseph E. Brown set the tone by warning that "a hungry swarm of abolition emissaries" was set to sweep over the South in the wake of Lincoln's election, flooding "the country with inflammatory abolition documents" and probably instigating violence.[44] Sounding a similar note, Senator Robert Toombs, one of the leading Georgia ultras, declared that the election of Lincoln had swept away "the last bulwark" of defense left to the South. The Republicans were determined to destroy slavery, charged Toombs: "They declare their purpose to war against slavery until there shall not be a slave in America, and until the African is elevated to a social and political equality with the white man." Equating Lincoln's party with the abolitionists who had allegedly plotted the destruction of slavery by the hand of black insurrectionists, Toombs asserted: "Hitherto they have carried on this warfare by State action, by individual action, . . . by the incendiary's torch and the poisoned bowl." But, warned the senator, after Lincoln's inauguration, there would be nothing to prevent them from realizing their goal of destroying slavery.[45]

41. Anonymous letter of October 22, 1860, in Charleston *Mercury,* November 3, 1860.

42. Scarborough, ed., *The Diary of Edmund Ruffin,* 1:463–464.

43. Mohr, *On the Threshold of Freedom,* 20.

44. William W. Freehling and Craig M. Simpson, eds., *Secession Debated: Georgia's Showdown in 1860* (New York, 1992), xi–xii; Mohr, *On the Threshold of Freedom,* 41.

45. Quoted in William E. Gienapp, ed., *The Civil War and Reconstruction: A Documentary Col-*

Thomas R. R. Cobb was more graphic when he solemnly asked his colleagues to:

> [r]ecur with me to the parting moment when you left your firesides, to attend upon your public duties at the Capitol. Remember the trembling hand of a loved wife, as she whispered her fears from the incendiary and the assassin. Recall the look of indefinable dread with which the little daughter inquired when your returning steps should be heard. And if there be manhood in you, tell me if this is the domestic tranquility which this "glorious Union" has achieved. Notice the anxious look when the traveling pedlar lingers too long in conversation at the door with the servant who turns the bolt—the watchful gaze when the slave tarries too long with the wandering artist who professes merely to furnish him with a picture—the suspicion aroused by a Northern man conversing in private with the most faithful of your negroes, and tell me if peace and tranquility are the heritage which this Union has brought to your firesides. Take up your daily papers, and see reports of insurrections in every direction. Hear the telegram read which announces another John Brown raid.[46]

Cobb said he was confident that a great majority of the South's slaves were loyal. "But a discontented few here and there, will become the incendiary or the poisoner, when instigated by the unscrupulous emissaries of Northern Abolitionists, and you and I cannot say but that your home or your family may be the first to greet your returning footsteps in ashes or in death.—What has given impulse to these fears, and aid and comfort to those outbreaks now, but the success of the Black Republicans—the election of Abraham Lincoln!"[47]

Even as they toiled to achieve the secession of their own states, disunionists of the Lower South also worked to convince the political leaders and voters of other slave states—especially those in the border region—of the dangers they faced, once a Republican administration had gained power. Five states—Mississippi, Alabama, South Carolina, Georgia, and Louisiana—dispatched "commissioners" to the other slave states on missions to persuade their leaders and citizens that a terrible fate awaited them under a Lincoln administration

---

lection (New York, 2001), 57–58.

46. Allen D. Candler, comp., *The Confederate Records of the State of Georgia*, 5 vols. (Atlanta, 1909–1911), 1:163–164. This speech may also be found in Freehling and Simpson, eds., *Secession Debated*, 11–12, and Mohr, *On the Threshold of Freedom*, 41–42.

47. Candler, comp., *The Confederate Records of the State of Georgia*, 1:164.

and that their only hope was to join their brethren of the Deep South in creating a southern confederacy. In all, some forty-two commissioners, whom historian Charles Dew has dubbed "Apostles of Disunion," combed the South, preaching their gospel to whomever would listen. They delivered their "sermons" in a variety of forums, including state legislatures, secession conventions, public meetings, and even on street corners.[48]

Regardless of the venue available to them, the missionaries of secession preached their message with great fervor. Their apocalyptic depictions of the fate that awaited the South under a Republican administration must have chilled the hearts of those southerners who had heard so much recently of the Texas Troubles. For example, addressing a large gathering in Baltimore, Mississippi judge Alexander Hamilton Hardy predicted that, under Lincoln, Republican appointees in the slave states would "excite the slave to cut the throat of his master." The only way to avoid widespread slave insurrections was by immediate secession.[49]

If neither legislatures nor secession conventions were in session, the commissioners often made their case in letters to the governors. Such was the case when Stephen Fowler Hale, of Alabama, wrote to Kentucky's governor, Beriah McGoffin. In a lengthy missive, Hale recounted all the wrongs against the South allegedly committed by the North from the founding of the Republic until the election of Abraham Lincoln. Long-suffering southerners had patiently tolerated these violations of their rights, he said, but "recent events" required the South to take drastic action in its own defense. First, John Brown's raid on Virginia, "slaughtering her citizens" and attempting to excite "servile insurrection among her slave population. . . . But the abolitionist fanatics did not cease their assault upon slavery after Harpers Ferry." "During the past summer," Hale continued, "the abolition incendiary has lit up the prairies of Texas, fired the dwellings of the inhabitants, burned down whole towns, and laid poison for her citizens, thus literally executing the terrible denunciations of fanaticism against the slave-holder, 'Alarm to their sleep, fire to their dwellings, and poison to their food.'"[50]

While the commissioners worked the other slave states and while the legislatures of the Lower South went about the business of laying the groundwork for secession, the eyes of the nation focused on Washington. The thirty-sixth

48. Charles B. Dew, *Apostles of Disunion: Southern Secession Commissioners and the Causes of the Civil War* (Charlottesville, Va., 2001), 1–21.

49. Ibid., 33–34.

50. Ibid., 94–95.

Congress convened for its second session on December 3, and when its members took their seats to hear President Buchanan's opening address, the unionists among them listened anxiously for some indication that the nation's chief executive would use his powers to discourage wavering slave states of the Lower South from following rash South Carolina, which everyone agreed would surely secede. The friends of the Union found little to cheer in the president's speech. They should not have been surprised. Buchanan, the "doughface" Democrat from Pennsylvania, had demonstrated throughout his presidency his belief that sectional peace could be maintained only by being concessionary to the South.

Although he now reaffirmed his devotion to the Union and denied that a southern state had the constitutional right to secede, Buchanan made it clear that he would not attempt to prevent a state from taking such action. Moreover, in analyzing the reasons why the Union was in jeopardy, he placed the blame not on the effort to exclude slavery from the territories, or even the attempts by some northern states to subvert the Fugitive Slave Law, but upon the "incessant and violent agitation of the slavery question throughout the North for the last quarter of a century." This ceaseless bombardment had "produced its malign influence on the slaves" and had "inspired them with vague notions of freedom. Hence a sense of security no longer exists around the family altar. This feeling of peace at home has given place to apprehensions of servile insurrections." Evoking imagery not unlike that of T. R. R. Cobb in the Georgia debates, Buchanan said: "Many a matron throughout the South retires at night in dread of what may befall herself and her children before morning. Should this apprehension of domestic danger, whether real or imaginary, extend and intensify itself, until it pervade the masses of the southern people, then disunion will become inevitable." The president went on to state his belief that the fear of insurrection had not yet become all-pervasive in the slave states, and he expressed his hope that it would not.[51]

Unfortunately, Buchanan was wrong, at least so far as the Lower South was concerned. The Texas Troubles had spread a malaise over much of the region and had greatly increased the likelihood that the cotton states would secede. Lincoln's election was decisive, since the party that allegedly had sponsored the insurrectionary conspiracies would now occupy the White House. On the eve of the presidential election, after it had become clear that Lincoln's election was inevitable, a Mississippi newspaper said that "the minds of the people are

51. James D. Richardson, comp., *Compilation of the Messages and Papers of the Presidents, 1789–1897*, 10 vols. (Washington, D.C., 1897), 5:628–637.

aroused to a pitch of excitement probably unparalleled in the history of the country."[52]

After listening to Buchanan's speech, Congress began its efforts to find a formula for a compromise that would save the Union. Early in the session, southern members clearly reflected the anxieties of their constituents. This was especially true in the Senate, where a testy debate broke out over the establishment of the Committee of Thirteen to consider possible compromise measures. During the course of the debate, lengthy references to the alleged abolitionist slave conspiracy, together with charges of Republican involvement made by southern senators and the incredulous and indignant reactions by their counterparts across the aisle, highlighted and dramatized the credibility gap that had developed between the sections. Several southern solons alluded to the insurrectionary allegations as evidence that the Republicans were planning to rid the nation of slavery, by violent means if necessary.[53]

Senator Louis T. Wigfall of Marshall, Texas, went to the greatest lengths in detailing the alleged conspiracy in the Lone Star State. Solemnly recounting his own harrowing experience of the previous summer, Wigfall said: "I returned home, sir, after the fatigues of the last session; I went there for peace and for quiet and consultation with my neighbors; and from the day I reached my home until I left—between six weeks and two months—there was a guard of twenty-four men every night in a small village of between two and three thousand inhabitants. I myself had to shoulder my gun, and stand guard." After describing the fear that had gripped his own community and state, the senator went on to blame the Republican party for the outrages in Texas, even alleging at one point that Senator William H. Seward had alerted "his John-Brown, Wide-Awake Praetorians" to remain organized following the election so that the fruits of victory could be ensured. "Over half million of men uniformed and drilled, and the purpose of their organization to sweep the country in which I live with fire and sword." At this point, with Wigfall in mid-sentence, Seward interrupted, strongly denying that he had said any such thing. Wigfall politely accepted the offended senator's denial but did not retract his main point that somehow the Republicans and their ancillary organizations were involved in a plot to destroy the South. "I would not misrepresent him [Seward]. But that this praetorian band is organized; that its members do undergo military drill;

52. Natchez (Miss.) *Daily Free Trader*, November 2, 1860.

53. For example, see the speeches of Robert Toombs and Thomas L. Clingman, *Congressional Globe*, 36th Cong., 2nd Sess., 4, 267.

that it is a military organization, no man who has looked upon them, *as I did this last summer,* and heard their regular military tramp, does or can doubt."[54]

Republican senator Benjamin Wade, like Seward, reacted with disbelief to the charges of Republican involvement in a plot to devastate Texas. Saying that he had listened patiently to the complaints of his southern colleagues, the Ohioan confessed, "I am now totally unable to understand precisely what it is of which they complain." He insisted that the Republicans had never done harm to the South, and he suggested that the southerners' fears over possible future abuses were "mere apprehensions—a bare suspicion; arising, I fear, out of their unwarrantable prejudices, and nothing else." Then he specifically addressed the question of insurrectionary violence to which Wigfall and others had alluded:

> Why, sir, I can hardly take up a paper—and I rely, too, upon southern papers—which does not give an account of the cruel treatment of some man who is traveling for pleasure or business in your quarter; and the lightest thing you do is to visit him with a vigilance committee, and compel him to return: "We give you so long to make your way out of our coast." "What is the accusation?" "Why, sir, you are from Ohio." They do not inquire what party he belongs to, or what standard he has followed. I say this is the case, if I may rely on the statements of your own papers; and many of these outrages occur under circumstances of cruelty that would disgrace a savage; and we have no security now in traveling in nearly one half of the Union, and especially the gulf States of this Confederacy. I care not what a man's character may be; he may be perfectly innocent of every charge; he may be a man who never has violated any law under heaven; and yet if he goes down into those States, and it is ascertained that he is from the North, and especially if he differs from them in the exercise of his political rights, if he has voted for Lincoln instead of for somebody else, it is a mortal offense, punishable by indignity, by tar and feathers, by stripes, and even by death; and yet you, whose constituents are guilty of all these things, can stand forth, and accuse us of being unfaithful to the Constitution of the United States! Gentlemen had better look at home.[55]

Answering the charge by southern fire-eaters like Wigfall and many southern newspapers that all members of his party were "John Brown men," Wade

54. Ibid., 74–75 (italics in the original).
55. Ibid., 99–100.

said the encouragement of racial violence in the South was "a thing no Republican ever dreamed of or ever thought about." Still, in spite of denials by all of the Republican party's leaders, the exasperated Ohioan continued, the southerners still believed the irresponsible charges. "No doubt they believe it because of a terrible excitement and reign of terror that prevails there. No doubt, they think so, but it arises from false information, or the want of information—that is all. Their prejudices have been appealed to until they have become uncontrolled and incontrollable."[56]

Senator Alfred O. P. Nicholson of Tennessee replied that Wade was correct in stating that there was a "deep and wide-spread conviction that the Republican party is the mortal enemy of the South, of the institutions and rights of the South." However, he denied that this conviction rested upon misapprehension or misinformation about that party's intentions, arguing instead that it was based upon "stubborn facts," derived from "authentic and reliable sources." Although he did not explicitly charge that the Republicans had actually supported the Brown raid or the recent "insurrection plot" in the South, Nicholson argued that Wade's party nevertheless represented social opinions that, if applied, would lead to "our final destruction." Since Republicans allegedly regarded slavery as a "social, moral, and political evil," said the Tennessee senator, they would undoubtedly use their control of the government, once gained, to bring about the ultimate destruction of the South's peculiar institution. Even if they did not endorse violence in the pursuit of their goal, what assurance could southern families take, knowing that "some misguided fanatic or monomaniac, who, feeling restive and unwilling to await the slow process of the Republican mode of liberating the slaves, chooses to resort to the torch and to insurrection? . . . Repose is the great object desired by the South."[57]

Southern radicals were not the only members of Congress to accept as true the allegations that Republicans had instigated race violence in the South. On December 10, amid debate on proposed concessions that might prevent the southern states from seceding, Jefferson Davis, perhaps the most moderate senator from the "Gulf squadron," criticized the proposals because they attacked the symptom, not the disease. "What though all the 'personal liberty bills' were repealed," he asked; "would that secure our rights? Would that give us the Union our fathers made? Would that renew good offices, or restrain raids and incendiarism, or prevent schools being founded to prepare missionaries to go into lands where they are to sow the seeds of insurrection, and, wearing the

56. Ibid., 104.
57. Ibid., 184–187.

livery of heaven, to serve the Devil by poisoning wells and burning towns?" No permanent remedy could be found unless there was a "mutual affection" between the people of the free and slave states, and if that no longer existed, then the South should secede, "instead of attempting to preserve a forced and fruitless Union." The Founding Fathers had created the Union "for domestic tranquility," Davis said, "not to organize within one State lawless bands to commit raids on another. . . . Who would keep a flower which had lost its beauty and its fragrance, and in their stead had formed a seed-vessel containing the deadliest poison?"[58]

Texas congressman John H. Reagan had already completed his remarkable metamorphosis from staunch unionist in 1859 to secessionist before the session of Congress began. During the panic he had stated his belief that there was indeed an abolitionist conspiracy and had told his brother about his participation in a vigilance meeting in Palestine. Nearer the election he demonstrated the effect of the Texas Troubles on his political position in a letter to George W. Paschal, with whose unionist views he had formerly agreed. On October 31 he wrote: "The success of the Republican doctrines would liberate among us this large number of negroes [and] involve us inevitably in a war of the races, which would result in the murder of many of the white race of all ages and of both sexes, and in the burning and destruction of a large amount of property, and the ultimate extinction of the negroe race among us."[59] Now, in a speech before the House, the one-time defender of the Union blamed the South's feeling of insecurity upon the alleged conspiracy in his state. Saying that no fewer than a dozen towns in his district lay in ashes and that the poisoning of wells was only prevented "by information, which came to light before the plan could be carried into execution," Reagan stopped just short of directly implicating the party of Lincoln in the affair. He nevertheless asserted, "These things . . . were the results of abolition teachings; a part of the irrepressible conflict; a part of the legitimate fruits of Republicanism."[60]

Oddly, in spite of the vicious comments made about him by the southern

58. Ibid., 29.

59. John H. Reagan, Palestine, to George W. Paschal, Austin, October 19, 1860, quoted in Dallas *Herald*, October 31, 1860. Reagan expressed a similar opinion in a letter of October 20, 1860, to Roger Q. Mills of Corsicana; see John H. Reagan Papers, Barker Texas History Center Archives, University of Texas, Austin, Texas.

60. *Congressional Globe*, 36th Cong., 2nd Sess., 393. Reagan had to know that the number of towns he cited was a wild exaggeration and that no poison had ever been discovered, yet like the ultras whom he had once disdained, he either closed his eyes to the facts or simply chose to ignore them.

rights press and fire-eaters in Congress, Lincoln seems not to have understood the extent of the South's hatred and distrust. There is no direct mention of the slave panic in his private papers or public utterances, but in a letter to Alexander H. Stephens, the Georgia unionist, the president-elect showed how out of touch he was with the southerners' hostile view of his impending presidency. Answering a letter of Stephens's that apparently had informed the president-elect of the southerners' fear that after assuming office he would take direct action against the South and its peculiar institution, Lincoln seemed incredulous: "Do the people of the South really entertain fears that a Republican administration would, *directly,* or *indirectly,* interfere with their slaves, or with them, about their slaves?" If so, he wrote, there was no cause to fear—the South would be in no more danger under his administration than they had been under George Washington's.[61]

Lincoln believed that the devotion to the Union of men like Stephens was much stronger than it actually was. After all, the president-elect had given public assurances to the South that he would not interfere with slavery where it legally existed and was even willing to support a proposed constitutional amendment that would guarantee his promise to dubious southerners. But what Lincoln failed to understand was that his offer fell upon deaf ears. Indeed, most southern newspapers did not bother reporting it. Editors and fire-eating politicians had waged their campaign to demonize the Illinois Republican ever since his nomination for president, and by the time of his election they had largely succeeded in making him synonymous in the Lower South with the "John Brownites" who had recently ravaged Texas.

Yet, curiously, Lincoln's self-delusion persisted, even after the Lower South had seceded. His naive misreading of the Deep South's mindset was succinctly demonstrated in the conclusion of his inaugural address, when he confidently said: "We are not enemies but friends. We must not be enemies. Though passion may have strained, it must not break our bonds of affection. The mystic chords of memory, stretching from every battle-field, and patriot grave, to every living heart and hearthstone, all over this broad land, will yet swell the chorus of the Union, when again touched, as surely they will be, by the better angels of our nature."[62]

By the time Lincoln was inaugurated, however, the "mystic chords of memory" had become a cacophonous dissonance to the ears of Americans living

61. Abraham Lincoln, Springfield, Ill., to Alexander H. Stephens, December 22, 1860, in *Abraham Lincoln: His Speeches and Writings,* ed. Roy P. Basler (New York, 1946), 576–568.

62. Roy P. Basler, ed., *Collected Works of Abraham Lincoln* (New Brunswick, N.J., 1953), 4:271.

in the Deep South. Indeed, well before the new president's eloquent address, events had already made Lincoln's earlier efforts to reassure southerners, as well as all the oratory in Congress, irrelevant. South Carolina had seceded on December 20, and five other states of the Lower South joined the Palmetto State in forming the Confederacy on February 4, 1861. Texas added a seventh star to the Confederate flag on March 2, after its voters ratified that state's secession ordinance. The eight remaining slave states hung in the balance until the bombardment of Fort Sumter forced them to choose allegiances. Four of those—Virginia, North Carolina, Tennessee, and Arkansas—would join the Confederacy, while Maryland, Delaware, Kentucky, and Missouri would remain in the Union.[63]

Although the secession ordinances generally were brief documents that did not spell out reasons for leaving the Union, several state conventions also wrote declarations explaining why separation from the United States was necessary. These documents invariably revealed a deep-seated fear that the North was committed to a policy that would destroy the South's way of life. As proof they cited the alleged attempts of abolitionists to burn and poison during the previous summer. These frightful events had happened under an administration friendly to the South. Since the secessionists believed that the Republicans were closely allied with those who had conspired to induce insurrections in the slave states, the occupation of the White House by Abraham Lincoln could only mean that abolitionist invasions would increase in frequency and intensity in the future.

South Carolina's convention complained that the northern states "have permitted open establishment among them of societies, whose avowed object is to disturb the peace and to eloign the property of the citizens of other States." The organizations had helped "thousands of our slaves" to escape to freedom, "and those who remain have been incited by emissaries, books and pictures to servile insurrection." But those acts were just a taste of that which awaited the South if it should accept Republican control of the White House, the South Carolinians argued. "On the 4th of March next, this party will take possession of the Government. It has announced . . . that a war must be waged against slavery until it shall cease throughout the United States."[64]

63. The largely nonslaveholding region of northwestern Virginia refused to accept that state's decision to secede. After months of political wrangling and after a Federal force under George B. McClellan had defeated Confederate attempts to occupy the area by military action, the West Virginians voted, on October 24, 1861, to separate from the Old Dominion. After its citizens agreed to abolish slavery, West Virginia was admitted to the Union on June 20, 1863 (McPherson, *Battle Cry of Freedom*, 297–304).

64. Quoted in John A. May and Joan R. Faunt, *South Carolina Secedes* (Columbia, S.C., 1960), 80–81.

Georgia charged that the abolitionists had for years worked "to subvert our institutions and to excite insurrection and servile war among us. They have sent emissaries among us for the accomplishment of these purposes." Moreover, "a majority" of leading Republicans, "the same men who are now proposed as our rulers," had sanctioned these efforts.[65]

Mississippi's state convention alleged that the Republican party "advocates negro equality, socially and politically, and promotes insurrection and incendiarism in our midst" to achieve its objective, which was: "to subvert our society and subject us not only to the loss of our property but the destruction of ourselves, our wives, and our children, and the desolation of our homes, our altars, and our firesides." To achieve its objective, that party had formed "associations" to carry out its schemes, "invaded a state," and lauded those who had applied "flames to our dwellings, and the weapons of destruction to our lives." Therefore, only one honorable choice was left to the Magnolia State: "To avoid these evils we resume the powers which our fathers delegated to the Government of the United States, and henceforth will seek new safeguards for our liberty, equality, security, and tranquility."[66]

Had there been no slave panic in 1860 it is likely that the course of secession at least would have been altered, although the end result might have been the same. The one state that definitely would *not* have acted differently was South Carolina, which already was determined to leave the Union upon the election of Lincoln. Indeed, immediately upon learning the result, that state's legislature voted to call a secession convention. When that convention met on December 20, it voted 169–0 to dissolve the states' ties to the Union. No one was surprised. Upon announcement of the vote, the Charleston *Mercury* took only five minutes to trumpet the news in an "extra."[67] It is probable that Florida and Mississippi would have followed the Palmetto State's example, just as they did in actuality. Beyond those states, however, the slave panic looms large as the key provocation that pushed the cause of secession over the top.

Understandably, Texas was the most immediately affected of the other Gulf States. Unionist candidates had virtually swept the Lone Star State in August 1859; a year and a half later the state would vote to secede by a three-to-one

65. U.S. War Department, comp., *War of the Rebellion: A Compilation of the Official Records of the Union and Confederate Armies* (Washington, D.C., 1880–1901), Ser. IV, 1:85.

66. State of Mississippi, *Journal of the State Convention, and Ordinances and Resolutions Adopted in January, 1861* (Jackson, Miss., 1861), 87–88. See also U.S. War Department, comp., *War of the Rebellion*, Ser. IV, 1:85.

67. Reynolds, *Editors Make War*, 161.

margin. Although other concerns aided the secessionists in Texas, notably the breakup of the national Democratic party and the federal government's failure to deal effectively with Indian raids on the frontier and banditry on the Mexican border, the slave panic was by far the dominant issue in the minds of the voters in the Lone Star State.[68] Listing the reasons for passing the secession ordinance, the convention demonstrated the importance that it attached to the alleged plot when it said: "They [the abolitionists] have, through the mails and hired emmissaries, sent seditious pamphlets and papers amongst us to stir up servile insurrection and bring blood and carnage to our firesides. They have sent hired emissaries among us to burn our towns and distribute arms and poison to our slaves for the same purpose."[69]

Texas aside, it is easy to forget that several states of the Deep South seceded only after fiercely contested battles in the legislatures and secession conventions. The key states of Louisiana, Alabama, and Georgia saw significant opposition to secession. John Bell and Stephen A. Douglas combined polled more votes than Breckinridge in both Louisiana and Georgia, and in Alabama the southern rights Democrat edged the other two candidates by only eight thousand votes. Moreover, although secessionists won majorities in the conventions of all three states, the vote for delegates was significantly lighter in each case than it had been in the recent presidential election, indicating that many unionists may have stayed at home.[70]

There is no question that the great slave panic of 1860 had a dramatic impact upon Louisiana, Alabama, and Georgia. Not only did secessionist editors and politicians in these key states use the Texas Troubles to great effect, but each one had its own smaller panic that served to dramatize and make even more immediate the danger of submitting to a Republican president. The avalanche of fear and emotion generally cowed those in the Lower South who wanted to preserve the Union or at least delay its destruction. Indeed, many conservatives succumbed to the horror stories told so fervently by the plot's publicists. Even though they often doubted the fearful tales, they seemed to have subscribed to the adage: where there is much smoke, there must be a little fire. Those who challenged outright the wild accounts of abolitionists running amok risked being branded as traitors who would put their own people in harm's way by counseling

68. Buenger, *Secession and the Union in Texas*, 37–39, 55–58, 75–77.

69. "A Declaration of the Causes which Impel the State of Texas to Secede from the Federal Union," in *Journal of the Secession Convention of Texas, 1861*, ed. Ernest W. Winkler (Austin, 1912), 64.

70. For a succinct survey of the post-election secession campaigns in the Lower South, see Craven, *The Growth of Southern Nationalism*, 349–390.

submission to an incendiary "Black Republican" president. Few could withstand such pressure.

Suppose only Mississippi and Florida had immediately followed South Carolina out of the Union. What then might have happened? First, it is unlikely that these three noncontiguous states could have formed a viable Confederacy; they would surely have waited until other states could be persuaded to join them. This would have bought time for the new administration, and time was its most pressing need. The cooperationists of the Deep South argued that Lincoln had been constitutionally elected and should be allowed to demonstrate that his administration would not harm the South or its peculiar institution. Given the caution with which Lincoln approached the South in general—and South Carolina in particular—after his inauguration, it is likely that he would have been even more circumspect had only three states initially seceded. If this were the case, the conservative position would have been vindicated, and it is even possible that the crisis would have passed without its bloody denouement.

Of course, any scenario outside the actual chain of events may be dismissed as groundless speculation. Even without a Confederate government to give it support, South Carolina undoubtedly would have tried to precipitate a crisis over Fort Sumter, in the hope of bringing all the slave states to its side. Without a central government to support it, however, the Palmetto State's task would have been more difficult. Lincoln could more readily have agreed to abandon the fort, as his cabinet wanted him to do anyway. Such a step would have sealed South Carolina's isolation and would have had the additional salutary effect of making Lincoln appear less threatening to the other slave states. In time, the few states that had seceded would have been forced by economic and political exigencies to make an accommodation with the federal government that would have brought them back into the Union.

This hypothesis admittedly accords well with the old-fashioned view that the Civil War was avoidable. Two generations ago, the "revisionists" argued that the Civil War was precipitated by a failure of leadership on both sides. Generally speaking, they asserted that northern and southern demagogues practiced the politics of extremism, magnifying real sectional differences and distorting events and issues for the purpose of inflaming the public and advancing their own agendas. After World War II, the revisionist argument faded from popularity as most Civil War historians generally came to accept the view that America's greatest conflict had arisen from fundamentally divisive issues.

While conceding that irresponsible extremists had deliberately stirred emotions to the breaking point, most scholars of the late twentieth century contended that it was the issues themselves, not the "heat" which they generated, that caused the war. Looked at in this way, even if the emotional frenzy whipped up by southern fire-eaters in the aftermath of the Texas fires were based upon false reports, it nevertheless reflected an accurate perception that the Republicans posed a very real threat to slavery in the long run. Thus the hobgoblins in the fevered southern mind represented a metaphor for what *could* happen in the future. Steven A. Channing neatly summed up this view: "Secession was the product of logical reasoning within a framework of irrational perception."[71] Even if Lincoln's inauguration would have had no immediate effect upon slavery, the disapproval by his party of the peculiar institution—clearly shown in the rhetoric of Republican leaders and in their determination to keep slavery from spreading—portended ultimate extinction for the South's labor system. From the white southerners' perspective, emancipation would mean the loss of social and economic control of blacks, and this, in turn, would not only wreck the southern economy, but would inevitably lead to a bloody race war. In effect, the Texas Troubles constituted a preview of what such a struggle might entail.

The view that southerners were right in assuming an aggressive Republican action against slavery, however, ignores both the racial and constitutional conservatism of that political party and of the North in general. Moreover, for all their differences, the southern and northern wings of the Democratic party would have continued to act as a powerful deterrent to any anti-slavery action by the Republicans. In addition, the Supreme Court, with its strong Democratic majority, promised to act as a bulwark in the defense of southern rights for some time to come. Although slavery was becoming a worldwide anachronism, its end would have come slowly in America, and it may be assumed that the longer a resolution of the problem was deferred, the less would be the likelihood that it had to be achieved through bloody conflict.

Even without the Texas Troubles of 1860, of course, sectional hatred and fear would have remained on both sides, and it is impossible to say that secession and war would not have occurred at some future point. But as C. Vann Woodward has reminded us, southerners have never been much influenced by abstractions.[72] Therefore, a fear of what the Republicans *might* do at some point in the distant future was insufficient to induce most of them to leave the Union of their fathers. The slave insurrection panic of 1860 provided a needed concrete example of the horrors that allegedly awaited the South under a Republican administration, and this gave the secessionists of the Lower South the

71. Steven A. Channing, *Crisis of Fear: Secession in South Carolina* (New York, 1964), 286.
72. Woodward, *The Burden of Southern History*, 22–24.

momentum they needed to put their cause over the top. Undoubtedly, as they celebrated their victory, they failed to appreciate the supreme irony of their success: their triumph helped seal the doom of the social system they thought they were saving.

CONCLUSIONS OF A MAD PEOPLE

On a July weekend in 1981 some two hundred descendants of Cato Miller, one of the three blacks hanged for allegedly setting the Dallas fire of 1860, met to commemorate the 121st anniversary of their ancestor's death. The object, according to the organizer of the meeting, was to keep alive awareness of the event and make sure future generations of the family would not forget.[1]

It was not just Cato Miller's descendants who needed reminding. Few Dallasites knew of the dramatic fire that led to the great panic of 1860, which set the stage for the secession of Texas, as well as six other states of the Lower South. In the late 1980s, in an effort to make the community more aware of the story, a group of Dallas citizens organized a "Committee for the Dallas Fire of 1860." The alleged incendiary plot and the hanging of the three blacks "has been talked about in a whisper," said one member of the multi-racial committee, and the group intended to see that the episode received the attention it deserved. Another committee member, a professor at Southern Methodist University, said: "We want to remember the deaths of these persons who were involved in the struggle for justice and the revolutionary spirit of the 1860s."[2] In conjunction with the Southern Christian Leadership Conference, the committee was able to secure passage by the Dallas City Council of a resolution recognizing that "Dallas was burned in an alleged 'slave uprising'" and noting the hanging of the three slaves "for their alleged part in setting fire to the city." The committee was less successful in its effort to place a state historical marker at the location of the hangings. The marker chairwoman reportedly thought such a

1. Dallas *Times Herald,* July 12, 1981.
2. Ibid., February 3, 1988.

commemoration might have a provocative effect upon the local citizenry and rejected the committee's application, which she considered "inflammatory."[3]

The prevailing public ignorance of the Dallas fire and its tragic repercussions probably stemmed from the failure of most Texas historians to deal with it. It may have been the "provocative" potential of the Texas Troubles that led many early historians of the period simply to leave the story out of their histories of the state.[4] Even those who wrote specifically about Dallas's past gave short shrift to the issue. For example, in his history of Dallas County, John H. Cochran said only that the fire destroyed Dallas and was "believed at the time to have been of incendiary origin." Philip Lindsley in his history of Dallas mentioned "the great fire of July 8, 1860," but he said nothing about its causes or an alleged abolitionist conspiracy.[5]

The fact is, the Texas slave panic of 1860 has posed problems for most of the historians who have dealt with it. In large measure this has been due to the adamant insistence of contemporary southern rights papers and politicians that there was indeed an abolitionist conspiracy and the equally strong-willed denials by their unionist opponents. An abundance of evidence and testimony on both sides of the argument has made it difficult for scholars to distinguish truth from fiction on the question of whether there actually was a plot. Perhaps it was for this reason that the most prominent national and southern historians who wrote about the Civil War era in the early to mid-twentieth century did not even mention the Texas slave insurrection panic.[6] Of all the early scholars

3. Karen Ray, "The Untold Story," *Dallas Life Magazine, Dallas Morning News,* July 8, 1990, 8–15.

4. For example, see Dudley G. Wooten, *A Complete History of Texas for Schools, Colleges and General Use* (Dallas, 1899); Louis J. Wortham, *A History of Texas, from Wilderness to Commonwealth,* 5 vols. (Fort Worth, Tex., 1924); Clarence Wharton, *History of Texas* (Dallas, 1935); Lewis W. Newton and Herbert P. Gambrell, *A Social and Political History of Texas* (Dallas, 1932); Frank X. Tolbert, *An Informal History of Texas, from Cabeza de Vaca to Temple Houston* (New York, 1961); Ralph W. Steen, *History of Texas* (Austin, 1939).

5. John H. Cochran, *Dallas County: A Record of Its Pioneers and Progress* (Dallas, 1928), 131; Philip Lindsley, *A History of Greater Dallas and Vicinity,* 2 vols. (Chicago, 1909). See also Frank M. Cockrell, *History of Early Dallas* (Chicago, 1944); George H. Santerre, *Dallas' First Hundred Years, 1856–1956* (Dallas, 1956).

6. For examples, see James Ford Rhodes, *History of the United States from the Compromise of 1850,* 9 vols. (New York, 1908–1928); James G. Randall and David H. Donald, *The Civil War and Reconstruction,* 2nd ed. (Lexington, Mass., 1969); Dwight L. Dumond, *The Secession Movement, 1860–1861* (New York, 1931); Bruce Catton, *The Centennial History of the Civil War,* vol. 1, *The Coming Fury,* 3 vols. (Garden City, N.Y., 1961); Avery O. Craven, *The Coming of the Civil War, 1848–1861,* rev. ed. (Chicago, 1957); Craven, *The Growth of Southern Nationalism;* Emerson D. Fite, *The Presidential Campaign of 1860* (New York, 1911); Stampp, *The Peculiar Institution.* Craven and Fite each devote considerable space to John Brown and his significance for the growth of southern national-

who studied the important events leading up to the Civil War, only Ollinger Crenshaw included a detailed analysis of the slave panic and its impact on the secession movement. Still, although his book, *The Slave States in the Presidential Election of 1860,* includes a critical and well-balanced account, he made no judgment as to whether the allegations of an abolitionist conspiracy had merit.[7]

Historians of the secession movement in Texas sometimes treated the issue of the supposed insurrection plot in a gingerly fashion. The distinguished scholar Charles W. Ramsdell, for example, wrote that the panic was an important reason for the triumph of secessionism in Texas; however, he begged the question of whether there was an abolitionist conspiracy, saying, "How much of fact and how much of invention were in the stories that circulated, it is impossible now to know and it is not worth while to ask."[8] Some hedged their conclusions with qualifying words that tended to soften their opinions. Ernest Wallace said the fires that greatly agitated Texans during the presidential campaign "were presumably the work of abolitionists," but he failed to offer an opinion on the validity of the presumption.[9]

---

ism, but neither scholar mentions the slave insurrection panic. Stampp curiously writes about the panic in Texas's Colorado County, in 1856, which he calls a "well authenticated conspiracy," but although he mentions the alleged plot of October 1860 in eastern North Carolina, which he calls "one of the last ante-bellum slave conspiracies," he says nothing at all about the more significant Texas Troubles of 1860, nor does he mention the other serious panics that broke out that summer in Mississippi, Alabama, and Georgia. Allan Nevins devoted two pages of his massive four-volume study of the Civil War to the slave panic, and concluded that there was no valid evidence to support the conspiracy theory, but he offered no documentation to support his view, and he erred in saying that "no modern Texas historian credits the wild rumors of the time" (Nevins, *The Emergence of Lincoln,* 2:306–308). In his important examination of vigilante movements in America, Richard Maxwell Brown included a table showing the eleven "Deadliest Vigilante Movements," but he omitted the Texas vigilante movement of 1860, even though it caused many more deaths than some of those he listed. See Brown, "The American Vigilante Tradition," 176. He repeated the oversight in his essay "The History of Vigilantism in America," in *Vigilante Politics,* ed. H. Jon Rosenbaum and Peter C. Sederberg (Philadelphia, 1976), 83–84. Other histories of the period that also have omitted the Texas slave insurrection panic from their studies are: Emory Thomas, *The American War and Peace, 1860–1877* (Englewood Cliffs, N.J., 1973), and David Potter, *The Impending Crisis, 1848–1861* (New York, 1976). Potter does include a short paragraph recognizing that there were reports of "dark conspiracies for slave revolts," but he does not discuss them, nor does he specifically mention the Texas Troubles.

7. Crenshaw, *The Slave States in the Presidential Election of 1860,* 92–111. See also Ollinger Crenshaw's "The Psychological Background of the Election of 1860 in the South," *North Carolina Historical Review* 19 (July 1942): 260–279.

8. Ramsdell, "The Frontier and Secession," 76.

9. Ernest Wallace, *Texas in Turmoil, 1849–1875* (Austin, 1965), 56.

Rupert N. Richardson, in a work that served for many years as the standard college textbook in Texas history, wrote: "Severe fires, apparently of incendiary origin," occurred in a number of Texas towns. The ensuing stories of slave uprisings, however, were "generally exaggerated if not altogether unfounded," and, he said, the tales of "wholesale poisonings . . . seem to have been almost wholly imaginary." Twenty years later, in his study of the frontier, Richardson seemed to have reconsidered his earlier opinion that incendiaries had even "apparently" been at work in the Lone Star State during the summer of 1860. He wrote that it was unlikely that abolitionists had caused the fires: "A more plausible explanation is that the fires, which flecked the map of Texas, started in the hot Texas summer through the spontaneous combustion of phosphorous matches, which were just at this time being extensively stocked by stores."[10] Still, in assessing the validity of the allegations of insurrectionary activity, the most recent edition of Richardson's textbook retained, almost verbatim, the phraseology of fifty years earlier, saying that the stories were "exaggerated if not wholly unfounded."[11]

T. R. Fehrenbach, whose book *Lone Star: A History of Texas and the Texans* replaced Richardson's text in many college classrooms, also dismissed the insurrectionary stories as false, but devoted only one of his 710 pages to that topic, and he neither bothered to explain the reasons for his conclusion nor provided documentation supporting it.[12]

Other Texas scholars embraced the conspiracy theory without equivocation. For example, Ben H. Procter, the biographer of John H. Reagan, accepted the conclusions of his subject when he wrote, "a wave of destructive fires, poisonings, and abortive slave insurrections—believed to be instigated by members of the Methodist Church North and by abolitionist agents, dedicated to wresting the western outpost of slavery from the South—terrified the people."[13] Eugene Hollon, the highly regarded historian of the Southwest, was even bolder, asserting, "The existence of an insurrection plot by abolitionist agents in Texas in 1860 is well supported by documentary evidence." He went on to explain that the plot failed only because it was poorly implemented and "covered too much territory."[14]

10. Rupert N. Richardson, *Texas, the Lone Star State* (New York, 1943), 244; Richardson, *The Frontier of Northwest Texas*, 223.

11. Rupert N. Richardson, Adrian Anderson, Cary D. Wintz, and Ernest Wallace, *Texas: The Lone Star State*, 9th edition (Upper Saddle River, N.J., 2005), 193.

12. T. R. Fehrenbach, *Lone Star: A History of Texas and the Texans* (Boulder, Colo.: Da Capo Press, 2000), 338.

13. Ben H. Procter, *Not Without Honor; The Life of John H. Reagan* (Austin, 1962), 118–119.

14. W. Eugene Hollon, *Frontier Violence; Another Look* (New York, 1974), 47.

Apparently it took little evidence to convince some scholars that arsonists had set the fires. An historian of the Henderson fire wrote, "It was caused by an incendiary, because it was not the first fire to take place in Texas during that year."[15] Another student of slave violence in the Lone Star State said, "It is inconceivable that there was nothing to the plot of 1860, because many slaves made similar confessions."[16]

Historians of American slave insurrections also have tended to accept the reports of the alleged abolitionist plot in Texas. Herbert Aptheker did admit that there was "exaggeration and distortion" in the reports. Specifically, he was skeptical of the many reports that "town after town" had burned and that "amazing quantities of poison" had turned up in the possession of slaves. Nevertheless, he stated, "It is not denied that conspiracies and outbreaks did occur [in Texas]," even though he conceded they had been embellished; moreover, he expressed no doubts whatsoever that insurrections occurred in the other southern states that summer.[17]

In his book, *Slave Insurrections in the United States, 1800–1865,* Joseph C. Carroll showed much less restraint than Aptheker. Sounding in tone and substance like the southern rights newspapers from which he drew most of his material, Carroll wrote: "Assisted by unscrupulous and fanatic whites, who called themselves Abolitionists, there was a well-laid plan of the slaves in the summer of 1860, for obtaining their freedom. Terror was spread through north Texas, Arkansas, Georgia, and portions of Alabama by the concerted efforts of the Negroes to destroy these regions by fire."[18]

Those who studied the Texas Troubles in greatest depth before the mid-1970s uniformly agreed that there was indeed an abolitionist-inspired insurrectionary plot. William W. White published the first of these detailed accounts in 1949. White concluded: "On the basis of the material studied thus far, it appears that a real plot of insurrection existed in 1860 in Texas. The plot, inspired by abolitionist agents, was inadequately organized and poorly executed due primarily to the vast extent of territory covered and to the scarcity of white leaders for carrying out the plan of actions."[19]

15. Winfrey, *A History of Rusk County, Texas,* 38–39.

16. Enda Junkins, "Slave Plots, Insurrections, and Acts of Violence in the State of Texas, 1828–1865" (Master's thesis, Baylor University, 1969), 83–84.

17. Aptheker, *American Slave Revolts,* 153, 353–357.

18. Carroll, *Slave Insurrections in the United States,* 195–199.

19. White, "The Texas Slave Insurrection of 1860," 285. For a less scholarly work that draws heavily upon White's article and presents the southern rights accounts of the alleged insurrection without contradiction, see David Stroud, *Flames and Vengeance: The East Texas Fires and the Presi-*

Wendell G. Addington also thought there had been a great slave uprising in 1860 and boldly asserted: "No other factor was more important in laying bare the impending doom of the slave system . . . than the tremendous upsurge of revolt in 1860 by the Negro people aided, in almost every case, by white allies." Although he admitted that "wild exaggeration" by the Texas press made it difficult to get a completely accurate picture, Addington averred: "Back of the exaggeration, however, can be discerned unmistakably an uprising of vast proportions against the slave system."[20]

Frank Smyrl, another student of Texas vigilantism, acknowledged the criticisms and denials of contemporary unionists; nevertheless, he concluded: "Yet the contention of the *Texas State Gazette* and other Democratic papers are based upon facts that are hard to ignore. There had indeed been a large number of fires in the state in a very short period, and separate confessions of Negroes and whites in different areas exposed very similar details of a supposed plot."[21]

Bill Ledbetter observed that most contemporary Texans believed the insurrection reports were accurate, "and no doubt many of them were. To think that only a few cases of Negro rebellion, arson or other forms of resistence [*sic*] occurred would be unrealistic." Elsewhere in the same article, the author wrote: "The series of insurrections and incendiary activities prior to the Black Republican's election was in all probability a part of an abolitionist plot, although it was poorly executed."[22]

During the last third of the twentieth century, a growing number of historians expressed much more skepticism with regard to the Texas Troubles than had their predecessors. In making the case that there was no abolitionist plot, they cited the large number of false reports of fires and poisonings, the lack of any eyewitness testimony, and the paucity of other credible evidence. These scholars generally accepted the view that the fires that actually occurred had originated accidentally. They argued that the spontaneous combustion of the unstable prairie matches, caused by the extreme heat, was the real culprit.[23]

---

dential Election of 1860 (Kilgore, Tex., 1992), 45–53, 63–74.

20. Addington, "Slave Insurrections in Texas," 414–418.

21. Smyrl, "Unionism, Abolitionism, and Vigilantism in Texas," 66–67. Richard Maxwell Brown in his study of mob violence and vigilantism said that the panic amounted to "social hysteria"; nevertheless, he stopped short of denying the validity of the plot allegations, citing Smyrl, "who has written the most detailed account of the Great Fear in Texas," and who "does not discuss the apprehensions of white Texans as groundless" (Richard Maxwell Brown, *Strain of Violence: Historical Studies of American Violence and Vigilantism* [New York, 1975], 239–241).

22. Ledbetter, "Slave Unrest and White Panic," 341, 342.

23. Campbell, *An Empire for Slavery,* 224–228; Campbell, *Gone to Texas,* 240; Buenger, *Seces-*

To address the allegations of contemporary advocates of the conspiracy theory and the historians who subsequently accepted their arguments, it is necessary to review their evidence. There can be no doubt that a number of fires occurred in North Texas on or around July 8, although they were not nearly so numerous as the press reported. The conspiracy theorists contended that the unusually large number of fires and their close proximity to each other, both geographically and temporally, ruled out any possibility that the fires were spontaneous or accidental in origin. And if one ruled out coincidence, they reasoned, the burnings must have been planned and coordinated. Since many Texans believed the newspaper stories charging that abolitionists already had been at work in their state during the previous half decade, it took no great leap of faith for them to accept the slaves' confessions that white abolitionists were behind a plan to use flames and poison to strike a blow against the peculiar institution throughout Texas. The extorted confessions, a profusion of rumors about other fires and poisonings, reported caches of weapons said to have been surreptitiously imported from the North, and the Bailey letter that purportedly laid out the master plan of the mysterious Mystic Red convinced a sizeable majority of Texans that they, and all southerners for that matter, were in dire danger from those who hated the South and its social system and were determined to destroy both.

The case for a conspiracy theory, built by southern rights editors and politicians, and subsequently supported by many historians, does not, however, stand up well under scrutiny. The cluster of fires that occurred on and around July 8 could be explained by a combination of extreme heat—the Dallas, Pilot Point, and Denton fires occurred on the hottest day of the summer in North Texas—and the presence in stores and homes of the new phosphorous matches, the unstable nature of which was not generally understood. A scientific analysis of the qualities of these matches, written in 1864, stated: "The too-great sensibility of [phosphorous] matches is the principal cause of those terrible explosions

---

sion and Union in Texas; William D. Carrigan, *The Making of a Lynching Culture: Violence and Vigilantism in Central Texas, 1836–1916* (Urbana, Ill., 2004), 48–49; Barr, *Black Texans*, 33–34; Jesús F. de la Teja, Paula Marks, and Ron Tyler, *Texas: Crossroads of North America* (New York, 2004); Phillips, "White Violence, Hegemony, and Slave Rebellion in Dallas, Texas," 25–35; Reynolds, *Editors Make War*, 108–110; Reynolds, "Vigilante Law During the Texas Slave Panic of 1860," 173–186; Donald E. Reynolds, "Reluctant Martyr: Anthony Bewley and the Texas Slave Insurrection Panic of 1860," *Southwestern Historical Quarterly* 96 (January 1993): 344–361; Donald E. Reynolds, "The Slave Insurrection Panic of 1860 and Southern Secession," in *A Mythic Land Apart: Reassessing Southerners and Their History*, ed. John David Smith and Thomas H. Appleton Jr. (Westport, Conn., 1993), 81–102.

and accidents, [and] their too great explosibility is the ordinary cause of the burns in the face and eyes. The sensibility is such that we have seen packages of matches take fire in the hand without knowing how it happens."[24] Writing in 1877, another author commented, "but a few years ago there occurred frequent examples of burns caused by the explosion of the match and the projection of its burning particles." To minimize the danger of spontaneous combustion, phosphorous matches were frequently packed in bran to insulate them from heat and placed in nonflammable metal boxes to prevent the spread of fire in case they ignited.[25] Western railroads flatly refused to carry "prairie matches" before the early 1860s because they deemed them too great a fire hazard.[26] The careless storage of these "Lucifers," as some called them, in conditions of extreme heat could endanger the homes and stores that had them.

The initial reports of the various fires in North Texas all tended to agree that the spontaneous combustion of prairie matches was the cause in each instance. Since most of the fires occurred in stores that would have stocked these matches, it was natural for them to reach such a conclusion. Attributing the outbreaks to combustion due to the heat and not to incendiaries also makes sense when the timing of the July 8 fires is considered. All of the fires occurred in early to mid-afternoon—when temperatures were at their peak—on what was generally agreed to have been the hottest day of the most torrid summer on record. If black arsonists had been the culprits, they would hardly have carried out their incendiary mission in broad daylight; rather, they would have worked under cover of darkness, when detection would have been less likely. Only after Charles Pryor's sensational letters were published did Texans come to believe that the fires were manmade. In subsequent weeks, southern rights editors printed every rumor alleging that the abolitionists and their black co-conspirators had burned numerous towns, although these later reports of burned towns almost always proved to be false.

Not only did the initial reports of the fires generally agree that they had originated accidentally, but many residents of North Texas who later discussed their recollections of the fires also testified to the accidental origins of the blazes. Thirty-two years after Dallas had burned, an enterprising reporter of the Dallas *Morning News* sought out Judge James Bentley, who had served on the vigilance committee, and asked him for his account of the city's destruction.

24. M. F. Crass Jr., "A History of the Match Industry," *Journal of Chemical Education*, part 3 (1941), 18:278.

25. Ibid.

26. Ibid., part 1, 118.

He at first refused to talk about the event, telling the reporter, "this was a bit of southern history that was not good." Finally agreeing to be interviewed, the judge said: "When the town was burned it was a hot day—so hot that matches ignited from the heat of the sun. Wallace Peak had just finished a new two-story frame building and in the building was a lot of boxes filled with shavings, and I think a cigar stump or a match was thrown into one of the boxes, and from that the fire started about 2 o'clock in the afternoon. Several fires had occurred; there was a great deal of excitement about the apprehended negro uprising; somebody had to hang; and the three negroes went."

Bentley also recalled that a Henderson merchant had written to a friend in Dallas and mentioned that on the same day Dallas burned, a box of matches ignited from the heat and that he barely had been able to save his store from destruction.[27] W. P. Overton, who had lived in Dallas County since 1844, agreed with Judge Bentley's version of the fire's inception. Overton later told an interviewer that a number of men had been smoking around the drugstore, "and I think the fire started from that." He also said, "I think the hanging of the three negroes for burning the town was unjust, because I don't believe they were guilty."[28]

C. A. Williams, of Denton, later wrote that the fire in that town "was caused by the igniting of what was then known as the 'prairie match.'" Williams went on to describe the characteristics of the match: "It was indeed a peculiar match, and whether they were dipped in some unctuous or resinous substance, or some peculiar chemical unknown to other matches, I do not know, but I do know that the match when ignited was very hard to be extinguished. The wind had but little or no effect upon it. . . . Another peculiarity about the match was that it was easily ignited in hot weather." Williams said that the local townspeople soon charged the abolitionists with the burning and their minds were not changed until they learned that in the nearby town of Lebanon, at about the same time that Denton's fire had occurred, "while a number of citizens were seated in front of stores in the day time, it was discovered that smoke and flames were emanating from a building, and upon diligent search and inquiry

27. "A Talk with one of the Jury men," Dallas *Morning News*, July 10, 1892. According to Bentley, those who believed the Dallas fire was accidental cited the merchant's experience to support their view. But the advocates of the conspiracy theory denounced the businessman, who had originally come from the North, as "being in collusion with the negroes." He had told his friend that he planned to come to Dallas, but the friend warned him that he would be in danger from the vigilantes, and he stayed away.

28. Quoted in *Memorial and Biographical History of Dallas County*, 177.

it was ascertained that no one had been around the back part of the building, and as the fire started at or near a place where the matches were kept the conclusion was reached that the fire originated from them." Williams mentioned the fires that had damaged Pilot Point, Dallas, Waxahachie, "and two places east from Denton," but instead of attributing those to incendiaries, he said, "The Day was an oppressively hot one and there is no doubt in my mind but what the fires were all caused from matches exploding by reason of the extremely hot weather."[29]

The citizens of Waxahachie came to the same conclusion as those of Lebanon, according to the recollections of a local minister. Reminiscing some thirty years after the panic, the Reverend R. M. White said the citizens of Waxahachie, like other North Texans, had been persuaded by observation that the fires had almost certainly resulted from the extreme heat, rather than arson. Initially, White said, "It was thought that the fires were the work of incendiaries, and in most instances no cause could be traced whereby the buildings could have taken fire from accidental causes, but finally matches in Old Uncle Billy Oldham's store in Waxahachie took fire whilst lying on the shelf, right under the sight of the clerks and proprietor, in broad daylight. The cat was out of the bag. The explanation of all the mysterious and alarming conflagrations of plain spontaneous ignition."[30]

George Jackson, who lived at Trinity Mills in northwest Dallas County and who had fought Indians in several counties of North Texas during his long residence in the region, later wrote, "The country at this time was very much excited and there were wild rumors afloat." Jackson told of "two Methodist preachers from Iowa" (Blunt and McKinney), who had previously been whipped and ordered to leave Texas, and he said that "men fresh from the North were looked on with suspicion, and some good men were threatened." The fire was "laid to the negroes," wrote Jackson, and three were hanged. Other blacks suffered, and "many of them were whipped. . . . I still thank the Lord that I took no part in it." Although he did not explicitly say so, Jackson implied that the fires were accidental when he wrote: "The summer of 1860 was very hot, 110 degrees in the shade, and in many places matches were known to take fire while on the mantel, or shelf. Some people thought that was the cause of many of the fires."[31]

29. Edmond F. Bates, *History and Reminiscences of Denton County* (Denton, Tex., 1918) 348–349.

30. "Reminiscences of Rev. R. M. White," *Memorial and Biographical History of Ellis County, Texas* (Chicago, 1892), 95–96.

31. George Jackson, *Sixty Years in Texas,* 2nd ed. (Dallas, 1908), 90–91.

A resident of Northeast Texas who published his memoirs just after the turn of the century said:

> The weather of that summer was distressingly hot and numbers of villages throughout Texas were burned, probably from spontaneous combustion, as the thermometer reached 114 degrees Fahrenheit in the shade at my father's house where I was staying, and sulphur matches caught fire and burned their heads off in the little wooden boxes in which they were kept. I here record this fact as it was under my own observation, and our house would have been burned had the fire not been discovered in time to prevent. So hot was politics that it was generally agreed that the burning was the work of incendiaries sent from the North to burn us out so that we could not resist invasion in the expected war. Such were the conclusions of a mad people.[32]

Other than the fires, the most frightening charges brought against the alleged abolitionists was that they had distributed strychnine to their black confederates, who supposedly were to use it to poison the food and water supply of unsuspecting whites. Secessionist editors and politicians, both in Texas and throughout the other slave states, continued to reiterate this allegation right down to the secession of the Lower South, long after it had become obvious that the reports were patently false. The vigilantes never produced any actual poison as evidence, nor was there a single confirmed report that anyone had suffered illness as a consequence of being poisoned. Not only was there an absence of eyewitness testimony or scientific analysis to support the accusations of arson and poisonings, but the only "evidence" of any kind was in the form of confessions wrung from terrified blacks by brutal whippings and threats. Such evidence would not have stood up even in a contemporary court, much less in a modern court of law.

Another problem for the proponents of the theory that there was a vast conspiracy was their inability to identify or produce any bona fide abolitionists. The whites who were hanged or expelled invariably had attracted the attention of the vigilantes because they were itinerant tradesmen or recent immigrants from the North. The only thing they had in common was a northern background and a relatively short tenure of residence in Texas. Charles Pryor's letters outlined a highly organized and detailed plot that the alleged black arsonists of Dallas had supposedly revealed, but he named no names other than the

32. A. W. Sparks, *The War Between the States, As I Saw It* (Tyler, Tex., 1901), 14.

ministers Solomon McKinney and William Blunt, who had been whipped and run out of the state the previous year. During the six-week period that followed Pryor's exposure of the plot, neither the Dallas editor nor anyone else identified the organization or mastermind responsible for planning and executing the destruction of the Lone Star State.

The vigilantes of Tarrant County apparently sought to correct this deficiency by producing the so-called Bailey letter, which laid out a comprehensive, ominous scheme for burning and poisoning under the auspices of an organization called the Mystic Red. Although the missive named sixteen "agents" of that mysterious organization, none was ever caught, or, with the single exception of Tom Willet, even identified.[33] When it came to the attention of the vigilantes that the notorious Methodist minister Anthony Bewley (a.k.a. William A. Buley) was not among those listed in the Bailey letter, the publicists of the letter lamely sought to correct the omission by saying that they had forgotten to mention that his name had been written on the back of the letter as the addressee. Although a careful analysis clearly demonstrates that the Bailey letter was a clumsy forgery and fraud, southern rights editors and politicians embraced it as authentic and used it to further their secessionist cause.[34]

Pryor's allegation that Parsons McKinney and Blunt were responsible for the Dallas fire, when closely examined, fares no better than the Bailey letter. The Dallas editor charged that the two preachers had returned to seek revenge for their ill treatment the previous year, and to that end had planned and organized the arson that destroyed Dallas. This allegation should have been received with skepticism, for no one reported that they had seen either man that summer in Dallas—or anywhere else in Texas for that matter. In fact, both men turned up in the North in early 1860, each protesting that they had been wrongly accused of holding anti-slavery opinions.

Wisconsin's Madison *State Journal* described William Blunt as a life-long Democrat, who was known for defending slavery from the pulpit. The anti-slavery *State Journal* saw irony in the preacher's mistreatment at the hands of the pro-slavery Texas mob, noting that Blunt "had distinguished himself by the

33. Although the elaborate network of agents and detailed account of procedures outlined in the Bailey letter indicated a highly organized, centrally controlled entity, there were no reports indicating that anyone, either in the North or the South, had ever heard of this clandestine fraternity before the missive surfaced. Since the Mystic Red subsequently was unmentioned in connection with any other alleged plots, there is no evidence, independent of the letter, that it ever existed.

34. For a full discussion of the letter and the author's argument that the Fort Worth vigilantes really thought they were forging a letter from Bewley, instead of the fictional Bailey, see chapter 6.

blatant character of his advocacy of slavery. . . . He was particularly 'gifted' in the Biblical argument in favor of slavery with long and flatulent speeches based upon Mosaic regulations." Indeed, Blunt had gone to Texas for his health and in the expectation that the Democrats there would receive him with open arms. Now, disabused of his illusion, Blunt was petitioning the Wisconsin legislature to seek redress from the state of Texas for the "wrongs and outrages" done to him in Dallas.[35]

Unlike his friend, Parson McKinney did not seek compensation for his mistreatment. Instead, he wrote a letter to a northern newspaper defending himself against charges that he was an abolitionist. Published accounts had attributed his harsh treatment to his comments about the inhumane treatment sometimes meted out to slaves,[36] but the preacher himself said the real cause had nothing to do with his sermon. According to McKinney, it was his attempt to collect a debt from a Dallas resident named Sprowle for an unnamed third party that led to his persecution. Sprowle denied that he owed the money and, for good measure, publicly denounced McKinney as an abolitionist. Although the accused preacher protested his innocence and his congregation defended him as well, a hastily formed citizens' committee ordered him to leave Texas. After receiving a death threat, McKinney and his family, along with Blunt, fled Dallas; however, they were pursued, caught twelve miles north of town, and brought back. The two men were then tied to trees and whipped with cowhide lashes by seven men taking turns. The mob then robbed the travelers of their money, but allowed them to leave and make their way to the North and safety.[37]

Judge James Bentley's recollection of the incident differed in no important respect with that of McKinney, but he supplied additional details, and his conclusion about both ministers' culpability and the alleged insurrection is worth noting. Bentley said:

> The two white preachers . . . I believe to have been guiltless of the charge laid against them. When the preachers were captured, one of them doubtless would have been shot in his buggy, but his wife threw her arms around his neck and threw herself in front of him, so that the vigilantes could not shoot him without shooting her. She made such a piteous plea for her husband's life that they decided to spare it. The elder

35. Madison (Wisc.) *State Journal*, n.d., quoted in Garrison, *The New "Reign of Terror,"* 30.
36. See chapter 1.
37. Unnamed Indiana journal, quoted in Galveston *Civilian and Gazette*, September 11, 1860. See also Grimsted, *American Mobbing*, 175.

of the preachers [Blunt] was not wanted, but he refused to leave his brother of the cloth. He said that he would return to Dallas and go to jail with him. The preachers were afterward whipped and told to leave the country. I think that about the extent of their connection with the negroes was that they had been seen perched on rail fences talking with negroes several times and once or twice they felt it their duty to preach to them. I don't believe they instigated an insurrection. In fact there was no insurrection. People became frightened and almost panic stricken.[38]

It would be easy to dismiss McKinney's claim of innocence as a lie to cover up his guilt, except for one thing. In a letter published in the Chicago *Times and Herald,* he refused to criticize those who had beaten him and driven him out of Texas. He did defend himself from the charges brought against him by the Dallas vigilantes, contending that the incident in Dallas originated from false accusations brought by "two or three designing men, whose personal dislike he had incurred." Nevertheless, instead of denouncing the citizens of Dallas for his mistreatment, he blamed the northern agitators of the slave question, who had made southerners suspicious of outsiders in general and northerners in particular. Southern papers saw McKinney's comments as vindication of their view that the fault for the recent aggressive treatment of northerners lay not with the vigilantes who carried them out, but with abolitionist agitators north of the Mason-Dixon Line. The *Times and Herald,* a Democratic paper, commended McKinney for his letter and took the opportunity to tweak its rivals. The Republican press, said the *Times and Herald,* had made much ado over McKinney's near martyrdom the previous year, calling it an illustration of the "'barbarism of slavery'": "Will the same Republican press now republish to the world the letter of that mobbed preacher, McKinney?"[39]

The Galveston *Civilian and Gazette,* in summing up McKinney's comments, said, "he reads a most biting lecture to Northern Abolitionists, and especially to the Northern Clergy, whom, from their prolonged and fanatical denunciations and aggressions against the Southern people and their domestic institutions, he declares to be solely responsible for the state of feelings which exists against all Northern men residing in Southern communities."[40] The *Civilian and Gazette* probably failed to realize that in accepting McKinney's assertion of his innocence

38. "A Talk with one of the Jury men," Dallas *Morning News,* July 10, 1892.

39. Chicago *Times and Herald,* n.d., quoted in Macon (Miss.) *Beacon,* September 12, 1860.

40. Chicago *Times and Herald,* n.d., quoted in Galveston *Civilian and Gazette,* September 25, 1860.

and his denunciation of abolitionists, it was effectively undermining the charge made by Pryor that the preacher was responsible for the burning of Dallas.

After the panic had passed, there were subtle indications that even those who had supported the conspiracy theory and helped fan the flames of terror experienced second thoughts about the dangers that abolitionists and black insurrectionists posed to the Lone Star State. Although most Texans supported the usurpation of the law by vigilance committees after the fires of July, some had wanted to tighten up the laws pertaining to slave tampering, and they asked the governor to call a special session of the legislature for that purpose. But Governor Houston had denied that abolitionists were behind the burning of Dallas and other towns in the state, and he ignored the request. After voting to secede in 1861, the Texas convention removed Houston from office, and that summer Texas voters elected Francis R. Lubbock, a secessionist, to replace him. From that point until the end of the war, men who stood foursquare for the Confederacy would remain firmly in control of the legislative process. Yet, although less than a year had passed since the slave panic had swept Texas, the legislature passed no laws to shore up the statutes concerning slave tampering, even though the existing laws concerning such crimes were relatively lenient.[41]

Addressing the Ninth Legislature in November 1861, Governor Lubbock went into great detail on matters that he thought the legislature needed to address, such as protection against a possible invasion of the state by the Union army and laws to strengthen the defense against marauding Indians on the frontier. The new chief executive said nothing, however, about the excitement of the previous year; nor did he ask the lawmakers to pass legislation that might diminish the danger of future abolitionist-inspired slave insurrections or to enact laws that would increase the severity of the relatively light legal penalties for slave tampering. Like the governor, the legislature saw no need to take action against the abolitionist threat. Neither House nor Senate journals reflect any qualms over these issues, although the legislature did show its concern for another security issue when it passed several acts shoring up the frontier defense against Indian raids.[42]

The excitement of secession and war made the Texas Troubles just a memory, but it did not end vigilantism in the Lone Star State. As the war dragged

41. For examples, see chapter 2.

42. "Governor Francis R. Lubbock's Address to a Joint Session of the Legislature, November 15, 1861," *House Journal of the Ninth Legislature, Regular Session of the State of Texas: November 4, 1861–January 14, 1862*, comp. and ed. James M. Day, et al. (Austin, 1964), 49–59.

deep into its second year, slaveholders from those areas that were threatened by invading northern armies fled westward into Texas, in the hope of preventing their bondsmen from falling into Yankee hands and becoming contraband of war. The influx of black and white refugees raised new fears among many whites. Anxiety was especially acute among Confederate loyalists in the northern counties, where a sizeable proportion of the population had opposed secession and where some still defiantly supported the Union. The rapid growth in the number of slaves in North Texas—Collin County's slave population alone grew by 70 percent—conjured up old fears of a possible slave insurrection, encouraged this time not by northern abolitionists but by local opponents of the war. The growing tension in the area ultimately culminated in the "Great Hanging" at Gainesville, Cooke County, which resulted in forty-two deaths.[43]

Influenced by the excitement over alleged disloyalty and a renewed concern over possible slave uprisings, the legislature, in February 1863, finally passed a law aimed at suppressing insurrections.[44] That the passage of this measure came two and a half years after the Texas Troubles, however, raises questions about the failure of the legislature to pass any anti-insurrectionary measures in 1861, in the aftermath of a conspiracy allegedly so sinister and so widespread that it had threatened to engulf the entire state. At the very least, this inaction demonstrated that the legislators were unconcerned that the agents of the Mystic Red, none of whom had been caught, might still be prowling about and inspiring blacks to rise against their masters. It may also show that the governor and lawmakers were now convinced that there had been no plot after all.

The legislature was not alone in evincing a short memory where the Texas Troubles were concerned. Key participants in the events of Texas's long, hot summer of 1860 who later published their reminiscences also demonstrated that the passage of time either had erased the Texas Troubles entirely from their memories or had diminished the panic's significance in their thinking. Lubbock's omission of any reference to abolitionists and black insurrectionists in his speech to the legislature carried over many years later to his memoirs,

---

43. Richard B. McCaslin, *Tainted Breeze: The Great Hanging at Gainesville, Texas, 1862* (Baton Rouge, 1994); Richard B. McCaslin, "Wheat Growers in the Confederacy: The Suppression of Dissent in Collin County, Texas, during the Civil War," *Southwestern Historical Quarterly* 96 (October 1993), 533. For other vigilante violence arising from conflict between Union sympathizers and Confederate loyalists, see David Pickering and Judy Falls, *Brush Men and Vigilantes: Civil War Dissent in Texas* (College Station, 2000).

44. Gammel, *The Laws of Texas*, 5:601–602.

in which he made no mention at all of the fiery excitement of 1860.[45] Another exemplar of selective memory loss concerning the alleged conspiracy was O. M. Roberts, who as president of the secession convention drafted the ordinance that had stressed the alleged efforts of abolitionist "emissaries" to "stir up servile insurrection and bring blood and carnage to our firesides." Nearly forty years later, however, in his lengthy political and legal history of the Lone Star State, Roberts made no mention of the "servile insurrection," or of its impact upon the politics of secession.[46]

Other than Louis T. Wigfall, arguably the most prominent Texan to justify secession by exploiting the alleged conspiracy on the national stage was Representative John H. Reagan, who soon became a member of Jefferson Davis's cabinet. It will be recalled that Reagan, the once ardent unionist, had personally participated in the vigilance movement and later powerfully reiterated the horror stories about arson and poisonings on the floor of the U.S. Congress. But in his later years, like Lubbock and Roberts, Reagan conveniently forgot his role in using the panic to further the cause of secession. In his memoirs he wrote in a general way about the northern violations of southern rights and devoted one paragraph to John Brown's raid on Harpers Ferry; significantly, however, he said nothing at all about the Texas Troubles of 1860 that once had so stirred him.[47]

John Henry Brown may represent the most interesting specimen among those who aided and abetted the conspiracy theorists and later wrote about the period. Brown was one of the three signers of the broadside containing the Bailey letter, attesting to its authenticity, and as editor of the Belton *Democrat* he was probably the individual responsible for its printing and distribution. Brown later wrote a lengthy history of Dallas County, and the single, rambling sentence he devoted to the Texas Troubles was not only ambiguous, but also demonstrated an obvious reluctance to reaffirm the strong support he had once given to conspiracy theory. In 1887, he wrote: "To recount the more recent events preceding the war, the destructive fire of July, 1860, the evidence of concerted incendiarism, the intense excitement and uprising of the people and the execution of several colored men considered the instruments of foreign fanatical

45. Francis R. Lubbock, *Six Decades in Texas; or, Memoirs of Francis Richard Lubbock, Governor of Texas in War Time, 1861–1863* (Austin, 1900).

46. Oran M. Roberts, "The Political, Legislative, and Judicial History of Texas for Its Fifty Years of Statehood, 1845–1895," in *A Comprehensive History of Texas, 1685 to 1897,* ed. Dudley G. Wooten (Dallas, 1898), 2:7–330.

47. Reagan, *Memoirs,* 90.

emissaries, would be to open a question, the discussion of which should be left to a later day—farther removed from the acrimonies of the war and of the actors in those scenes."[48]

Since we are "farther removed from the acrimonies of the war and of the actors in those scenes," it should be possible to arrive at a dispassionate assessment of the allegations and recriminations made in the heat of battle. In truth, it is impossible to prove conclusively that there was no validity at all to the allegations brought by Charles Pryor and elaborated on by other secessionists. There was no ironclad proof on either side of the argument, although the vigilantes and their editorial allies tried to manufacture such proof in the form of the Bailey letter. Nevertheless, the total absence of any convincing evidence that there *was* a plot, together with much circumstantial evidence and testimony indicating that none existed, strongly suggests that there was no conspiracy.

The images of lustful and vindictive blacks prowling the South and acting under the direction of nefarious white abolitionists to commit arson, murder, and rape almost certainly were produced by the fevered imagination of a public driven to distraction by a long-festering fear of anti-slavery zealots, an emotional presidential campaign, and the summer's suffocating heat. Shrewdly playing upon the public's fears and anxieties, secessionist editors and politicians were able to parlay the fires of July 8 into a psychological conflagration that became the most widespread—and most disastrous—mass panic in southern history.

48. John Henry Brown, *History of Dallas County, Texas: From 1837 to 1887* (Dallas, 1887), 102. Born in Missouri, Brown worked for various newspapers in his native state as well as Texas before settling for good in the Lone Star State in the 1840s. A staunch Democrat, he became a secessionist in the 1850s. He used his newspaper, the Belton *Democrat,* to oppose Sam Houston and trumpet the cause of secession. Brown served as a member of the secession convention and chaired the committee that drafted the articles of secession. In his later years he wrote prolifically on various historical topics (Sibley, *Lone Stars and State Gazettes,* 210–211; see also *Handbook of Texas Online,* s.v., www.tsha.utexas.edu/handbook/online/articles/BB/fbr94.html [accessed July 18, 2006]).

BIBLIOGRAPHY

PRIMARY SOURCES

Manuscripts

Arkansas Historical Commission, Little Rock, Arkansas
    Kellan, Robert F., Diary. General Microfilm Collection.
Austin Public Library, Austin, Texas
    Pease-Graham-Niles Family Papers.
Emory University, Woodruff Library Special Collections, Atlanta, Georgia
    Thompson, William Sydnor, Papers.
    "Ulysses," Letters.
    Wadley, Sarah L., Diary, Microfilm Typescript.
Fort Worth, Texas, Public Library
    Mitchell, Charles Ellis, "Reminiscences of Charles Ellis Mitchell," Texas Writers' Project, Research Data, Fort Worth and Tarrant County, Texas, Typescript, 6:2002, 1941.
Library of Congress, Washington, D.C.
    Stephens, Alexander H., Papers.
Texas A&M University-Commerce, James G. Gee Library Archives, Commerce, Texas
    "E. D.," Letter, August 11, 1860.
    Delling, Violet C., Letter, September 4, 1860.
Texas State Archives, Austin, Texas
    Donathan Family Correspondence.
University of North Carolina at Chapel Hill, Southern Historical Collection, Chapel Hill, North Carolina
    Gervin, David, Diary, Typescript.
    Miles, William Porcher, Papers.

University of North Texas Library, Denton, Texas
    Moore Papers.
University of Texas, Barker Texas History Center Archives, Austin, Texas
    Addison, Oscar Murray, Papers.
    Baker, James H., Diary, Typescript.
    Bryan, Guy M., Papers.
    Barry, James Buckner, Diary, Typescript. James Buckner Barry Papers.
    Campbell Papers.
    Ballinger, Will Pitt, Papers.
    Enloe Collection.
    Huling Papers.
    Reagan, John H., Papers.
    South, Walter S., Diary, Typescript.
    Winfrey Collection.

Published Documents and Published Memoirs, Letters, Interviews,
Speeches, and Histories by Contemporaries

Basler, Roy P., ed. *Abraham Lincoln: His Speeches and Writings.* New York: World Publishing Company, 1946.

———. *Collected Works of Abraham Lincoln.* 8 vols. New Brunswick, N.J.: Rutgers Univ. Press, 1953–1955.

Barron, S. B. *The Lone Star Defenders: A Chronicle of the Third Texas Cavalry, Ross Brigade.* New York: Neal Publishing Company, 1908.

Brown, John Henry. *History of Dallas County, Texas: From 1837 to 1887.* Dallas: Mulligan, Cornett and Farnham, Printers, 1887.

———. *History of Texas: From 1685 to 1892.* St. Louis: L. E. Darnell, 1892.

Candler, Allen D., comp. *The Confederate Records of the State of Georgia.* 5 vols. Atlanta: C. P. Byrd, 1909–1911.

Clinton, Catherine, ed. *Fanny Kemble's Journals.* Cambridge, Mass.: Harvard Univ. Press, 2000.

Dallas Morning News.

"First Account of an Old Settler in Dallas," July 10, 1892.

"Judge Nat M. Burford's Version," July 10, 1892.

"A Talk with one of the Jury Men," July 10, 1892.

"Reminiscences of Mrs. Addie K. McDermett," June 21, 1925.

Day, James M., comp. and ed., et al. *House Journal of the Ninth Legislature, Regular Session of the State of Texas: November 4, 1861–January 14, 1862.* Austin: Texas State Library, 1964.

———. *House Journal of the Ninth Legislature, First Called Session of the State of Texas: February 2, 1863–March 7, 1863.* Austin: Texas State Library, 1963.

Elliott, Charles. *South-Western Methodism: A History of the M. E. Church in the South-West, from 1844 to 1864.* Cincinnati: Poe and Hitchcock, 1868.

Freehling, William W., and Craig M. Simpson, eds. *Secession Debated: Georgia's Showdown in 1860.* New York: Oxford Univ. Press, 1992.

Gammel, H.P.N., comp. *The Laws of Texas, 1822–1897.* 10 vols. Austin: Gammel Book Company, 1898–1902.

Garrison, William Lloyd. *The New "Reign of Terror" in the Slaveholding States, for 1859–1860.* New York: American Anti-Slavery Society, 1860. Reprint, New York: Arno Press, 1969.

Gienapp, William E., ed. *The Civil War and Reconstruction: A Documentary Collection.* New York: Norton, 2001.

Graf, LeRoy P., and Ralph W. Haskins, eds. *The Papers of Andrew Johnson.* 16 vols. Knoxville: Univ. of Tennessee Press, 1967–2000.

Hofstadter, Richard, and Michael Wallace, eds. *American Violence: A Documentary History.* New York: Knopf, 1970.

Jackson, George. *Sixty Years in Texas,* 2nd ed. Dallas: Wilkinson Printing Company, 1908.

Kerner Commission. *Report of the National Advisory Commission on Civil Disorders.* New York: E. P. Dutton, 1968.

Lincecum, Jerry B., Edward H. Phillips, and Peggy A. Redshaw, eds., *Gideon Lincecum's Sword: Civil War Letters from the Home Front.* Denton, Tex. Univ. of North Texas Press, 2001.

Lubbock, Francis R. *Six Decades in Texas; or, Memoirs of Francis Richard Lubbock, Governor of Texas in War Time, 1861–1863.* Austin: B. C. Jones and Company, Printers, 1900.

Martin, Isabella D., and Myra Lockett Avary, eds. *A Diary from Dixie, as written by Mary Boykin Chesnut.* New York: Appleton, 1906.

Memorial and Biographical History of Ellis County, Texas. Chicago: Lewis Publishing Company, 1892.

"Reminiscences of Rev. R. M. White."

Memorial and Biographical History of Dallas County. Chicago: Lewis Publishing Company, 1892.

"Reminiscence of Emma Baird Brown."

"Reminiscence of W. P. Overton."

Mississippi, State of. *Journal of the State Convention, and Ordinances and Resolutions Adopted in January, 1861.* Jackson: E. Barksdale, State Printer, 1861.

Morrell, Z. N. *Flowers and Fruits from the Wilderness; or Thirty-six Years in Texas and Two Winters in Honduras.* Boston: Gould and Lincoln, 1872.

Olmsted, Frederick Law. *A Journey in the Back Country.* New York: Mason Brothers, 1860. Reprint, Williamstown, Mass.: Connor House Publishers, 1972.

Reagan, John H. *Memoirs, With Special Reference to Secession and the Civil War.* New York: Neale Publishing Company, 1906.

Richardson, James D., comp. *Compilation of the Messages and Papers of the Presidents, 1789–1897.* 10 vols. Washington, D.C.: Government Printing Office, 1897.

Roberts, Oran M. "The Political, Legislative, and Judicial History of Texas for Its Fifty Years of Statehood, 1845–1895." In *A Comprehensive History of Texas, 1685 to 1897,* edited by Dudley G. Wooten. Dallas: Scarff, 1898.

Rowland, Kate M., and Mrs. Morris L. Croxall, eds. *The Journal of Julia LeGrand, New Orleans, 1862–1863.* Richmond, Va.: Everett Waddey Company, 1911.

Ruffin, Edmund. *Anticipations of the Future, To Serve as Lessons for the Present Time.* Richmond, Va.: J. W. Randolph, 1860.

Scarborough, William K., ed. *The Diary of Edmund Ruffin.* 3 vols. Baton Rouge: Louisiana State Univ. Press, 1972–1989.

Sparks, A. W. *The War Between the States, As I Saw It.* Tyler, Texas: Lee and Burnet Printers, 1901.

Speer, William S., and John Henry Brown, eds. *The Encyclopedia of the New West.* Marshall, Tex.: U.S. Biographical Publishing Company, 1881.

Townsend, John. *The Doom of Slavery in the Union: Its Safety Out of It; An Address to the Edisto Island Vigilant Association, October 29th, 1860.* Charleston, S.C.: Evans and Cogswell, 1860.

U.S. Bureau of the Census. *Population of the United States in 1860: Compiled from the Original Returns of the Eighth Census.* Washington, D.C.: Government Printing Office, 1864.

U. S. Congress. *The Congressional Globe, 36th Congress, 2nd Session, 1860.* Washington, D.C.: Blair and Rives, 1873.

U. S. Riot Commission. *Report of the National Advisory Commission on Civil Disorders.* New York: Bantam Books, 1968.

U. S. War Department, comp. *War of the Rebellion: A Compilation of the Official Records of the Union and Confederate Armies.* 70 vols. in 128. Washington, D.C.: Government Printing Office, 1880–1901.

Waldstreicher, David, ed. *Notes on the State of Virginia, with Related Documents.* New York: Bedford/St. Martin, 2002.

Wigfall, Louis T. *Speech of Hon. Louis T. Wigfall, of Texas, In Reply to Mr. Douglas, and on Mr. Powell's Resolution, Delivered in the Senate of the United States, December 11th and 12th 1860.* Washington, D.C.: Lemuel Towers, 1860.

———. *Speech of Louis T. Wigfall on the pending political issues; delivered at Tyler, Smith County, Texas, September 3, 1860.* Washington, D.C.: Lemuel Towers, 1860.

Williams, Amelia W., and Eugene C. Barker, eds. *The Writings of Sam Houston, 1813–1863.* 8 vols. Austin: Univ. of Texas Press, 1938–1943.

Winkler, Ernest W., ed. *Journal of the Secession Convention of Texas, 1861.* Austin: Austin Printing Company, 1912.

Newspapers.

Texas Journals
    Anderson *Central Texian.*
    Anderson *Texas Baptist.*

Austin *Southern Intelligencer.*
Austin *Texas State Gazette.*
Bastrop *Advertiser.*
Bellville *Texas Countryman.*
Belton *Democrat.*
Bonham *Era.*
Bonham *Independent.*
Brenham *Texas Ranger.*
Cameron *Sentinel.*
Centerville *Times.*
Clarksville *Northern Standard.*
Columbia *Democrat and Planter.*
Columbus *Colorado Citizen.*
Columbus *Times.*
Corpus Christi *Ranchero.*
Corsicana *Navarro Express.*
Crockett *Printer.*
Dallas *Herald.*
Dallas *Morning News,* July 8, 1990.
Dallas *Times Herald,* July 12, 1981; February 3, 1988.
Fairfield *Pioneer.*
Fort Worth *Chief.*
Galveston *Civilian and Gazette.*
Galveston *News.*
Galveston *Texas Christian Advocate.*
Henderson *Times.*
Houston *Petrel.*
Houston *Telegraph.*
Houston *True Southron.*
Huntsville *Item.*
Indianola *Bulletin.*
Indianola *Courier.*
Jacksboro *White Man.*
Jacksonville *Republican.*
Jasper *Clarion.*
Jefferson *Herald.*
La Grange *True Issue.*
McKinney *Messenger.*
Marshall *Harrison Flag.*
Marshall *Texas Republican.*
Matagorda *Gazette.*

Mount Pleasant *Union*.
Nacogdoches *Chronicle*.
Palestine *Trinity Advocate*.
Paris *Press*.
Quitman *Herald*.
Rusk *Enquirer*.
San Antonio *Alamo Express*.
San Antonio *Herald*.
San Antonio *Ledger and Texan*.
San Augustine *Red Land Express*.
Sherman *North Texian*.
Sherman *Patriot*.
Seguin *Mercury*.
Seguin *Union Democrat*.
Sulphur Springs *Independent Monitor*.
Tyler *Reporter*.
Tyler *Sentinel*.
Waco *Democrat*.
Weatherford *News*.

Journals of Other States

Alabama
Carrollton *West Alabamian*.
Centre *Coosa River Argus*.
Clayton *Banner*.
Florence *Gazette*.
Greensboro *Alabama Beacon*.
Grove Hill *Clarke County Democrat*.
Hayneville *Chronicle*.
Hayneville *Watchman*.
Jacksonville *Republican*.
Montgomery *Weekly Advertiser*.
Montgomery *Weekly Post*.
Montgomery *Mail*.
Opelika *Southern Era*.
Prattville *Autauga Citizen*.
Prattville *Southern Statesman*.
Selma *Issue*.
Talladega *Alabama Reporter*.
Troy *Advertiser*.
Tuscumbia *States Rights Democrat*.

Wetumpka *Enquirer.*
Arkansas
    Des Arc *Weekly Citizen.*
    Fayetteville *Arkansian.*
    Fort Smith *Herald.*
    Fort Smith *Times.*
    Little Rock *Old-Line Democrat.*
    Little Rock *True Democrat.*
    Van Buren *Press.*
Connecticut
    Hartford *Weekly Times.*
District of Columbia
    Washington *Constitution.*
    Washington *Daily National Intelligencer.*
Florida
    Tallahassee *East Floridian.*
    Tallahassee *Floridian and Journal.*
Georgia
    Athens *Southern Banner.*
    Atlanta *Daily Intelligencer.*
    Augusta *Chronicle and Sentinel.*
    Carrollton *Advocate.*
    Columbus *Sun.*
    Hamilton *Harris County Enterprise.*
    Macon *Daily Telegraph.*
    Milledgeville *Federal Union.*
    Milledgeville *Southern Recorder.*
    Rome *Weekly Courier.*
    Sandersville *Central Georgian.*
    Savannah *Republican.*
    Waynesboro *Independent South.*
Illinois
    Chicago *Press and Tribune.*
    Chicago *Times and Herald.*
Kentucky
    Louisville *Courier.*
Louisiana
    Alexandria *Constitutional.*
    Baton Rouge *Daily Advocate.*
    False River *Pointe Coupée Democrat.*
    New Orleans *Bee.*

New Orleans *Daily Delta*.
New Orleans *Picayune*.
Opelousas *Courier*.

Massachusetts
Boston *Journal*
Boston *Liberator*.
Boston *Zion's Herald*.

Maine
Bath *Sentinel*.

Mississippi
Columbus *Mississippi Democrat*.
Jackson *Mississippian*.
Macon *Beacon*.
Natchez *Daily Courier*.
Natchez *Free Trader*.
Paulding *Eastern Clarion*.
Raymond *Hinds County Gazette*.
Vicksburg *Whig*.

Missouri
St. Louis *Central Christian Advocate*.
St. Louis *Daily Missouri Advocate*.
St. Louis *Daily Missouri Republican*.
St. Louis *Express*.

New York
New York *Christian Advocate and Journal*.
New York *Day Book*.
New York *Herald*.
New York *Times*.
New York *Tribune*.
New York *World*.

North Carolina
Asheville *News*.
Charlotte *Whig*.
Fayetteville *North Carolinian*.
Greensboro *Times*.
Hillsborough *Recorder*.
Newbern *Weekly Progress*.
Raleigh *North Carolina Christian Advocate*.
Raleigh *Register*.
Salisbury *Carolina Watchman*.

Wadesborough *North Carolina Argus.*
Wilmington *Daily Journal.*
Ohio
Cincinnati *Christian Luminary.*
Cincinnati *Daily Commercial.*
South Carolina
Anderson *Intelligencer.*
Charleston *Daily Courier.*
Charleston *Mercury.*
Spartanburg *Carolina Spartan.*
Tennessee
Clarksville *Jeffersonian.*
Knoxville *Whig.*
Memphis *Avalanche.*
Memphis *Daily Appeal.*
Nashville *Christian Advocate.*
Nashville *Republican Banner.*
Nashville *Union and American.*
Paris *Sentinel.*
Virginia
Alexandria *Gazette.*
Barbour *Jeffersonian Democrat.*
Kanawha *Valley Star.*
Lynchburg *Daily Virginian.*
Norfolk *Southern Argus.*
Richmond *Daily Dispatch.*
Richmond *Enquirer.*
Richmond *Examiner.*
Richmond *Whig.*
Shepherdstown *Register.*
Wellsburg *Herald.*
Wheeling *Daily Intelligencer.*
Wisconsin
Madison *State Journal.*

SECONDARY SOURCES

Addington, Wendell G. "Slave Insurrections in Texas." *Journal of Negro History* 35 (October 1950): 408–434.
Aptheker, Herbert. *American Negro Slave Revolts.* New York: Columbia Univ. Press, 1943.

Baker, Robin E., and Dale Baum. "The Texas Voter and the Crisis of the Union, 1859–1861." *Journal of Southern History* 53, no. 3 (August 1987): 395–420.

Baillio, Ferdinand B. *A History of the Texas Press Association.* Dallas: Southwestern Printing Company, 1916.

Barney, William L. *The Road to Secession: A New Perspective on the Old South.* New York: Praeger Publishers, 1972.

———. *The Secessionist Impulse: Alabama and Mississippi in 1860.* Princeton: Princeton Univ. Press, 1974.

Barr, Alwyn. *Black Texans: A History of African Americans in Texas, 1528–1995.* Norman: Univ. of Oklahoma Press, 1996.

Bates, Edmond F. *History and Reminiscences of Denton County.* Denton, Tex.: McNitsky Printing Company, 1918.

Baum, Dale. *The Shattering of Texas Unionism: Politics in the Lone Star State during the Civil War Era.* Baton Rouge: Louisiana State Univ. Press, 1999.

Bender, Averam. *The March of Empire: Frontier Defense in the Southwest, 1848–1860.* Lawrence: Univ. of Kansas Press, 1952.

Brown, Richard Maxwell. "The American Vigilante Tradition." In *The History of Violence in America: Historical and Comparative Perspectives,* edited by Hugh D. Graham and Ted R. Gurr, 121–180. New York: F. A. Praeger, 1969.

———. "The History of Vigilantism in the United States." In *Vigilante Politics,* edited by H. Jon Rosenbaum and Peter C. Sederberg, 79–109. Philadelphia: Univ. of Pennsylvania Press, 1976.

———. *Strain of Violence: Historical Studies of American Violence and Vigilantism.* New York: Oxford Univ. Press, 1975.

Bruce, Dickson D. *Violence and Culture in the Antebellum South.* Austin: Univ. of Texas Press, 1979.

Buenger, Walter L. *Secession and the Union in Texas.* Austin: Univ. of Texas Press, 1984.

Campbell, Randolph B. *An Empire for Slavery: The Peculiar Institution in Texas, 1821–1865.* Baton Rouge: Louisiana State Univ. Press, 1989.

———. *Gone to Texas: A History of the Lone Star State.* New York: Oxford Univ. Press, 2003.

Carrigan, William D. *The Making of a Lynching Culture: Violence and Vigilantism in Central Texas, 1836–1916.* Urbana: Univ. of Illinois Press, 2004.

Carroll, Joseph C. *Slave Insurrections in the United States, 1800–1865.* Boston: Chapman and Grimes, 1938.

Catton, Bruce. *The Centennial History of the Civil War.* 3 vols. Garden City, N.Y.: Doubleday, 1961.

Channing, Steven A. *Crisis of Fear: Secession in South Carolina.* New York: Simon and Schuster, 1970.

Cochran, John H. *Dallas County: A Record of Its Pioneers and Progress.* Dallas, Tex.: A. S. Mathis, Service Publishing Company, 1928.

Cockrell, Frank M. *History of Early Dallas.* Chicago: Privately printed, 1944.

Coulter, E. Merton. *The Confederate States of America, 1861–1865*. Baton Rouge: Louisiana State Univ. Press, 1950.

Crass, M. F., Jr. "A History of the Match Industry." *Journal of Chemical Education,* part 3, vol. 18 (1941): 116–120, 277–282

Craven, Avery O. *The Coming of the Civil War, 1848–1861,* rev. ed. Chicago: Univ. of Chicago Press, 1957.

———. "Coming of the War Between the States, An Interpretation." *Journal of Southern History* (August 1936): 321–322.

———. *The Growth of Southern Nationalism, 1848–1861*. Baton Rouge: Louisiana State Univ. Press, 1953.

Crenshaw, Ollinger. "The Psychological Background of the Election of 1860 in the South." *North Carolina Historical Review* 19 (July 1942): 260–279.

———. *The Slave States in the Presidential Election of 1860.* Baltimore: Johns Hopkins Press, 1945. Reprint, Gloucester, Mass.: Peter Smith, 1969.

DeLeon, Arnaldo. *They Called Them Greasers: Anglo Attitudes toward Mexicans in Texas, 1821–1900*. Austin: Univ. of Texas Press, 1983.

Dew, Charles B. *Apostles of Disunion: Southern Secession Commissioners and the Causes of the Civil War*. Charlottesville: Univ. Press of Virginia, 2001.

Dubois, Laurent. *Avengers of the New World: The Story of the Haitian Revolution*. Cambridge, Mass.: Belknap Press of Harvard Univ. Press, 2004.

Du Bose, John W. *The Life and Times of William Lowndes Yancey: A History of Political Parties in the United States, from 1834 to 1864*. 2 vols. Birmingham, Ala.: Roberts and Son, 1892. Reprint, New York: Peter Smith, 1942.

Dumond, Dwight L. *The Secession Movement, 1860–1861*. New York: Macmillan, 1931.

Eaton, Clement. *The Freedom-of-Thought Struggle in the Old South*. New York: Harper and Row, 1964.

———. "Mob Violence in the Old South." *Mississippi Valley Historical Review* 29 (December 1942): 351–370.

Faust, Drew Gilpin, ed. *The Ideology of Slavery: Proslavery Thought in the Antebellum South, 1830–1860*. Baton Rouge: Louisiana State Univ. Press, 1981.

Fehrenbach, T. R. *Lone Star: A History of Texas and the Texans*. Boulder, Colo.: Da Capo Press, 2000.

Finkelman, Paul. "Manufacturing Martyrdom: The Antislavery Response to John Brown's Raid." In *His Soul Goes Marching On: Responses to John Brown and the Harpers Ferry Raid,* edited by Paul Finkelman, 41–66. Charlottesville: Univ. Press of Virginia, 1995.

Fite, Emerson D. *The Presidential Campaign of 1860*. New York: Macmillan, 1911.

Fredrickson, George M. *The Black Image in the White Mind: The Debate on Afro-American Character and Destiny, 1817–1914*. New York: Harper and Row, 1971.

Freehling, William W., and Craig M. Simpson, eds. *Secession Debated: Georgia's Showdown in 1860*. New York: Oxford Univ. Press, 1992.

Gage, Larry J. "The Texas Road to Secession: John Marshall and the *Texas State Gazette*, 1860–1861." *Southwestern Historical Quarterly* 62 (October 1958): 191–226.

Gallaway, B. P. *The Ragged Rebel: A Common Soldier in W. H. Parsons' Texas Cavalry, 1861–1865.* Austin: Univ. of Texas Press, 1988.

Genovese, Eugene D. *Roll, Jordan, Roll: The World the Slaves Made.* New York: Pantheon Books, 1974.

Goodman, Louis S., and Alfred Gilman. *The Pharmacological Basis of Therapeutics,* 2nd ed. New York: Macmillan, 1958.

Griffitt, William, and Russell Veitch. "Hot and Crowded: Influence of Population Density and Temperature on Interpersonal Affective Behavior." *Journal of Personality and Social Psychology* 17 (1971): 92–98.

Grimsted, David. *American Mobbing, 1828–1861: Toward Civil War.* New York: Oxford Univ. Press, 1998.

Haley, James L. *Passionate Nation: The Epic History of Texas.* New York: Free Press, 2006.

Hollon, W. Eugene. *Frontier Violence, Another Look.* New York: Oxford Univ. Press, 1974.

Jenkins, William Sumner. *Pro-Slavery Thought in the Old South.* Chapel Hill: Univ. of North Carolina Press, 1935.

Johnson, Michael. *Toward a Patriarchal Republic: The Secession of Georgia.* Baton Rouge: Louisiana State Univ. Press, 1977.

Jordan, Winthrop D. *White Over Black: American Attitudes Toward the Negro, 1550–1812.* Chapel Hill: Univ. of North Carolina Press, 1968.

———. *The White Man's Burden: Historical Origins of Racism in America.* New York: Oxford Univ. Press, 1974.

Junkins, Enda. "Slave Plots, Insurrections, and Acts of Violence in the State of Texas, 1828–1865." Master's thesis, Baylor University, 1969.

Kelley, Sean. "'Mexico in His Head': Slavery and the Texas-Mexico Border, 1810–1860." *Journal of Social History* 37, no. 3 (2004): 709–723.

Kesselus, Kenneth. *History of Bastrop County, Texas, 1846–1865.* Austin: Jenkins Publishing, 1987.

King, Alvy L. *Louis T. Wigfall: Southern Fire-Eater.* Baton Rouge: Louisiana State Univ. Press, 1970.

Lack, Paul D. "Slavery and Vigilantism in Austin, Texas, 1840–1860." *Southwestern Historical Quarterly* 85 (July 1981): 1–20.

Ledbetter, Billy D. "Politics and Society: The Popular Response to Political Rhetoric in Texas, 1857–1860." *East Texas Historical Journal* 13 (fall 1975): 11–24.

———. "Slave Unrest and White Panic: The Impact of Black Republicanism in Ante-Bellum Texas." *Texana* 10 (1972): 335–350.

Lindsley, Philip. *A History of Greater Dallas and Vicinity.* 2 vols. Chicago: Lewis Publishing Company, 1909.

Marten, James. "Slaves and Rebels: The Peculiar Institution in Texas, 1861–1865." *East Texas Historical Journal* 28, no. 1 (1991): 29–36.

———. *Texas Divided: Loyalty and Dissent in the Lone Star State, 1856–1874.* Lexington: Univ. Press of Kentucky, 1990.

May, John A., and Joan R. Faunt. *South Carolina Secedes.* Columbia: Univ. of South Carolina Press, 1960.

McCaslin, Richard B. "Conditional Confederates: The Eleventh Cavalry West of the Mississippi River." *Military History of the Southwest* 21 (spring 1991): 87–99.

———. *Tainted Breeze: The Great Hanging at Gainesville, Texas, 1862.* Baton Rouge: Louisiana State Univ. Press, 1994.

———. "Wheat Growers in the Confederacy: The Suppression of Dissent in Collin County, Texas, during the Civil War." *Southwestern Historical Quarterly* 96 (October 1993): 526–539.

McPherson, James M. *Battle Cry of Freedom.* New York: Oxford Univ. Press, 1988.

———. *Ordeal by Fire: The Civil War and Reconstruction.* New York: Knopf, 1982.

Mohr, Clarence L. *On the Threshold of Freedom: Masters and Slaves in Civil War Georgia.* Athens: Univ. of Georgia Press, 1986.

Nevins, Allan. *The Emergence of Lincoln.* 2 vols. New York: Scribner, 1950.

Newton, Lewis W., and Herbert P. Gambrell. *A Social and Political History of Texas.* Dallas: Southwest Press, 1932.

Norton, Wesley. "The Methodist Episcopal Church and the Civil Disturbances in North Texas in 1859 and 1860." *Southwestern Historical Quarterly* 68 (January 1965): 317–341.

Oates, Stephen B. *The Fires of Jubilee: Nat Turner's Fierce Rebellion.* New York: Harper and Row, 1975.

———. *To Purge This Land with Blood: A Biography of John Brown.* Amherst: Univ. of Massachusetts Press, 1984.

Oldham, W. S. "Colonel John Marshall." *Southwestern Historical Quarterly* 20 (October 1916): 132–138.

Oltorf, Frank C. *The Marlin Compound: Letters of a Singular Family.* Austin: Univ. of Texas Press, 1968.

Phelan, Marcus. *A History of Early Methodism in Texas, 1817–1866.* Dallas, Tex.: Cokesbury Press, 1924.

Phillips, Michael. *White Metropolis: Race, Ethnicity, and Religion in Dallas, 1841–2001.* Austin: Univ. of Texas Press, 2006.

———. "White Violence, Hegemony, and Slave Rebellion in Dallas, Texas, before the Civil War." *East Texas Historical Journal* 37, no. 2 (1999): 25–35.

Phillips, Ulrich B. *American Negro Slavery: A Survey of the Supply, Employment and Control of Negro Labor as Determined by the Plantation Regime.* New York: Appleton, 1918.

Pickering, David, and Judy Falls. *Brush Men and Vigilantes: Civil War Dissent in Texas.* College Station: Texas A&M Univ. Press, 2000.

Potter, David. *The Impending Crisis, 1848–1861.* New York: Harper and Row, 1976.

Procter, Ben H. *Not Without Honor; The Life of John H. Reagan.* Austin: Univ. of Texas Press, 1962.

Rainwater, Percy L. *Mississippi: Storm Center of Secession, 1856–1861.* Baton Rouge, La.: O. Claitor, 1938.

Ramsdell, Charles W. "The Frontier and Secession." In *Studies in Southern History and Politics, inscribed to William Archibald Dunning, Ph.D., LL.D., Lieber Professor of history and political philosophy in Columbia University, by his former pupils, the authors.* 63–79. New York: Columbia Univ. Press, 1914.

Randall, James G., and David H. Donald. *The Civil War and Reconstruction,* 2nd ed. Lexington, Mass.: Heath, 1969.

Reynolds, Donald E. *Editors Make War: Southern Newspapers in the Secession Crisis.* Nashville, Tenn.: Vanderbilt Univ. Press, 1970.

———. "Reluctant Martyr: Anthony Bewley and the Texas Slave Insurrection Panic of 1860." *Southwestern Historical Quarterly* 96 (January 1993): 344–361.

———. "The Slave Insurrection Panic of 1860 and Southern Secession." In *A Mythic Land Apart: Reassessing Southerners and Their History,* edited by John David Smith and Thomas Appleton Jr., 81–102. Westport, Conn.: Greenwood Press, 1993.

———. "Smith County and Its Neighbors during the Slave Insurrection Panic of 1860." *Chronicles of Smith County* 10 (fall 1971): 1–8.

———. "Vigilante Law during the Texas Slave Panic of 1860." *Locus: An Historical Journal of Regional Perspectives* 2 (spring 1990): 173–186.

Rhodes James Ford. *History of the United States from the Compromise of 1850.* 9 vols. New York: Macmillan, 1900–1928.

Richardson, Rupert N. *The Frontier of Northwest Texas, 1846–1876; Advance and Defense by the Pioneer Settlers of the Cross Timbers and Plains.* Glendale, Calif.: A. H. Clark, 1963.

———. *Texas, the Lone Star State.* New York: Prentice-Hall, 1943.

Richardson, Rupert N., Adrian Anderson, Cary D. Wintz, and Ernest Wallace. *Texas: The Lone Star State,* 9th edition. Upper Saddle River, N.J.: Pearson-Prentice Hall, 2005.

Roach, Hattie J. *A History of Cherokee County.* Dallas, Tex.: Southwest Press, 1934.

Robertson, Robert J. "Slavery and the Coming of the Civil War, as Seen in the Beaumont *Banner.*" *East Texas Historical Journal* 34, no. 1 (1996): 129–138.

Sandbo, Anna I. "Beginnings of the Secession Movement in Texas." *Southwestern Historical Quarterly* 18 (July 1914): 41–73.

Santerre, George H. *Dallas' First Hundred Years, 1856–1956.* Dallas, Tex.: Book Craft, 1956.

Sibley, Marilyn M. *Lone Stars and State Gazettes: Texas Newspapers before the Civil War.* College Station: Texas A&M Univ. Press, 1983.

Simkins, Francis B., and James W. Patton. *The Women of the Confederacy.* Richmond, Va.: Garrett and Massie, 1936.

Simkins, Francis B., and Charles P. Roland. *A History of the South,* 4th ed. New York: Knopf, 1972.

Smith, David Paul. *Frontier Defense in the Civil War: Texas' Rangers and Rebels.* College Station: Texas A&M Univ. Press, 1992.

Smyrl, Frank H. "Unionism, Abolitionism, and Vigilantism in Texas, 1856–1865." Master's thesis, University of Texas, 1961.

Stampp, Kenneth M. *The Peculiar Institution: Slavery in the Ante-Bellum South.* New York: Knopf, 1956.

Steen, Ralph W. *History of Texas.* Austin: Steck, 1939.

Stroud, David. *Flames and Vengeance: The East Texas Fires and the Presidential Election of 1860.* Kilgore, Tex.: Pinecrest Publishing, 1992.

Sydnor, Charles S. "The Southerner and the Laws." *Journal of Southern History* 6 (February 1940): 3–23.

Teja, Jesús F. de la, Paula Marks, and Ron Tyler. *Texas: Crossroads of North America.* New York: Houghton Mifflin, 2004.

Thomas, Emory. *The American War and Peace, 1860–1877.* Englewood Cliffs, N. J.: Prentice Hall, 1973.

———. *The Confederate Nation, 1861–1865.* New York: Harper and Row, 1979.

Thornton, J. Mills. *Politics and Power in a Slave Society: Alabama, 1800–1861.* Baton Rouge: Louisiana State Univ. Press, 1978.

Timmons, Joe T. "Texas on the Road to Secession." Ph. D. diss., University of Chicago, 1973.

Tolbert, Frank X. *An Informal History of Texas, from Cabeza de Vaca to Temple Houston.* New York: Harper, 1961.

Wallace, Ernest. *Texas in Turmoil, 1849–1875.* Austin, Tex.: Steck-Vaughn, 1965.

Wallenstein, Peter. "Incendiaries All: Southern Politics and the Harpers Ferry Raid." In *His Soul Goes Marching On: Responses to John Brown and the Harpers Ferry Raid,* edited by Paul Finkelman, 149–174. Charlottesville: Univ. Press of Virginia, 1995.

Walther, Eric H. *The Fire-Eaters.* Baton Rouge: Louisiana State Univ. Press, 1992.

Webb, Walter Prescott, H. Bailey Carroll, and Eldon S. Branda, eds. *The Handbook of Texas.* 3 vols. Austin: Texas State Historical Association, 1952–1976.

Wharton, Clarence. *History of Texas.* Dallas, Tex.: Turner, 1935.

White, Laura A. *Robert Barnwell Rhett: Father of Secession.* New York: Century, 1931.

White, William W. "The Texas Slave Insurrection of 1860." *Southwestern Historical Quarterly* 52 (January 1949): 259–285.

Winfrey, Dorman H. *A History of Rusk County, Texas.* Waco, Tex.: Texian Press, 1961.

Wish, Harvey. "American Slave Insurrections before 1861." *Journal of Negro History* 22 (July 1937): 299–320.

———. "The Slave Insurrection Panic of 1856." *Journal of Southern History* 5 (May 1939): 206–222.

Woodward, C. Vann. *The Burden of Southern History,* 3rd. ed. Baton Rouge: Louisiana State Univ. Press, 1993.

Wooster, Ralph A. *The Secession Conventions of the South.* Princeton: Princeton Univ. Press, 1962.

Wooten, Dudley G. *A Complete History of Texas for Schools, Colleges and General Use.* Dallas, Tex.: Texas Historical Company, 1899.

Wortham, Louis J. *A History of Texas, from Wilderness to Commonwealth.* 5 vols. Fort Worth, Tex.: Wortham-Molyneaux, 1924.

Wyatt-Brown, Bertram. *Southern Honor: Ethics and Behavior in the Old South.* New York: Oxford Univ. Press, 1982.

Young, Thomas Daniel, Floyd C. Watkins, Richmond C. Beatty, *The Literature of the South,* rev. ed.: Glenview, Ill.: Scott, Foresman, 1968.

INDEX

abolitionists (alleged), 4, 6–7, 24, 73, 75, 111, 114, 118, 125, 128, 136, 141, 155, 173–76, 210–11; and blacks, 35–37, 44, 48–49, 52, 80, 113, 204, 214; and "Bailey letter," 156–57; blamed for fires and poisoning, 23, 37, 40, 41–44, 112, 117, 191, 193, 199, 201, 203, 204, 205, 207; difficulty identifying, 65, 107, 160, 207; expulsion of, 90–96; fears of, 6, 21, 23, 98, 104–5, 183, 212, 214; hanging of, 7, 62, 79, 84–89, 90; and Indians, 35, 49; laws regarding, 56, 58; linked to Republicans, 13, 62, 132, 173, 179, 180, 182, 191, 192; organization of, 36–37, 156; preachers suspected as, 66, 69–72; targeting North Texas, 36–37

Addington, Wendell G., 202

Addison, J. H., 131

Addison, Malcolm H., 90

Addison, Oscar M., 70, 131

African Americans. *See* blacks

Alabama, 27, 174, 201; absence of confirmed terrorist attacks in, 111; alleged plots in, 108–10; banning of northern teachers, 20; commissioners sponsored by, 183–84; unionist strength in, 193; women's fears in, 109

Anderson *Texas Baptist,* 71, 80

Anthon, Frederick, escapes mob, 95

anti-slavery movement, 4, 114, 140, 155, 171, 179, 214. *See also* abolitionists

Aptheker, Herbert, on insurrections in the Old South, 1n, 201

Arkansas, 29, 94, 129–30, 164, 191, 201; and Bewley's capture, 149–51; fears of abolitionists in, 100–101; Marsh incident, 101–5

Athens, Ga., *Southern Banner,* 115

Austin *Southern Intelligencer,* 44, 120, 128, 132, 133; attacked by southern rights press, 142–44; defends Texans of northern background, 65–66; deplores appeals to passion, 132; initial acceptance of plot stories, 44; on reassertion of judicial authority, 128–29; on Texas Troubles and the economy, 130

Austin *Texas State Gazette,* 34, 39, 43, 47, 49, 86, 113, 123, 141, 158, 162, 171, 202; attacks unionists, 144; "Bailey letter" broadside, 155, 157; publishes Pryor's first letter, 35

Bailey, William H., 156; and Bewley's name, 164–65; identity of questioned, 160, 165

Bailey letter, 157, 159, 160; Bewley's omission from, 161, 208; critical analysis of, 159–60; summarized, 156–57

Baker, Robin, 176–77

Barkley, Benjamin F., 59, 83, 96–97

Barney, William L., 4, 98, 111

Barron, S. B., 26, 53

Barry, James Buckner, 87, 90